POSTCARD HISTORY SERIES

Cincinnati Landmarks

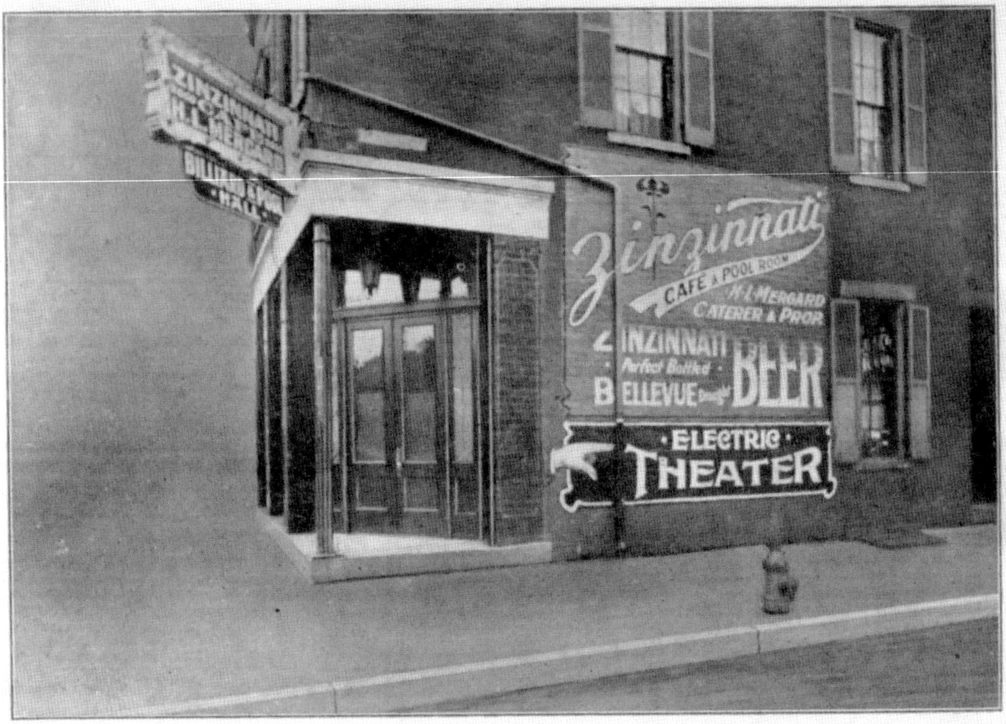

N. E. COR. COLERAIN AND MARSHALL AVENUES

The Zinzinnati Café is now boarded up with no hint of its great heritage. The Zinzinnati beer advertised on the side of the building was made by the Bellevue Brewery. Begun by George Klotter in 1866, it was, like many local breweries, a casualty of Prohibition. The old brewery building can still be seen on McMicken Avenue. (From the Collection of the Public Library of Cincinnati and Hamilton County.)

On the Cover: Music Hall on Elm Street is considered by many to be the greatest work of architect Samuel Hannaford. Hannaford was an Englishman who immigrated to the United States in 1844. From 1857 to 1896, he created many of Cincinnati's most endearing landmarks, from city hall to the Probasco Fountain in Clifton (on the back cover). (From the Collection of the Public Library of Cincinnati and Hamilton County.)

POSTCARD HISTORY SERIES

Cincinnati Landmarks

Steven J. Rolfes

ARCADIA PUBLISHING

ISBN 978-0-7385-9395-1

Published by Arcadia Publishing
Charleston, South Carolina

Printed in the United States of America

Library of Congress Control Number: 2012939214

For all general information contact Arcadia Publishing at:
Telephone 843-853-2070
Fax 843-853-0044
E-mail sales@arcadiapublishing.com
For customer service and orders:
Toll-Free 1-888-313-2665

Visit us on the Internet at www.arcadiapublishing.com

To Hallie Burnett, Gilbert Crawford Sr., and Willie J. Crawford, and to Theodore Rolfes and family, who came to Cincinnati from Hanover, Germany, in the 1800s

Contents

Acknowledgments		6
Introduction		7
1.	Beneath the Rhine	11
2.	Over and Above the Rhine	27
3.	Riding the Inclines to the Summits	47
4.	A Day in the Park	69
5.	A Trip to the Zoo	87
6.	A Day of Fun	99
7.	Zinzinnati	113

ACKNOWLEDGMENTS

This book would not have been possible without the efforts of many helping hands. Many thanks go to my acquisitions editor, Sandy Shalton, for her patience and encouragement, and to Jeff Reutsche. I would like to thank the great people at the Cincinnati and Hamilton County Library and the SWON (SouthWest Ohio and Neighboring) library system for providing permission to use their marvelous collection of vintage postcards and scanning the many images in this book.

I would particularly like to commend Kimber Fender, Diane Mallstrom, Nathan Swartzendruber, and all of the others who helped to assemble the materials for this book. I would also like to thank Elaine Kuhn and all the folks at the Kenton County Library System for their help, and Ken and Tammy Galyon with the Souvenir Factory for their postcard of Cincinnati Chili.

Endless thanks are extended for the technical assistance given to me by my family, my wife, Terri, and my daughter Selena. A special thank-you goes to Jordan Rolfes for computer assistance and taking photographs. Photographer Doug Weise should receive a medal for photographic bravery—instead of capturing the Chicken Dance from afar, he charged right into the middle of the action and was in imminent peril of being trampled by chickens! As always, we thank the Lord for His many blessings.

INTRODUCTION

Landmarks always have stories behind them, and there is no better story from old Cincinnati than that of the gazebo in Eden Park. Built in 1904, it resembles something from the *Arabian Nights*. However, the story is not in the Moorish design, but rather, in what happened there.

It was the Jazz Age—the days of Prohibition and gangsters. A young German immigrant named George Remus, who was both a pharmacist and an attorney, was practicing law in Chicago. As a defense attorney, he catered to clients who were mostly bootleggers. Remus was amazed at the rather ignorant and uncultured men who were becoming wealthy overnight as a result of this new law. He was certain that, with his brains and ambition, he could do even better. He studied the Volstead Act, the law instituting Prohibition He then left Chicago for Cincinnati, a city filled with thirsty Germans who did not like Washington, DC, telling them that they could not drink their beloved beer.

Remus set up shop, and using the loopholes that he had discovered in the law, quickly became known as the "King of the Bootleggers." He also became one of the wealthiest men in the country. At a New Year's Eve party in 1922, he gave new automobiles and diamond jewelry away as party favors. However, it all came crashing down when he was arrested and sent to a federal penitentiary in Georgia.

While he was incarcerated, he instructed his wife, Imogene, to "get in good" with the man who arrested him, hoping that he might get out of jail through the back door. Imogene then began a torrid affair with Frank Dodge, the same federal agent who had locked her husband up. When the bootlegger was finally released, he returned to his Price Hill mansion on Hermosa Avenue only to find that his beloved wife and her new boyfriend had literally cleaned him out, taking even the carpeting from the floors.

On October 6, 1927, Imogene left the Alms Hotel in Walnut Hills, heading downtown to finalize the divorce. Behind her taxi came George Remus, driven by his chauffeur, George Klug. When they reached that beautiful gazebo in Eden Park, Klug ran the taxi off the road and an enraged Remus jumped out of the car. Imogene tried to escape, and then turned to her husband, begging for her life. Remus pulled a revolver out of his coat, and as she desperately pleaded for mercy, the enraged gangster shot her.

Imogene died a few hours later at a nearby hospital. Remus threw the gun into the bushes—the police's "thorough search" was unable to find it, but months later, a child on an Easter egg hunt did—and headed to a nearby train station. On the way, he reached a strange conclusion. Rather than fleeing and living life as a fugitive, he decided that he could beat the case in court.

In an act of what many considered total foolishness, Remus went to trial for the admitted murder of his wife. Even more surprising, he had the audacity to act as his own attorney. This was quite brave considering that the prosecutor was none other than Charles Taft, the son of former president and then US Supreme Court chief justice William Howard Taft.

Charles Taft should have been able to put away this notorious bootlegger for life, or maybe even send him to the electric chair. But he overlooked just how unpopular Prohibition was in Cincinnati and the fact that Remus was a hero to the common people, some of whom made up the jury.

Remus's defense was that he was not legally responsible for his actions due to an all-consuming rage. The jury bought it, and he was found not guilty by temporary insanity and confined for a very short time to a mental hospital. He was released soon after, but he was never able to restore his bootlegging empire or his power. In anger, he had his Price Hill mansion, once known as the Marble Palace, razed. Today, a series of very plain apartment buildings occupies the site.

Ever since then, many people have reported seeing the ghost of a woman in 1920s clothing near the gazebo in Eden Park. She begs for her life for a moment and then vanishes.

Cincinnati has many such landmarks, which people can still visit and remember stories of the old days. Being a very old city, Cincinnati also has landmarks that no longer exist—and one that never existed at all.

Probably the most beloved landmarks of all are those that can be enjoyed by the entire family. Going to an amusement park is one of the few occasions that busy parents spend a full day with their children for the purpose of just having fun. This is where fond memories of childhood are made.

Cincinnati had two major amusement parks, Coney Island and Chester Park. Chester Park is one of the landmarks that no longer exists, having been closed because of an unpaid water bill in 1932. The only surviving trace of it is a spot where Spring Grove Avenue suddenly becomes wider. This was so that streetcars could turn around after letting people off for a day of fun.

It was almost put out of business in 1911, when a pair of crossed wires in the storeroom underneath the Tickler ride shorted out, causing a fire that quickly spread throughout the many wooden structures of the park. As terrified patrons fled to safety, a number of trained bears from a vaudeville animal act became panicked. Employees rushed in to save them. Soon, these bears were being taken away on leashes to safety, except for one. A policeman had been leading him when a female singer came running up to him and, as soon as she was close to the officer, fainted. In an act of chivalry, the policeman caught the girl. Of course, the bear promptly escaped, but it was quickly recaptured and taken to join his companions in safety.

Although incredible damage was done to the park, no lives were lost in the inferno. A nearby lumberyard also caught fire and quickly turned into one of the most horrific blazes in the city. While the park was saved and soon reopened, the lumberyard was a total loss.

Most Cincinnatians today have no memory of Chester Park, but many childhood reminiscences include family outings at Coney Island. It was only two years after the Civil War that James Parker first allowed picnickers to pay to use his groves for outings. As more and more people escaped the heat and smoke of the city for a pleasant afternoon in the country, this simple orchard quickly grew into a thriving entertainment park, particularly after he allowed a Sunday school group to charter a steamboat to bring them to his facility. The park grew quickly with the addition of a dance hall and a mule-powered merry-go-round. Parker proclaimed it "Ohio Grove, the Coney Island of the West."

Managing the park was hard and Parker had to contend with drunken brawls, pickpockets, and horrendous floods. By 1886, the growing park was sold to William McIntyre, a retired steamboat captain.

It went through a series of owners until 1925, when it was purchased by George Schott and Rudolph Hynicka, who was already quite famous in Cincinnati as the heir apparent to "Boss" Cox, the powerful city boss. By riding Cox's coattails, Hynicka had become a wealthy power broker. He was one of the select few men who ran the city from the round table in Weilert's Biergarten. Nine years after his patron's death, he was a part owner of Coney Island.

Hynicka, known to his friends as "Rud," had little to do with the day-to-day running of the facility and died unexpectedly two years later while on a trip to St. Petersburg, Florida. The man who had ridden to power from newspaper reporter to wealthy wheeler and dealer was eulogized by Raymond Kunkel of the Blaine Club. "Without friends," said Kunkel, "without influence, without family background to buoy him up, he began life's pilgrimage, with strength of mind and charm of personality his only assets." There was likely more than a little coughing in the room at these words.

Schott, a former shoe merchant, loved Coney Island and was there every day. On one hot July night in 1935, while walking through Moonlight Gardens after closing, he fell over dead from a heart attack. It was only fitting that he died in the place that he, and so many Cincinnatians, loved.

Cincinnati also possesses a very unique landmark, one that never actually existed. In the late 1800s, the Miami-Erie Canal wound its way towards the Ohio River, past the then German neighborhood of Over-the-Rhine, to the east side of the city. With the advent of the railroads, the canal was doomed.

As long ago as 1877, the Cincinnati Chamber of Commerce studied the waterway, which even then was a filthy mess, and came to some surprising conclusions. Seeing that the canal was no longer feasible, they suggested draining the waterway and putting a modern highway on the top and a subway in the already-dug depression. In its report, the chamber states, "The General Assembly which passed the Canal Act had no more idea that within twenty years steam cars would be thundering down the Miami Valley . . . than we have today that within the next score of years all the traffic will be conducted by balloons through the free and pathless air."

We never did get the balloons in the "pathless air," but the more practical recommendations were adopted. It took another 50 years, but finally the open sewer known as the Miami-Erie Canal was officially drained and construction began on the ill-fated Cincinnati subway system. In 1920, ground was broken and the ambitious project began. It quickly became a fiasco. Few Cincinnatians today know that there is a Cincinnati subway.

The other recommendation of the chamber of commerce report, using the top for a modern street, has been realized in the form of Central Parkway. On a traffic island in the midst of Central Parkway near Vine Street, there is a simple metal cover on the sidewalk. Beneath this is the entrance to a subway that has never had even a single passenger. After decades of squabbling in city hall and a miscalculation leading to the collapse of a number of hillside houses in Brighton, the project was abandoned.

The marvelous Chamber of Commerce Building, from which the report was rendered, was itself quite a landmark. The site, on Fourth and Race Streets, was originally the home of Reuben Springer and later became the post office. Architect H.H. Richardson designed the massive Romanesque Revival building with prominent turrets. In January 1911, a small grease fire erupted in the ceiling over a busy kitchen. As everyone was preparing for a banquet, one of the cooks simply tossed some water up and thought that the problem was ended; it was not.

Later, an exhausted fire department returning from a distant fire in Avondale received word that the Chamber of Commerce Building was being consumed by an out-of-control blaze, and another landmark was lost. While the building may be gone, parts of it can still be seen. The picturesque Arch Bridge in Eden Park is graced by eagles from the building. A curious modernist sculpture on the northern edge of Burnet Woods is entirely composed of stones left over from the fire, which had been rescued and assembled by engineering students at the nearby University of Cincinnati.

Another landmark was the Hotel Sinton, on the corner of Fourth and Vine Streets and one of the most luxurious and opulent hotels of its day. There was plenty of history in the hotel over the decades. In 1919, the infamous Chicago "Black Sox" players met here with ex-prizefighter Abe Attell. The players were angry at not receiving enough cash in advance from the underworld gamblers who were pulling the strings to throw the World Series. Attell was able to smooth their ruffled feathers, thereby giving the Sinton a place in one of the greatest scandals in American sports history.

It was also at the Sinton, in the 1920s, that rising star Rudy Vallee sang for a luncheon of wealthy fans. Before he could put down his trademark megaphone, the sophisticated debutantes mobbed the stage, overturning tables and shattering expensive china.

In 1964, the last guest checked out of the Sinton, remarking that it was rather eerie to walk out of the once thriving hotel through an empty, dark lobby. Soon after, the wrecking ball came.

Thousands of people visit Cincinnati each year, but most only *think* that they have been here. The truth is, if you haven't tried the chili, you haven't really been to Cincinnati. Created by Macedonian immigrants Tom and John Kiradjieff in 1922, this unique food is certainly one of the most beloved landmarks of Cincinnati. Below is the recipe that is printed on the postcard on page 113, so that you can enjoy a Cincinnati landmark no matter where you live.

Ingredients:
1 1/2 pounds ground beef
1 (29-ounce can) tomato sauce
1 (14.5-ounce can) peeled whole tomatoes
Small onion, chopped
1/2 teaspoon cinnamon
1/2 teaspoon allspice
1 teaspoon salt
1/2 teaspoon pepper
1 1/2 tablespoon chili powder
1 tablespoon white vinegar
1 clove garlic
3 bay leaves

Directions:
Brown meat; cook onions with meat; drain grease. Place meat and onions in large pan or crock pot. Add rest of ingredients. Cook slowly 4–5 hours, covered. Remove bay leaves and garlic before serving. Serve on a bed of spaghetti and top with grated cheddar cheese. Serves 6–8.

This recipe is courtesy of, but not exclusive to, the Souvenir Factory.

One

BENEATH THE RHINE

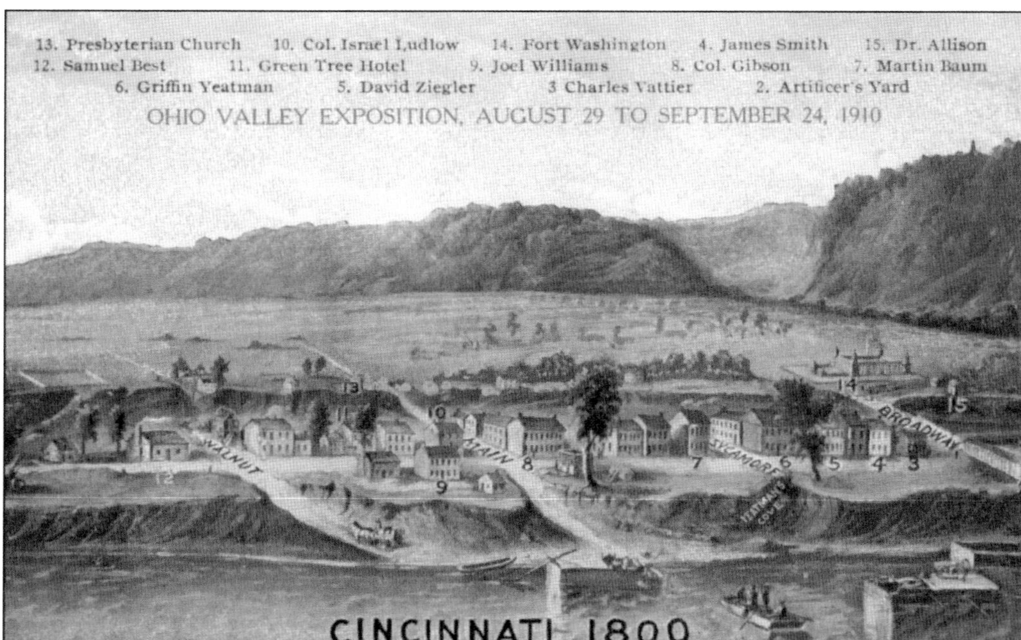

Although there were few landmarks at this time, the sight of Cincinnati was welcome to weary and thirsty river travelers. The very first tavern was located at Front and Sycamore Streets, roughly the site of the current Great American Baseball Park. Erected by Griffin Yeatman in 1793, the tavern was a popular stop for rivermen piloting flatboats down the Ohio. (From the Collection of the Public Library of Cincinnati and Hamilton County.)

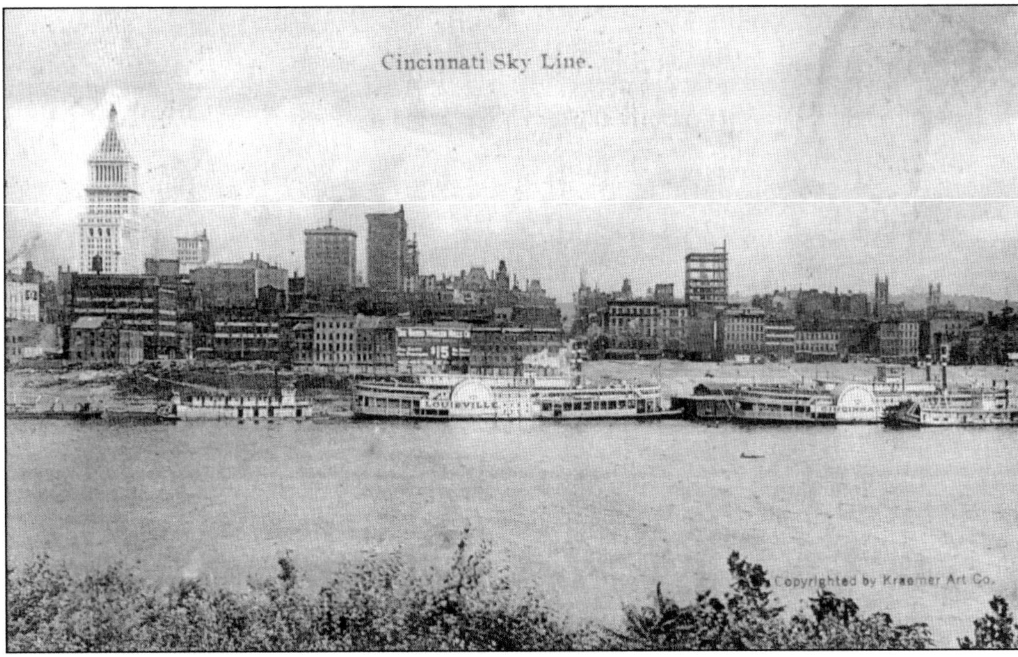

There is no better landmark in Cincinnati than its magnificent skyline. It has changed drastically from this 1918 image, but the words of Dr. Daniel Drake still ring true: "From Newport and Covington [Kentucky] the appearance of the town is beautiful . . . and promises to become magnificent." (From the Collection of the Public Library of Cincinnati and Hamilton County.)

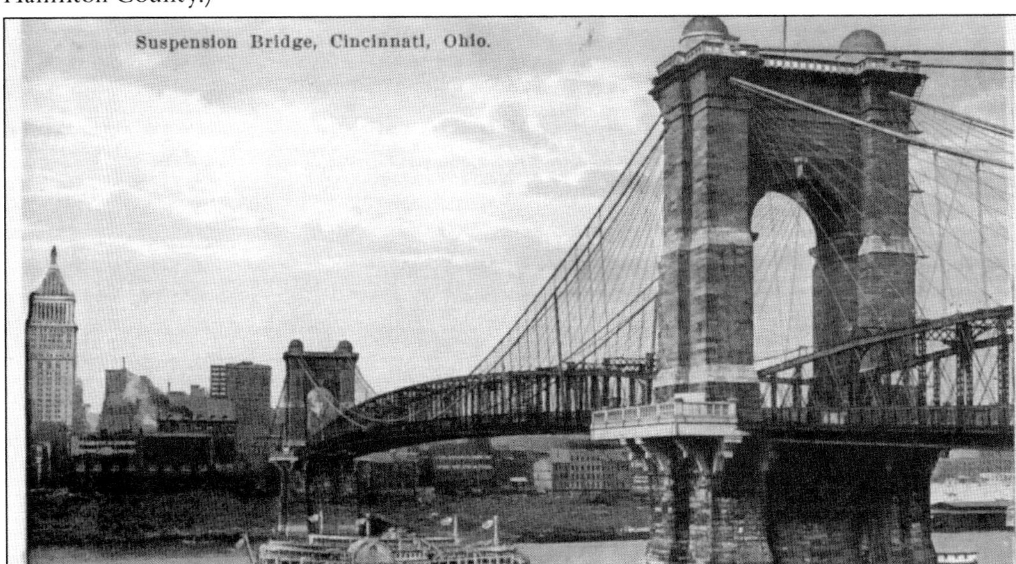

John Roebling, the son of a tobacconist in Mülhausen, Germany, immigrated to the United States in 1831. He built two great bridges: the Brooklyn Bridge and the Suspension Bridge in Cincinnati. In 1867, while building the Brooklyn Bridge, his foot was crushed. He attempted "water treatment," or pouring water on the wound, but unfortunately died within a month from tetanus. (From the Collection of the Public Library of Cincinnati and Hamilton County.)

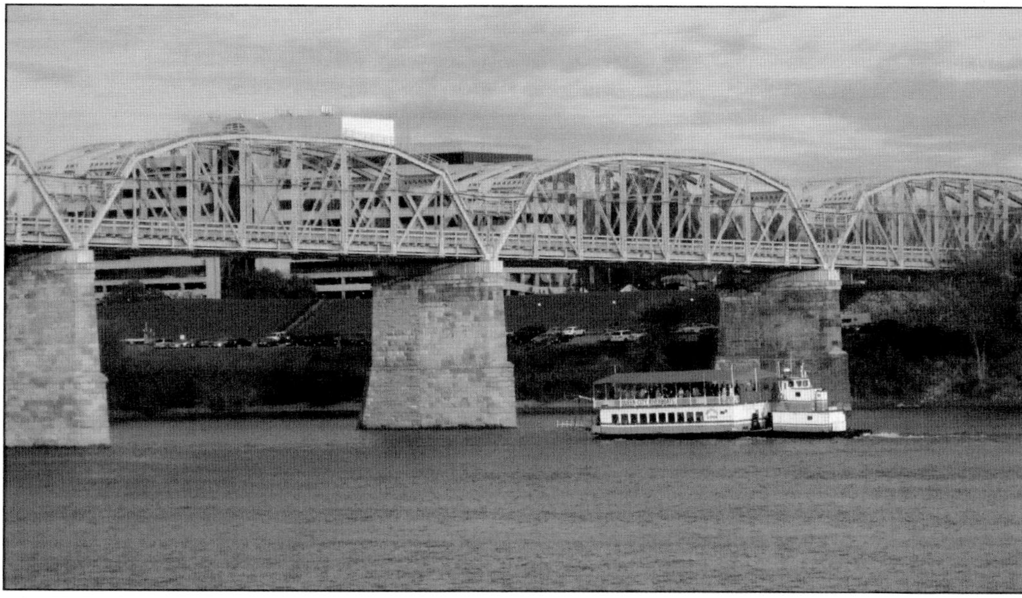

This is a Cincinnati landmark that refuses to die. Built in 1896, the Louisville &Nashville Bridge was the first railroad bridge connecting Newport and Cincinnati. With the decline of the railroads, it was neglected and finally closed in 1987. In 2001, painted purple, the span was transformed into a pedestrian walkway, whimsically called the Purple People Bridge.(Photograph by Jordan Rolfes.)

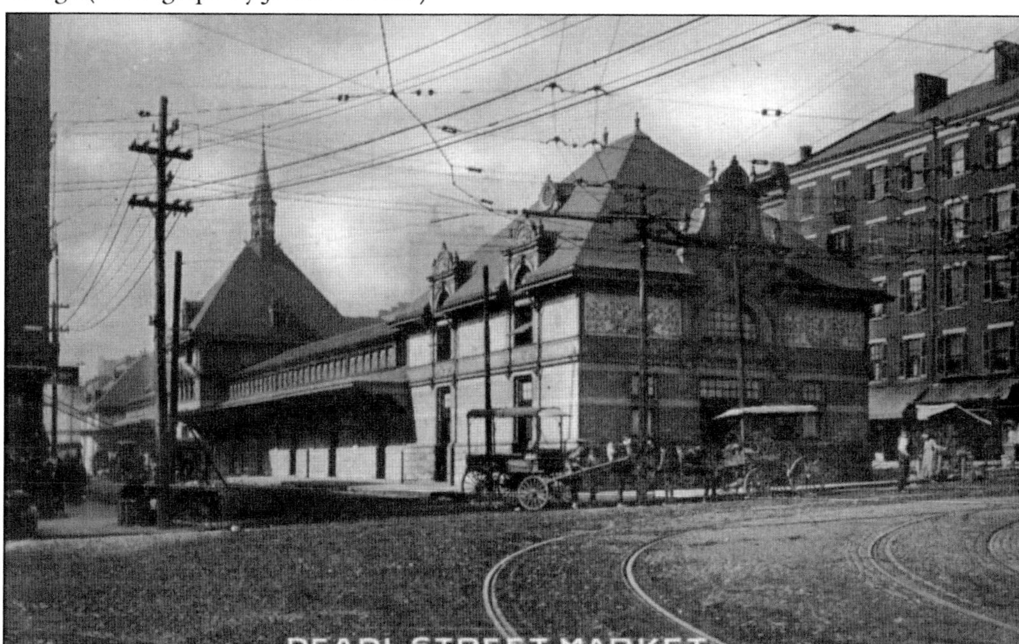

Pres. James Monroe, Charles Dickens, and the Marquis de Lafayette were just a few of the thousands who pushed carts through the Pearl Street Growers' Market. Since 1816, women would race to the market before sunrise to grab the freshest foodstuffs. Shopping had to be completed by 9:00 a.m. It was closed in 1934, and its famous bells were moved to Findlay Market. (From the Collection of the Public Library of Cincinnati and Hamilton County.)

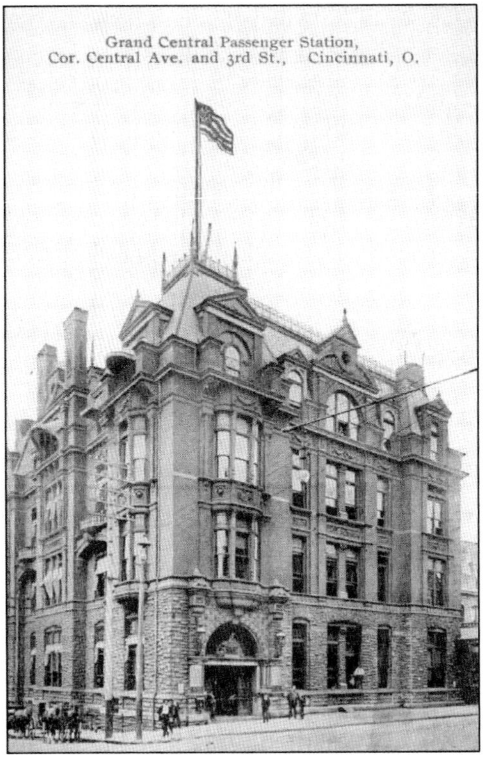

By 1873, it was obvious that there were too many depots along the often flooded riverfront. It took until 1881 to purchase the land at Third Street and Central Parkway and another two years to build this ornate Romanesque depot, the Union Central. Right across the street was the magnificent Grand Hotel, thus giving the depot the nickname "Grand Central Station." (From the Collection of the Public Library of Cincinnati and Hamilton County.)

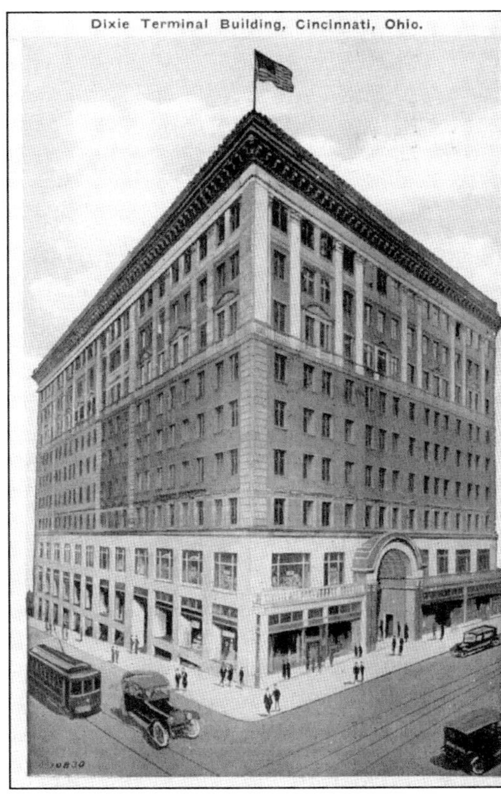

Dixie Terminal, built in 1921, was originally the Kentucky bus station. Hidden in plain sight amidst the hundreds of baroque figures in the arcade—alongside centaurs and cherubs—are the faces of the architects, Fred Garber and Clifford Woodward. (From the Collection of the Public Library of Cincinnati and Hamilton County.)

This luxurious hotel may be considered the world's fanciest speakeasy. In 1929, the Chatterbox Club opened on the ninth floor. Everyone there brought his or her own refreshments in hip flasks, and as the couples danced below, the black ceiling was illuminated by the "Aurora Borealis," a multicolored light show. (From the Collection of the Public Library of Cincinnati and Hamilton County.)

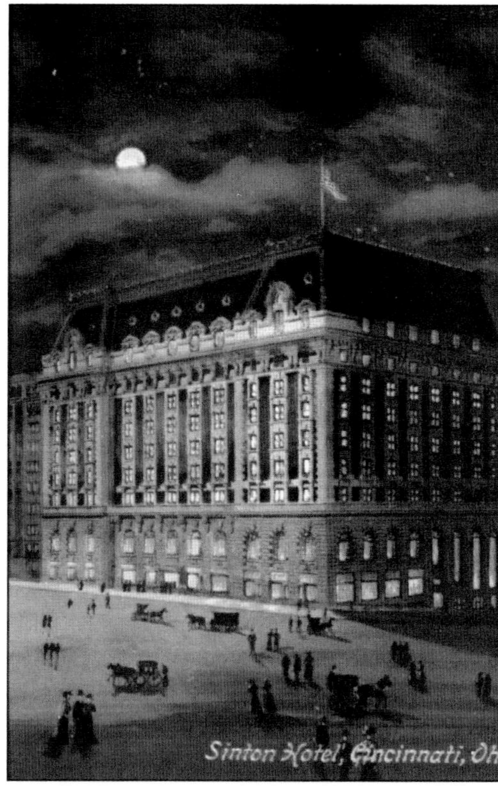

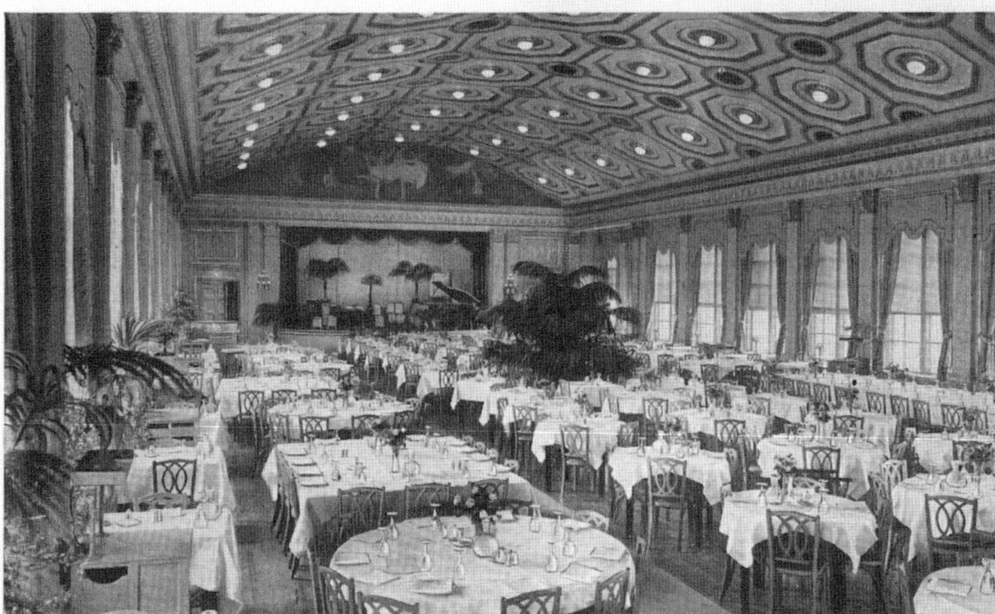

PORTION OF ROOF DINING ROOM, HOTEL GIBSON, CINCINNATI, OHIO.

The Gibson Hotel hosted countless elegant banquets over its many years of operation. Perhaps the most memorable was in 1869, when the hotel hosted the undefeated Cincinnati Red Stockings. (From the Collection of the Public Library of Cincinnati and Hamilton County.)

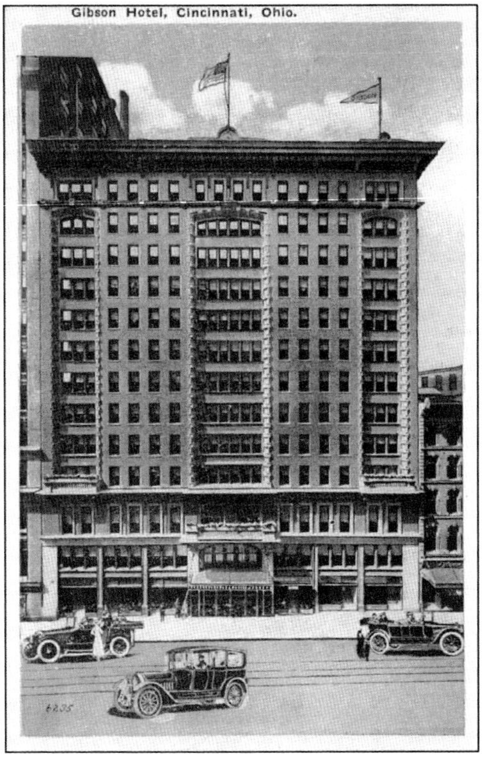

Peter Gibson endured laughter from his peers when he built this hotel far out in the wilderness of Fifth Street in 1849. The area was so remote that it was actually located on Hezekiah Flint's cornfield. But Gibson was a visionary and knew that the city would grow out to his location. (From the Collection of the Public Library of Cincinnati and Hamilton County.)

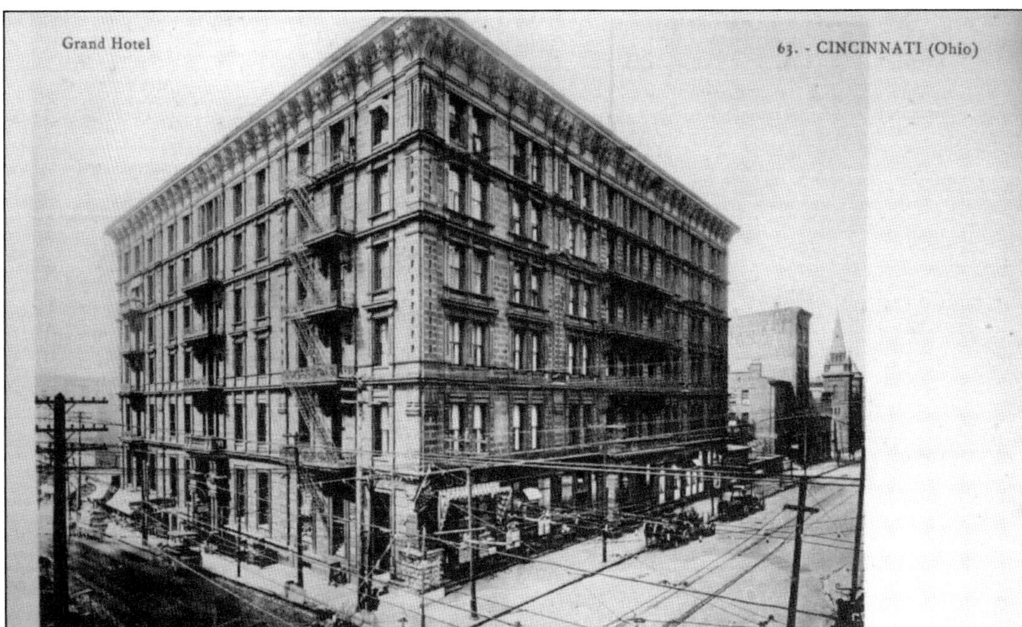

The registry of the Grand Hotel provides a lesson in civics. The names included presidents Theodore Roosevelt, James Garfield, William McKinley, and Grover Cleveland. President Grant loved the billiard room, and Pres. Rutherford B. Hayes gave a speech on the staircase of the lobby. The hotel closed in 1933 with the opening of Union Terminal. (From the Collection of the Public Library of Cincinnati and Hamilton County.)

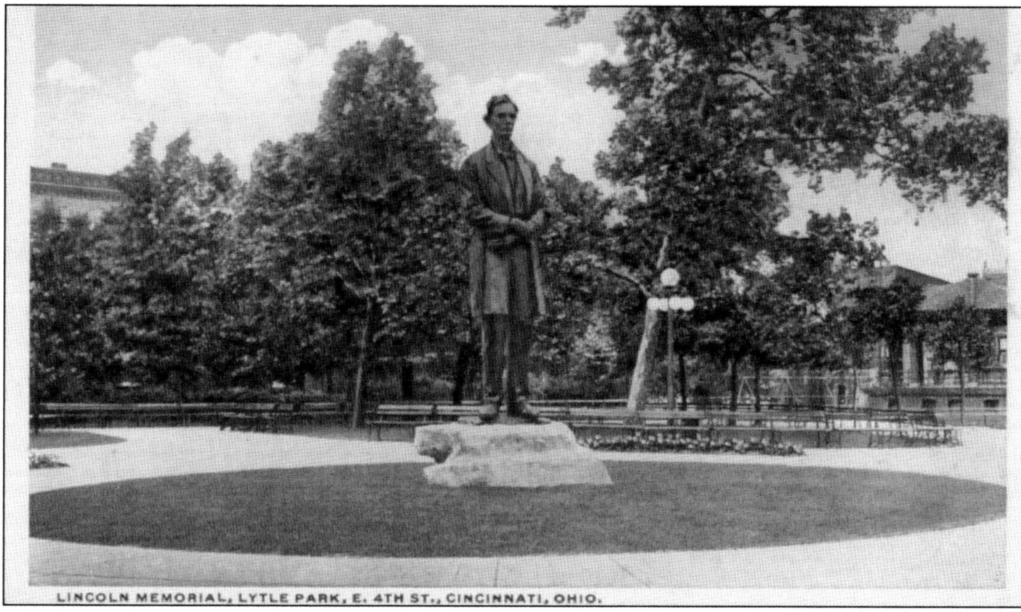

Art often provokes controversy. One example of this occurred when George Grey Barnard's 11-foot-tall statue of Abraham Lincoln in Lytle Park omitted his beard. Some call it hideous, while others declare it a masterpiece. It was presented to the city in 1917 by Charles Taft, whose half brother, former president William Howard Taft, gave the speech at the unveiling. (From the Collection of the Public Library of Cincinnati and Hamilton County.)

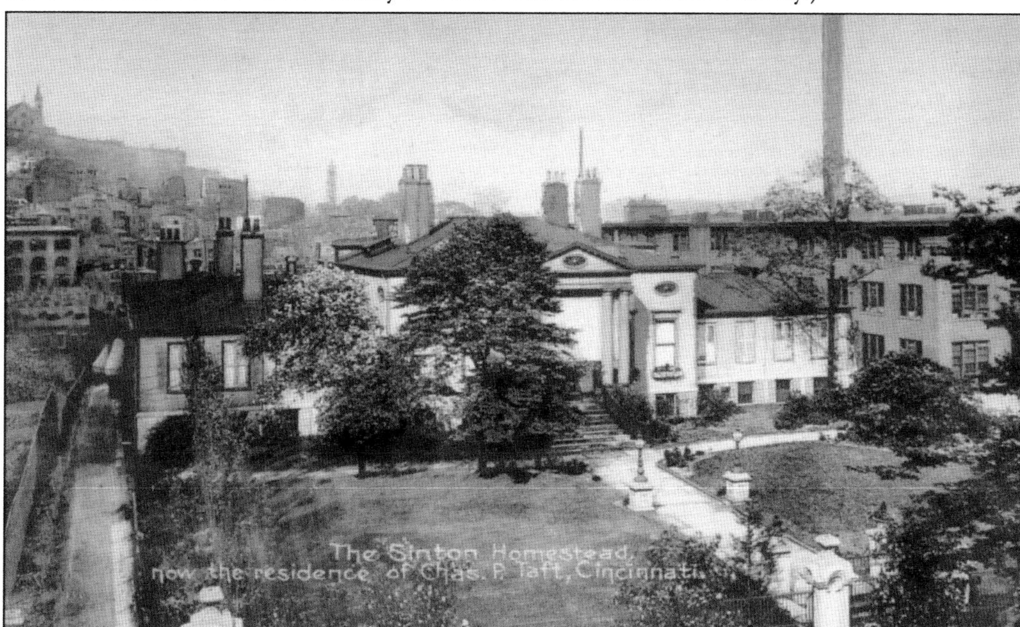

This Pike Street mansion was originally owned by Martin Baum, a former mayor who had fought alongside Anthony Wayne. It was purchased by Nicholas Longworth and later sold to David Sinton, who made a fortune in iron during the Civil War. Sinton's daughter married Charles Taft. The house has since been converted into the Taft Museum of Art. (From the Collection of the Public Library of Cincinnati and Hamilton County.)

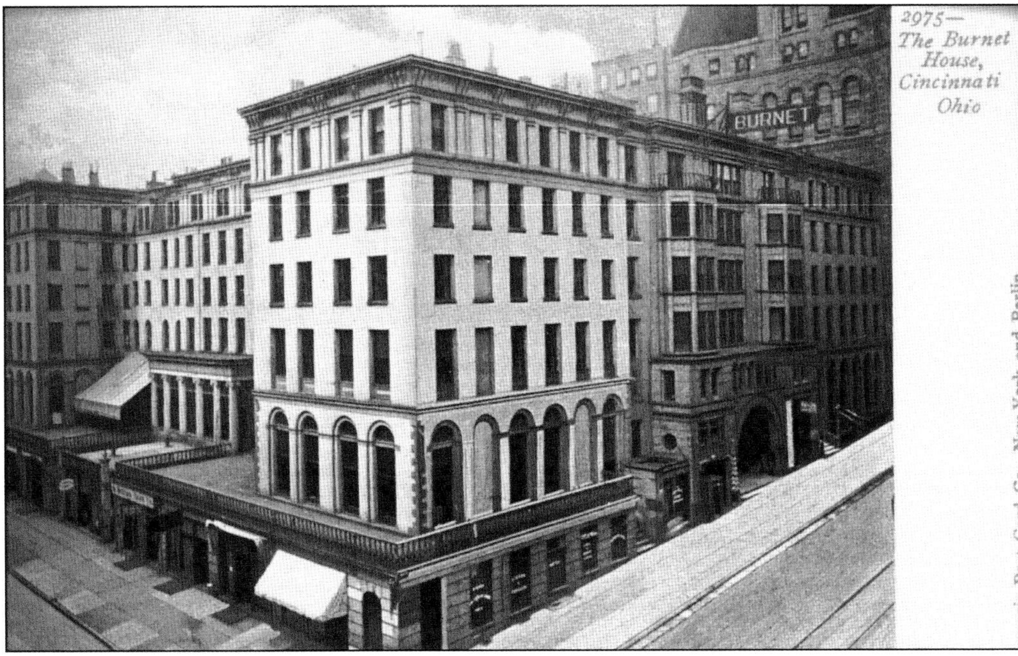

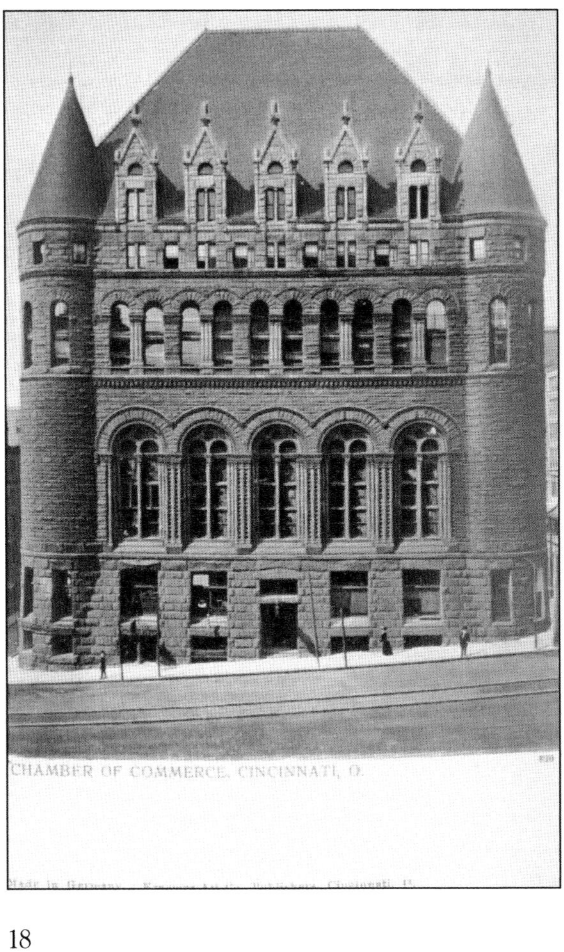

One of the most famous hotels in the Midwest, the Burnet House was located a few blocks from the river at Third and Vine Streets. It had quite an impressive roster of guests including the presidents on both sides of the Civil War—Abraham Lincoln and Jefferson Davis. (From the Collection of the Public Library of Cincinnati and Hamilton County.)

Celebrated architect H.H. Richardson died in 1886 and did not live to see his Chamber of Commerce Building erected. His designs—he also designed the Allegheny County Courthouse—are praised by architectural writer Vincent Scully as giving "the power of a building to embody a heroic attitude." (From the Collection of the Public Library of Cincinnati and Hamilton County.)

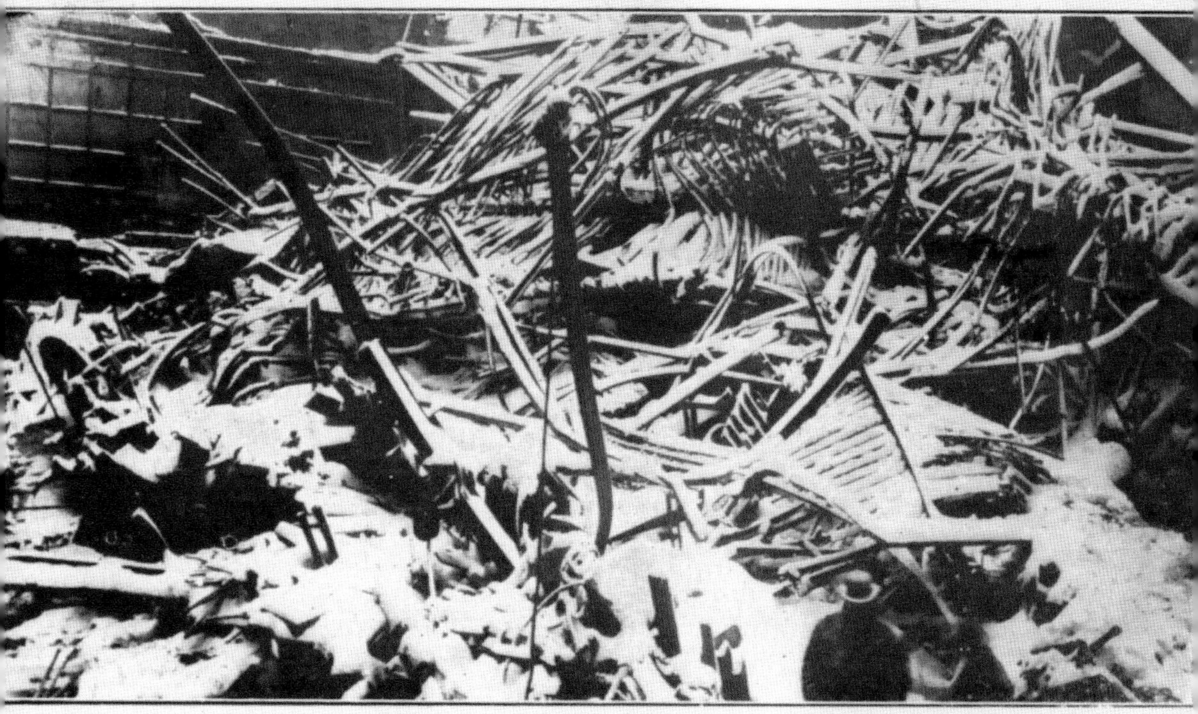

CINCINNATI CHAMBER OF COMMERCE FIRE, JAN. 10, 1911

operty Loss $1,000,000, Six Lives Sacrificed — Snow Covered Ruins a Week Later

"There is a little fire here. You had better come down. It doesn't amount to much but you had better . . ." Those were the last words of bookkeeper Charles Sibbald, spoken to a colleague in the Chamber of Commerce Building on January 10, 1911. A small fire in the ceiling of the kitchen was not dealt with quickly, allowing it to spread. On the floor beneath was a banquet for the Business Men's Club. At first, the waiters told the guests to ignore the commotion, that there was a small fire upstairs but it was being taken care of. Later, the group was asked to evacuate. They did so in an orderly manner until the lights went out and they smelled smoke. If the group had waited only a few minutes more before leaving, the ceiling would have collapsed upon them. Cincinnati mayor Louis Schwab had been scheduled to give a speech there, but another commitment in Northside prevented him from attending. (From the Collection of the Public Library of Cincinnati and Hamilton County.)

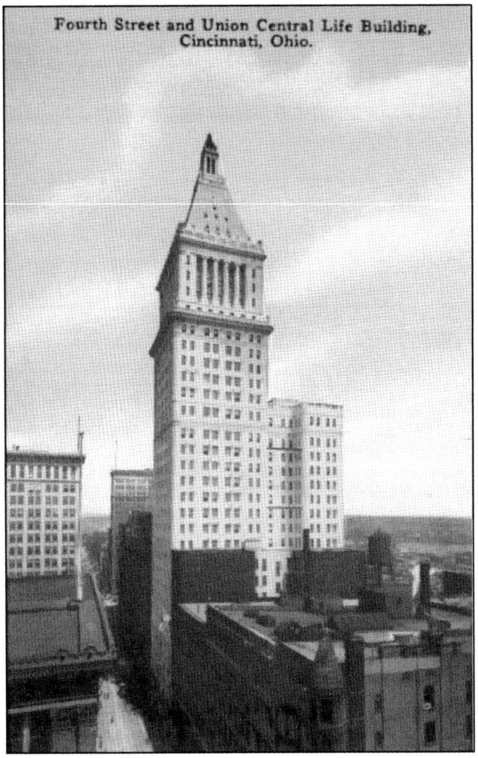

The most recognizable skyscraper in downtown Cincinnati, the Union Central Tower, was originally intended to be a train station. The building's unique design dates from 1903, when a new train station was being proposed. When the Chamber of Commerce Building burned down in 1911, the old building plans were resurrected like a phoenix from the ashes. (From the Collection of the Public Library of Cincinnati and Hamilton County.)

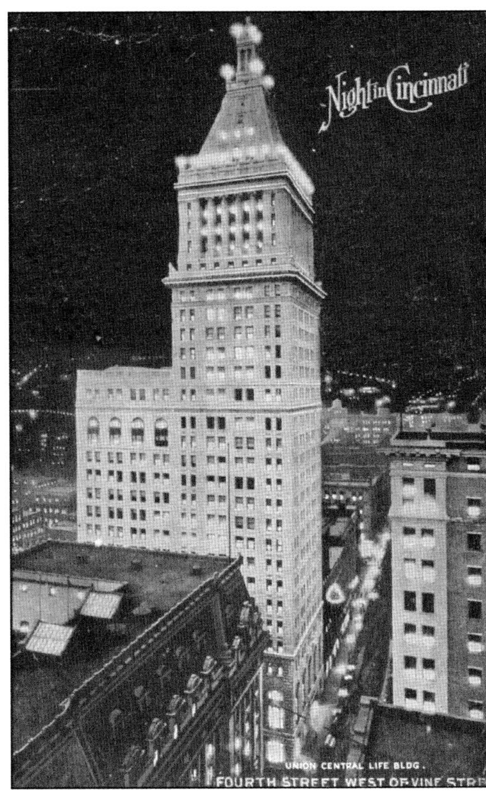

While the skyline is impressive in daytime, it is stunning at night. The lights of the skyscrapers beckoned people to the city for evenings of theater and dining. This vintage postcard image shows the Union Central Tower (now the PNC Building) dramatically illuminated against the night sky. (From the Collection of the Public Library of Cincinnati and Hamilton County.)

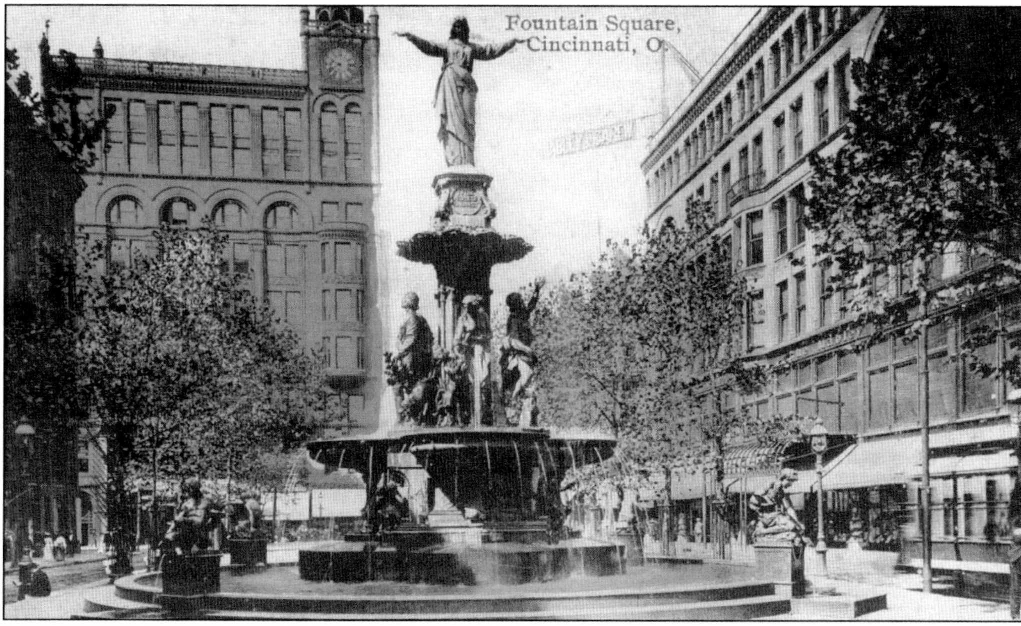

The most recognizable landmark in Cincinnati is the Tyler Davidson fountain. Located at Fifth and Vine Streets, it was born of conflict—finally built in 1871 after court battles with butchers who had their stalls on this site. The statue itself, August von Kreling's *Genius of Water*, was fashioned with brass from old cannons. (From the Collection of the Public Library of Cincinnati and Hamilton County.)

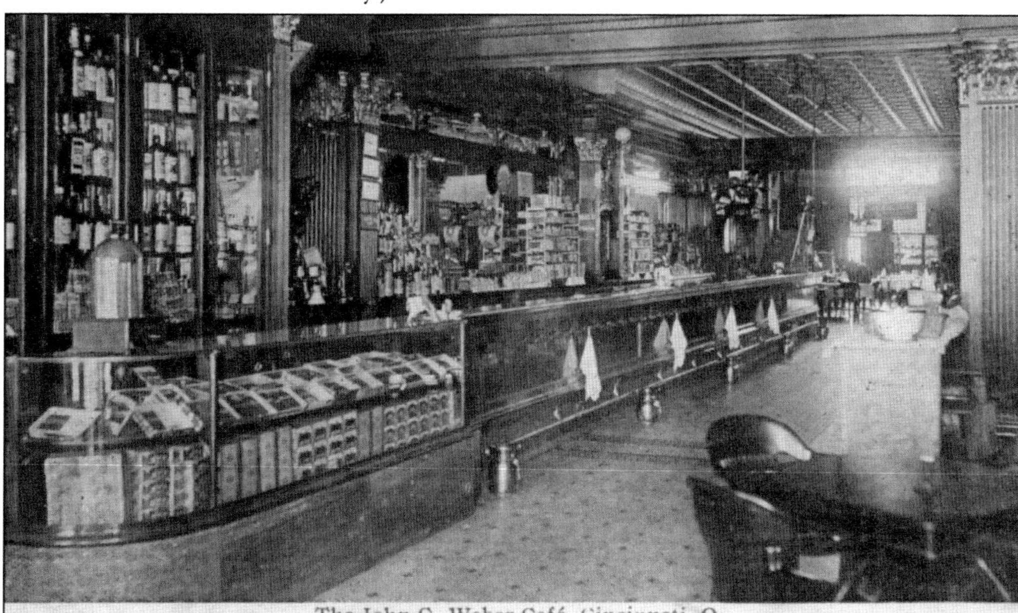

Downtown Cincinnati had numerous drinking establishments that became landmarks over the years. "Boss" Cox ran the city from Wielert's Biergarten in Over-the-Rhine and the Mecca on Walnut Street. Most of these establishments catered to the theater crowd. Weber's Café on Vine Street was located close to the Grand Opera House and the fountain. (From the Collection of the Public Library of Cincinnati and Hamilton County.)

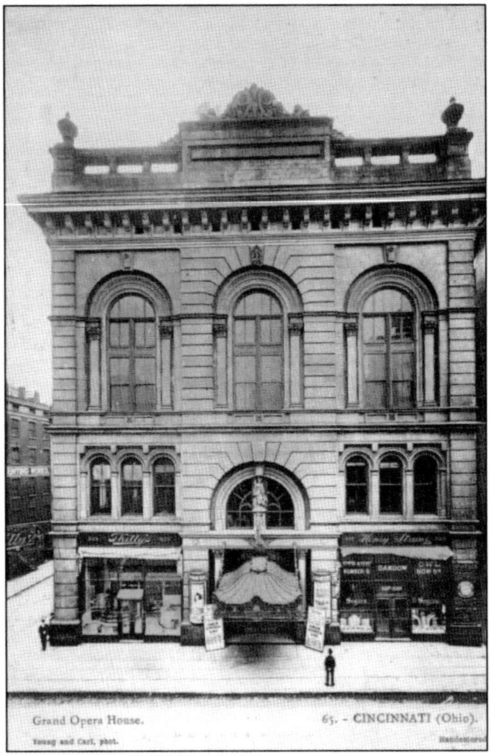

This opulent theater, where the likes of Lily Langtry and Sarah Bernhardt performed, began as a Catholic university. Trouble came in 1867 when an antichurch play was performed, followed by a speech from the famous agnostic Bob Ingersoll. Archbishop John Baptist Purcell severed all church relationships with the institution, after which David Sinton purchased the building and converted it into a theater. (From the Collection of the Public Library of Cincinnati and Hamilton County.)

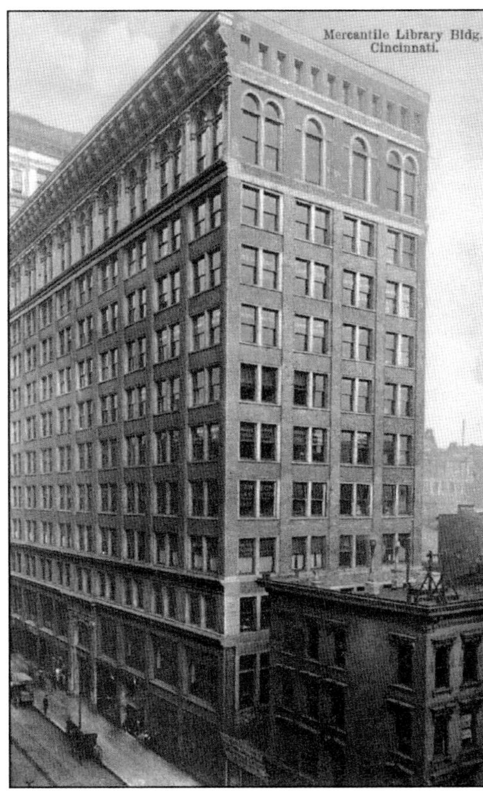

The Mercantile Library on Walnut Street, located on the site of the first courthouse, was Cincinnati's first library. Erected in 1835, the building burned down 10 years later, but the rare books were saved by five fire companies. Over the years, notables such as Ralph Waldo Emerson, Harriet Beecher Stowe, and William Thackeray lectured there. The current structure was built in 1902. (From the Collection of the Public Library of Cincinnati and Hamilton County.)

The Cincinnati and Hamilton County Public Library began in 1855 at Sixth and Vine Streets with only 1,500 volumes and is now one of the largest in the nation. The librarians have not always approved of the selection of reading material. One librarian even complained about popular novels, stating that, "Such reading has given us much pain." (From the Collection of the Public Library of Cincinnati and Hamilton County.)

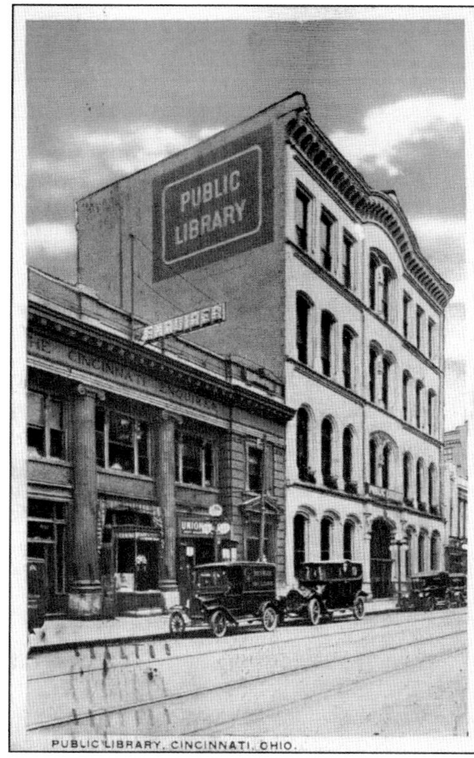

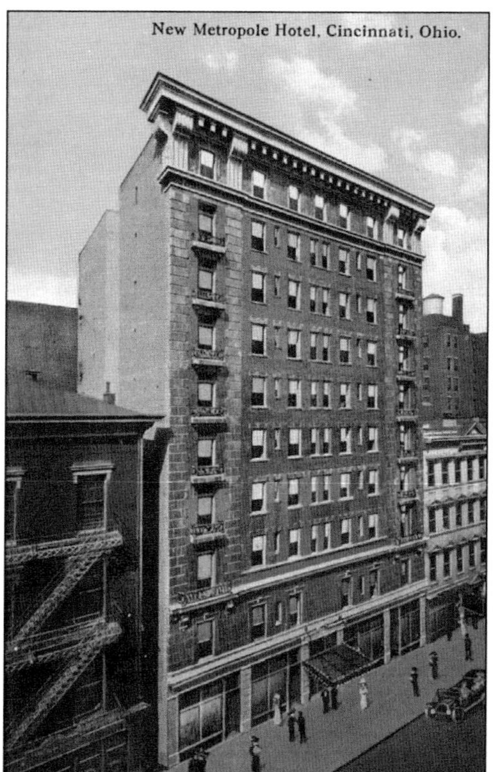

The Metropole was opened in 1912 as a luxury hotel. With its grand ballroom, massive lobby, and decorated ceilings, it was soon considered to be one of the finest hotels in the city. By 1971, it was converted into low-income housing. It is now being restored as a hotel and museum. (From the Collection of the Public Library of Cincinnati and Hamilton County.)

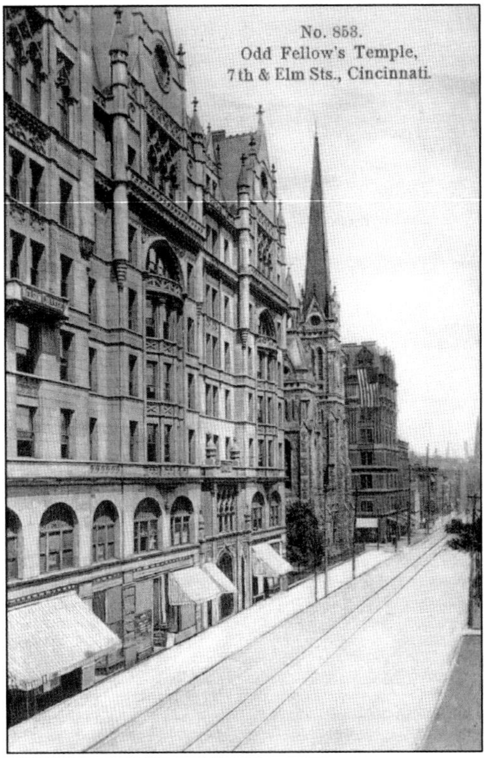

The architecture of Samuel Hannaford is visible throughout Cincinnati. While most of his buildings are still standing, a few, such as this ornate Odd Fellows Temple at Seventh and Elm Streets, are now long gone. (From the Collection of the Public Library of Cincinnati and Hamilton County.)

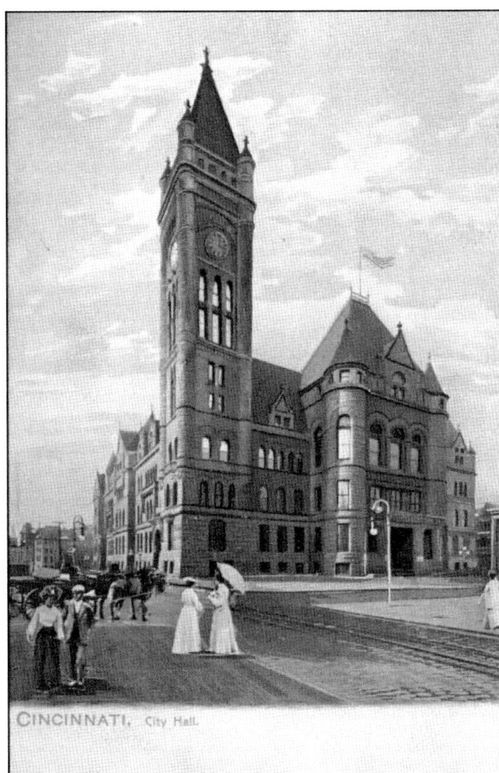

Cincinnati's city hall, a massive Romanesque structure on Plum Street, is Samuel Hannaford's masterpiece. The giant complex, opened in 1893, replaced an earlier city hall that was only two stories tall. Despite the beauty of this classic building, there were serious proposals to close it in the 1950s and 1960s. Thankfully, the architectural landmark is still functioning today. (From the Collection of the Public Library of Cincinnati and Hamilton County.)

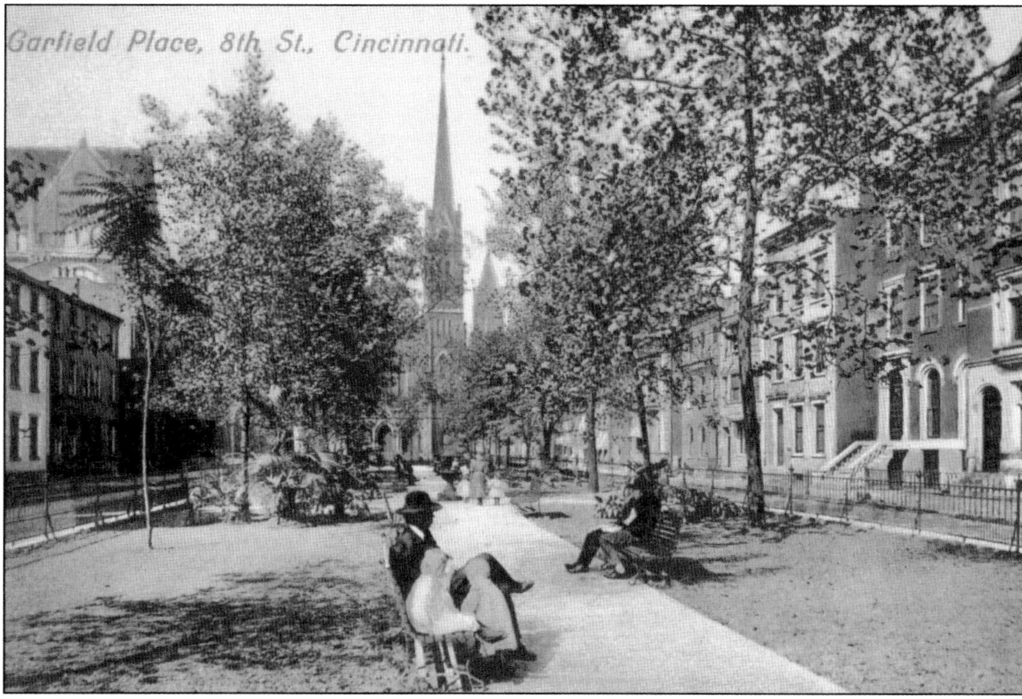

Piatt Park is an island of tranquility in downtown Cincinnati, bordered by the library on the east end and a magnificent Presbyterian church on the west. It was a gift from the two Piatt brothers, Benjamin, a judge and member of the state legislature, and John, a steamboat manufacturer. (From the Collection of the Public Library of Cincinnati and Hamilton County.)

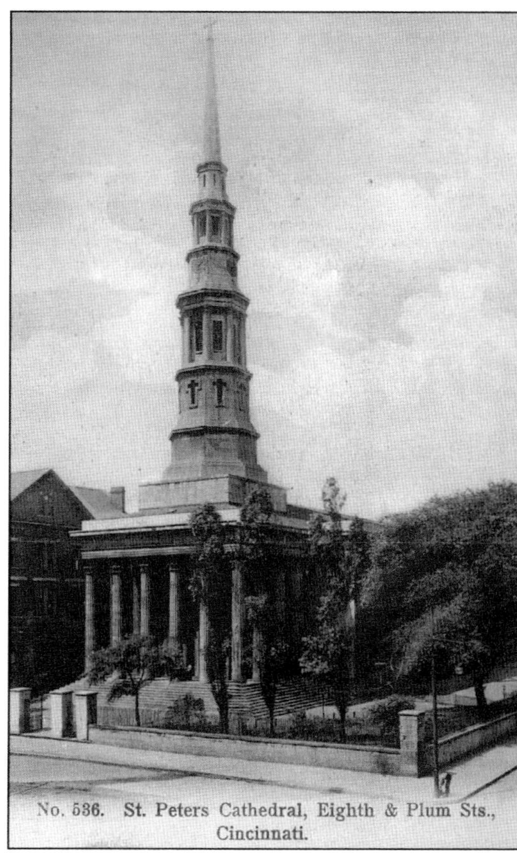

One of the first artistic European sculptures imported to Cincinnati, a pair of angels by Odoardo Fantachiotti, once graced the St. Peter in Chains Cathedral. The angels can now be viewed at the Cincinnati Art Museum. Works of such artists as Anton Wendling and Benvenuto Cellini can still be seen in the church. (From the Collection of the Public Library of Cincinnati and Hamilton County.)

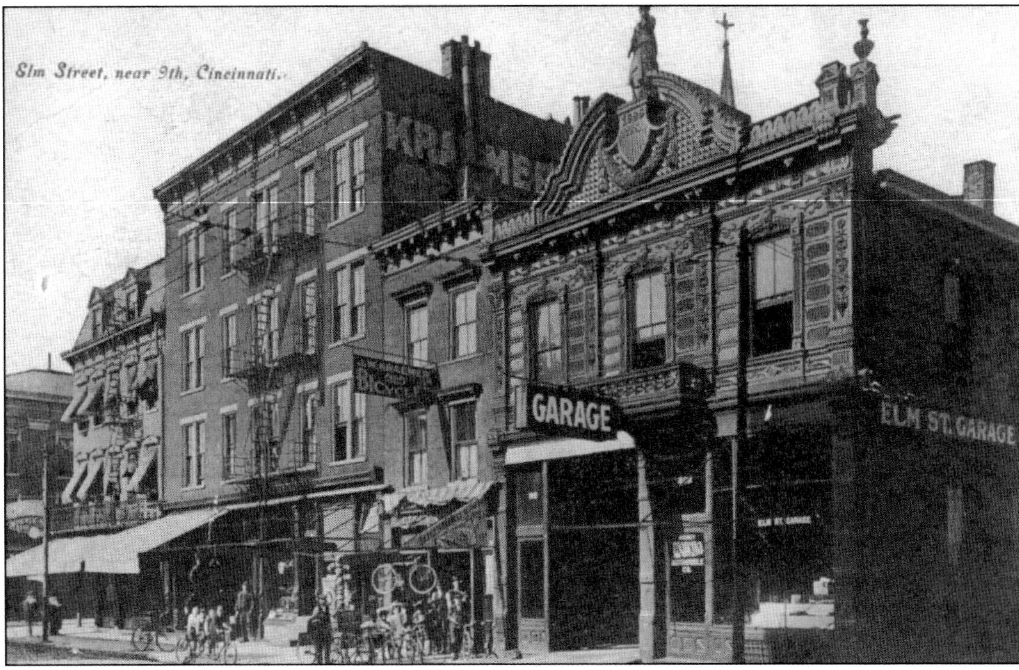

This bizarre building on Elm Street close to Ninth Street is no longer in existence. It was likely the most gothic place one could go to have his or her automobile repaired. This area was known as Crosley Square for many years and now houses a school. (From the Collection of the Public Library of Cincinnati and Hamilton County.)

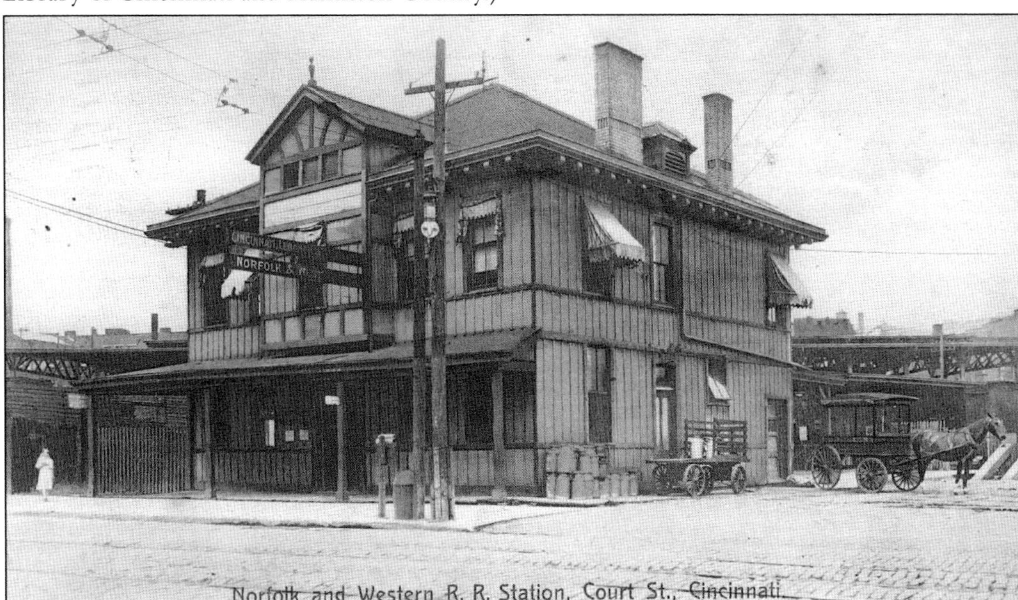

This 1909 image shows the Norfolk & Western Railway depot in its heyday. A romantic piece of Americana, the station was built in 1872. As it was located on the east end of Court Street near Broadway Street, it was spared from the ravages of floods. This picturesque building deteriorated after the construction of Union Terminal and closed in 1933. (From the Collection of the Public Library of Cincinnati and Hamilton County.)

Two

Over and Above the Rhine

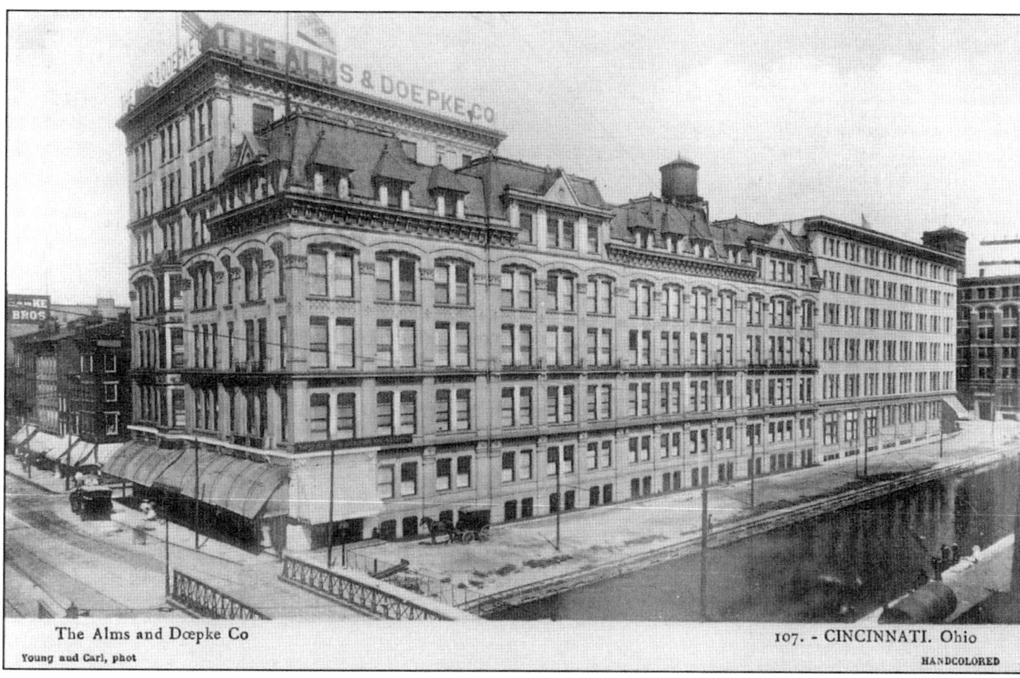

Founded at the end of the Civil War, the Alms and Doepke department store was one of the nation's largest retailers. In 1878, it relocated to Main Street just above the Miami-Erie Canal. However, as the Over-the-Rhine area deteriorated, business fell off. The once proud store closed forever in 1955. The Samuel Hannaford Building is now used for government offices. (From the Collection of the Public Library of Cincinnati and Hamilton County.)

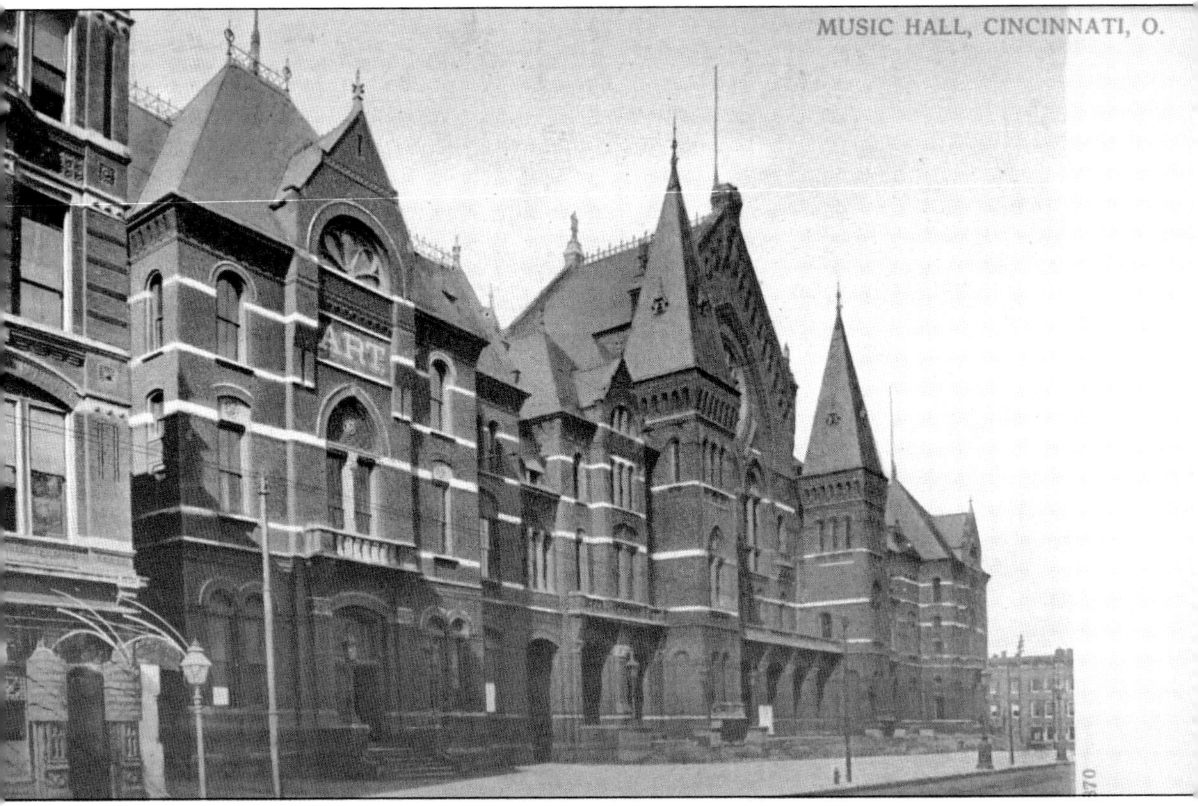

Cincinnati's Gothic Revival Music Hall is considered by many to be architect Samuel Hannaford's crowning achievement. Replacing the earlier Gesang Hall, the building was erected in 1878 as a home for the German music festival Saengerfest. The site, however, has a dark history—Ohio's first lunatic asylum was housed here. Later, it was an orphanage, and it was converted into a pest house during the horrific cholera epidemic of 1832. Afterwards, the land became a potter's field. To this day, construction occasionally unearths remains of the forgotten poor. One electrician working underneath the stage claimed that he saw the apparition of a poor, barefoot girl quietly watching him as he worked. The stone carvings are the work of artist Isaac Graveson. A marvelous baroque ceiling mural, *Allegory of the Arts*, was painted by Conrad Arthur Thomas. The mural had been so covered in residue from cigars and weathering that it had to be "rediscovered" in 1941 and painstakingly restored to its former glory. (From the Collection of the Public Library of Cincinnati and Hamilton County.)

This massive organ once serenaded the ghosts of years past, as Music Hall is reported to be haunted. One often-experienced haunting involves a freight elevator. Some people using the device report hearing an eerie music box playing "Let Me Call You Sweetheart." To no one's surprise, many employees refuse to use that elevator. (From the Collection of the Public Library of Cincinnati and Hamilton County.)

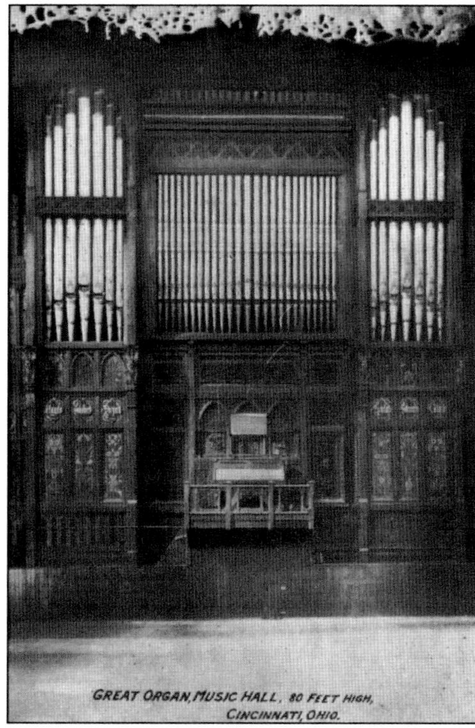

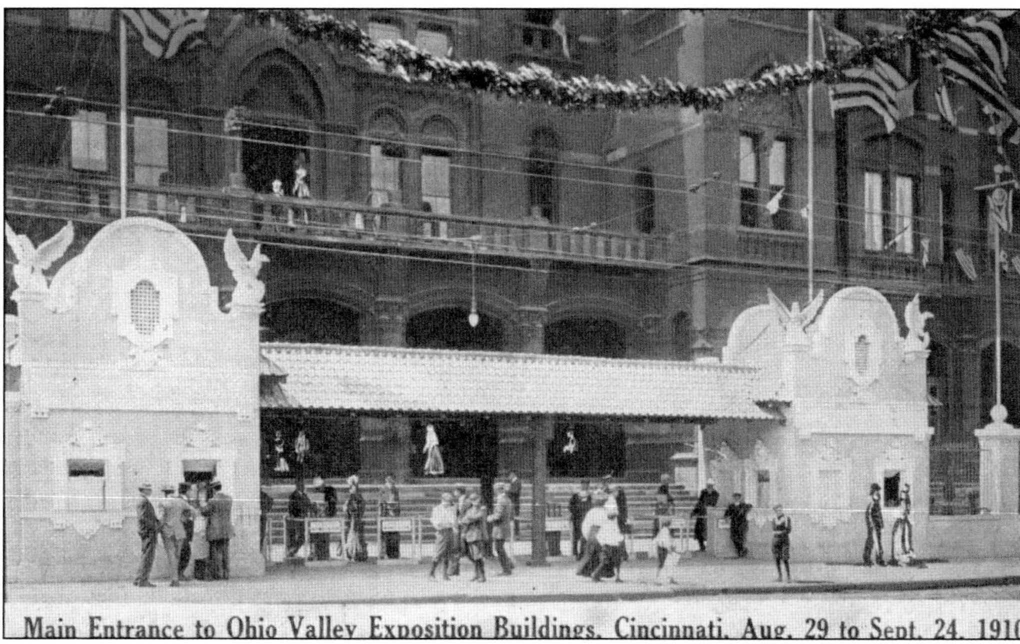

Cincinnati has hosted countless conventions, one of the largest being the Ohio Valley Exposition. To encourage attendance, the promoters even brought in Pres. Theodore Roosevelt for a special "Roosevelt Day." At one point, they even had a "Commercial Travelers' Day." Apparently, this did not work, for when the figures were added up, the event had lost a whopping $30,000. (From the Collection of the Public Library of Cincinnati and Hamilton County.)

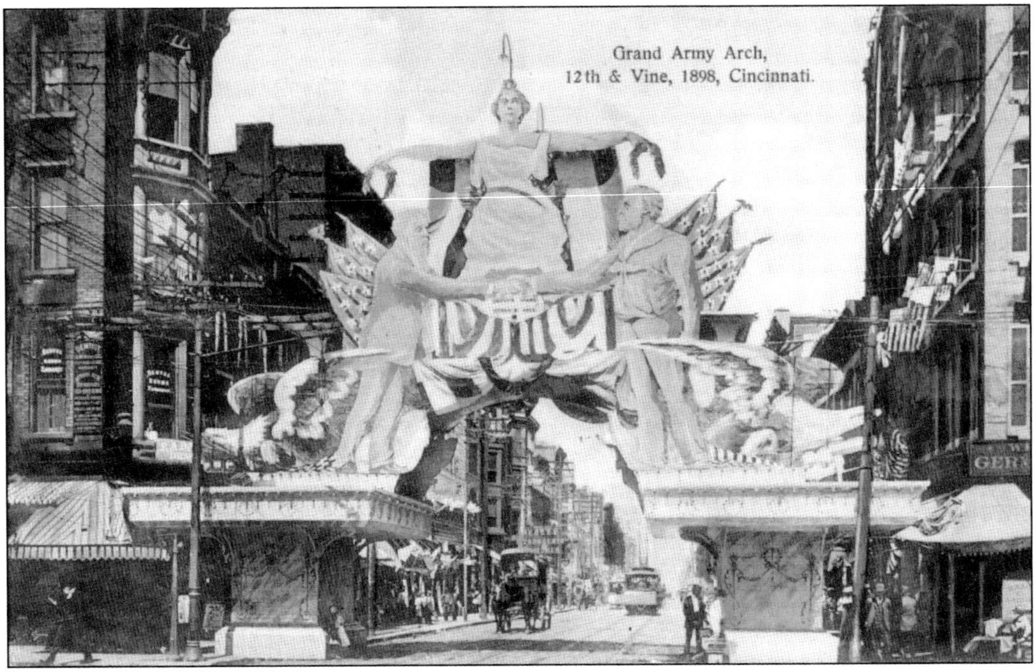

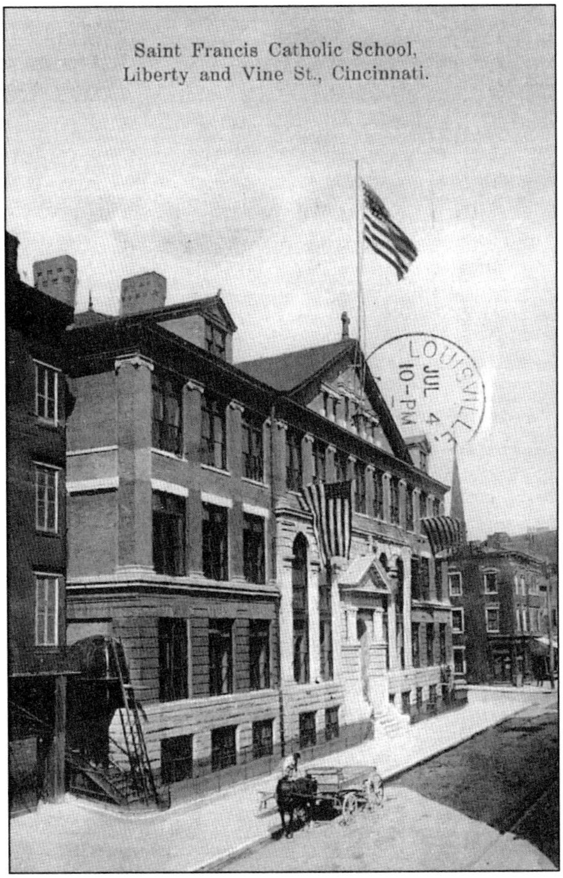

In 1898, Cincinnati hosted an encampment of the Grand Army of the Republic. Although there was an actual camp near the Mill Creek, most of the aging Civil War veterans preferred the comforts of hotels. Despite the image on the great arch, very few Confederate veterans joined in the celebration. (From the Collection of the Public Library of Cincinnati and Hamilton County.)

The corner of Liberty and Vine Streets has housed a Catholic church since 1819. The first Catholic church in the city was built there and then literally rolled downtown, leaving the former site as a cemetery. In 1859, St. Francis Seraph Church was built there, the bodies were moved into a crypt, and the tombstones were used for the floor of the new church. (From the Collection of the Public Library of Cincinnati and Hamilton County.)

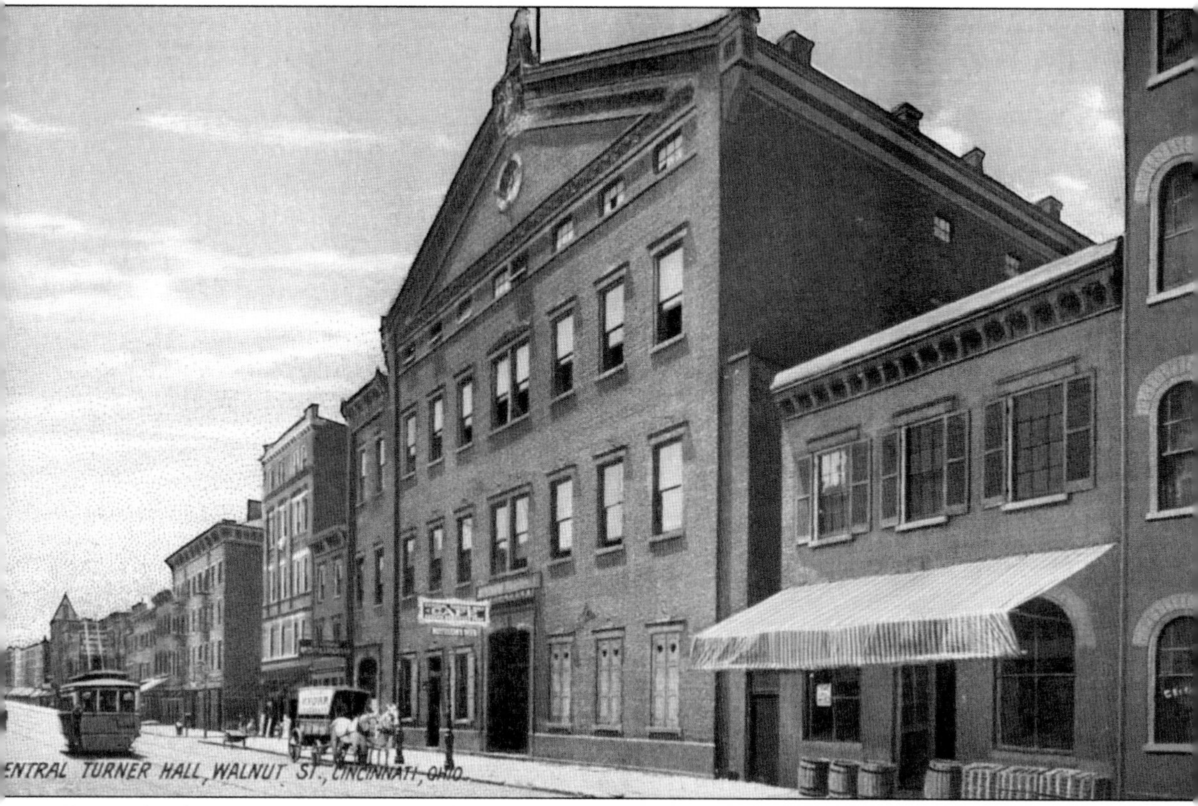

Begun in Germany as a society of resistance fighters against Napoleon, the Turners' motto was *Frisch, Fromm, Froelich, Frei*—or "Fresh, Pious, Merry, Free" in English. Thus, it was no surprise that the Turner Hall at 1410 Walnut Street was a center of German cultural activity in Over-the-Rhine. The facility included a dance hall and a gymnasium. The celebrations often became rowdy, calling for the services of "Big" Mike Arnold, "Happy" Sam Saffin, Cap Bell, and other bouncers who would give the errant partygoers a quick trip to the cobblestones of Walnut Street, very often airborne. Besides social and athletic events, the Turner Hall hosted many political conventions and meetings. The back of the hall led to Wielert's Biergarten, where "Boss" Cox, Rudolph Hynicka, August Hermann, and others sat at their usual large, round table. Messengers would carry results of conventions, running out of the back door of the hall right up to the table, giving Cox news that he had already known before the convention began. (From the Collection of the Public Library of Cincinnati and Hamilton County.)

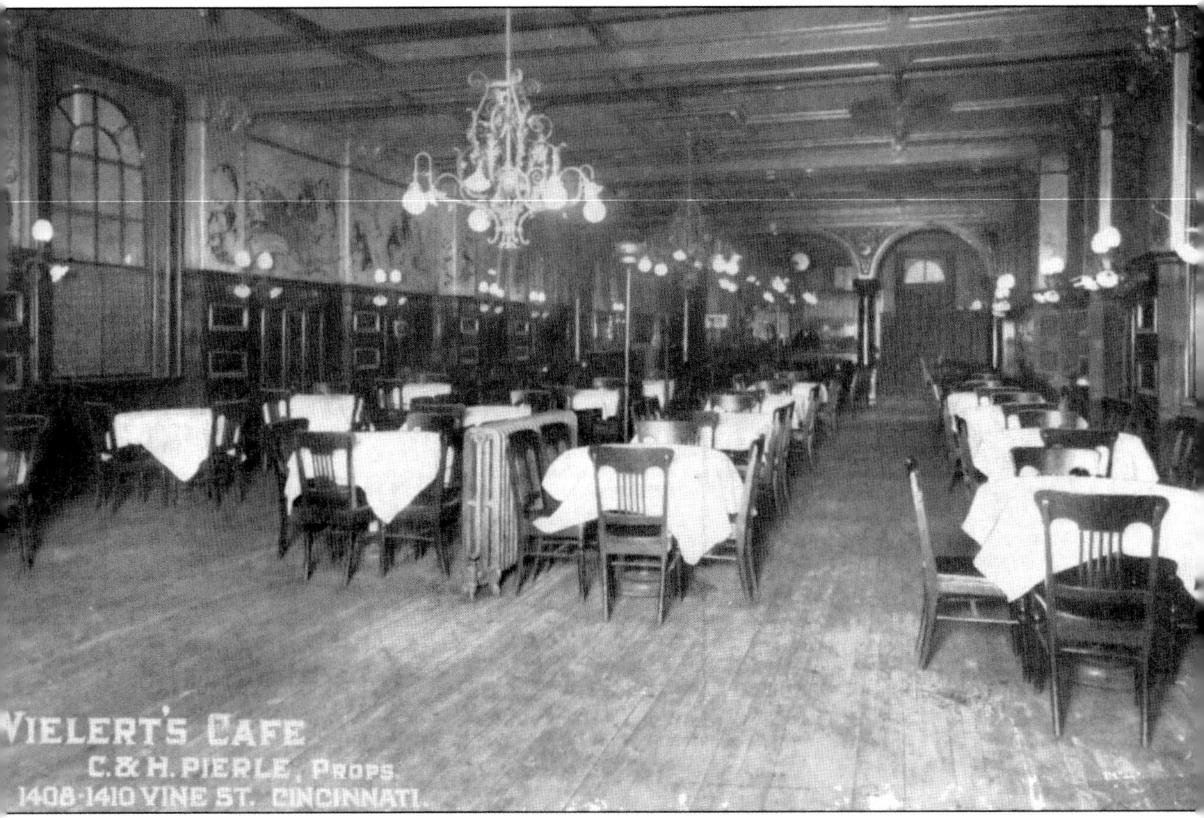

In the early 1900s, Wielert's Biergarten on Vine Street was the de facto city hall. It was a massive establishment with an outdoor garden that extended for an entire block. Begun in 1873 by Heinrich Wielert, the establishment grew to be the finest of many drinking establishments in Over-the-Rhine. Unless they had specifically requested something else, all guests were automatically served Wiener schnitzel, German fried potatoes, and beer. The music was supplied by Michael Brand's Orchestra, which was part of the Cincinnati Symphony. "Boss" Cox and his lieutenants—August Hermann, Rudolph Hynicka, and others—would meet promptly at 5:00 p.m. at his *Stammtisch*, a huge round table. There, sitting like a king on his throne, surrounded by his court, Cox would make the decisions affecting the city. This historic landmark, so long a vital part of Cincinnati, was yet another casualty of Prohibition. (From the Collection of the Public Library of Cincinnati and Hamilton County.)

The McMicken Avenue Protestant church was built because of an argument. In 1890, a group from nearby St. Matthew's was literally locked out. Undaunted, they formed their own church. The famous steeple of this new church shows not a cross, but a hand and finger pointing upwards to heaven. (From the Collection of the Public Library of Cincinnati and Hamilton County.)

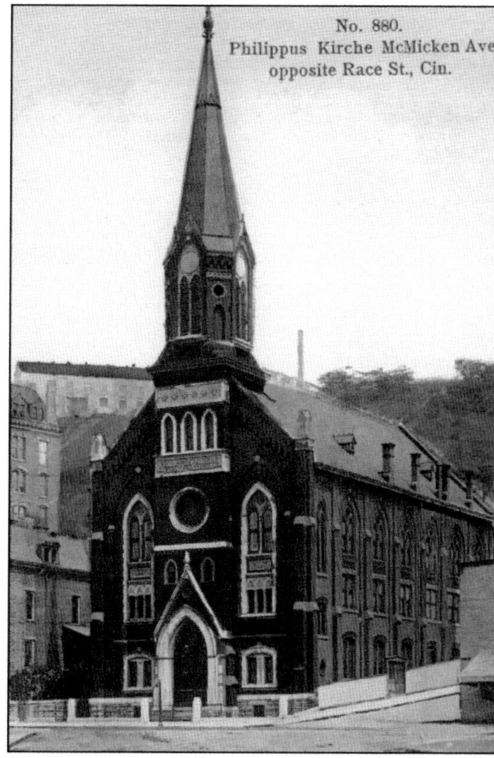

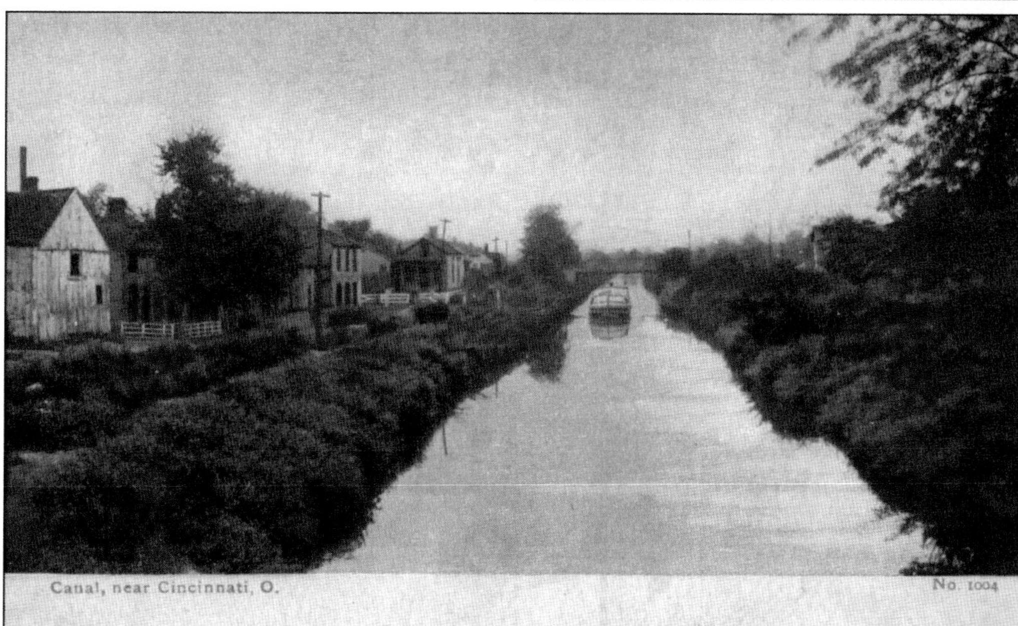

Once during Saengerfest, an enterprising canalboat owner purchased some kegs of beer and tied up right next to the festival. Thirsty Germans, with songs in their hearts, were delighted at this novel way to have a drink. That boat owner made a great deal of money as he brought a bit of Venice to Cincinnati. (From the Collection of the Public Library of Cincinnati and Hamilton County.)

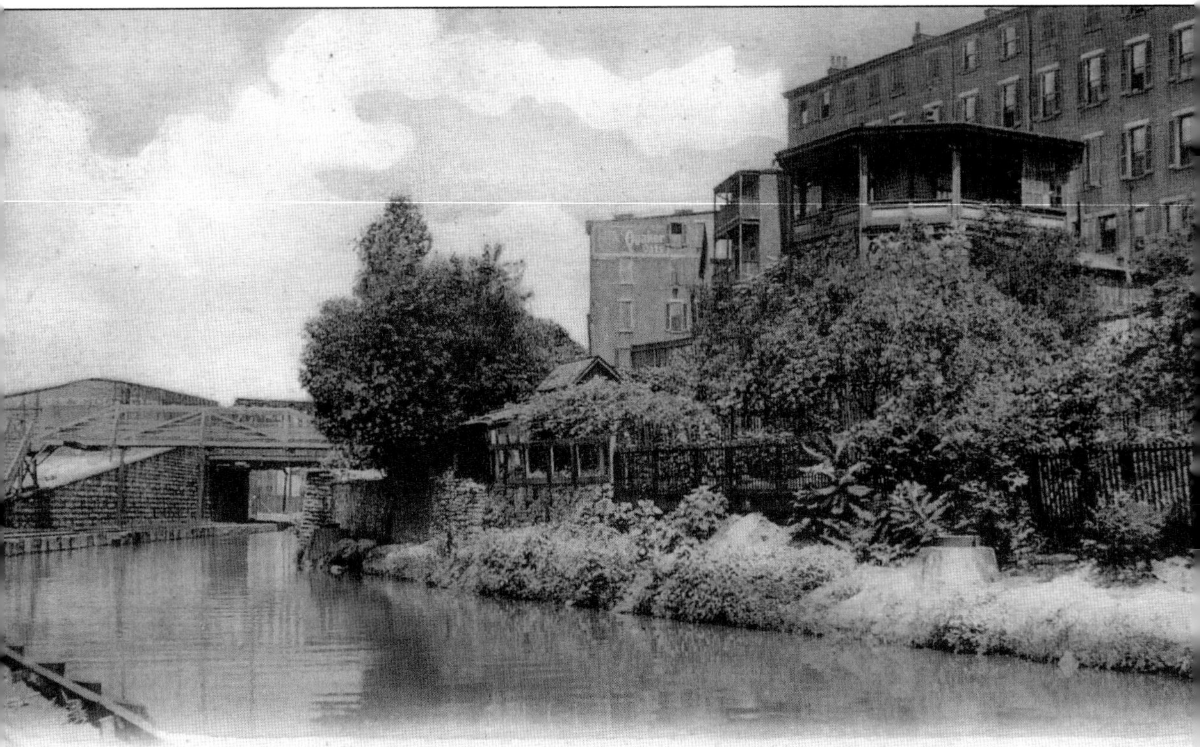

No. 539. Miami & Erie Canal at Brighton, Cincinnati.

Many famous Cincinnatians swam in the Miami-Erie Canal as boys, including Cincinnati mayor Murray Seasongood, Nicholas Longworth, and even William Howard Taft. These happy memories of childhood are recalled in the Charles Ludwig book *Playmates of the Towpath: Memories of the Canal Swimmers Society*: "Off to the Canal we trooped as boys, shouting and laughing, what sweet noise!" The law required bathing suits when swimming in the canal, but boys preferred "more natural" attire. One group of naked youths fled to Findlay Market, where all but one dressed; Adolph Smith lost his clothing and was given a duster by the police. Years later, he became a policeman himself, rising to the rank of lieutenant. On another occasion, having seen a picture of a life preserver in a magazine, some adventurous boys constructed one out of cork from Gerke's Brewery. What they did not notice was how heavy the beer-soaked cork was. Judd Brown, who could not swim, jumped in with it, promptly sank to the bottom, and was saved by a passing fireman. (From the Collection of the Public Library of Cincinnati and Hamilton County.)

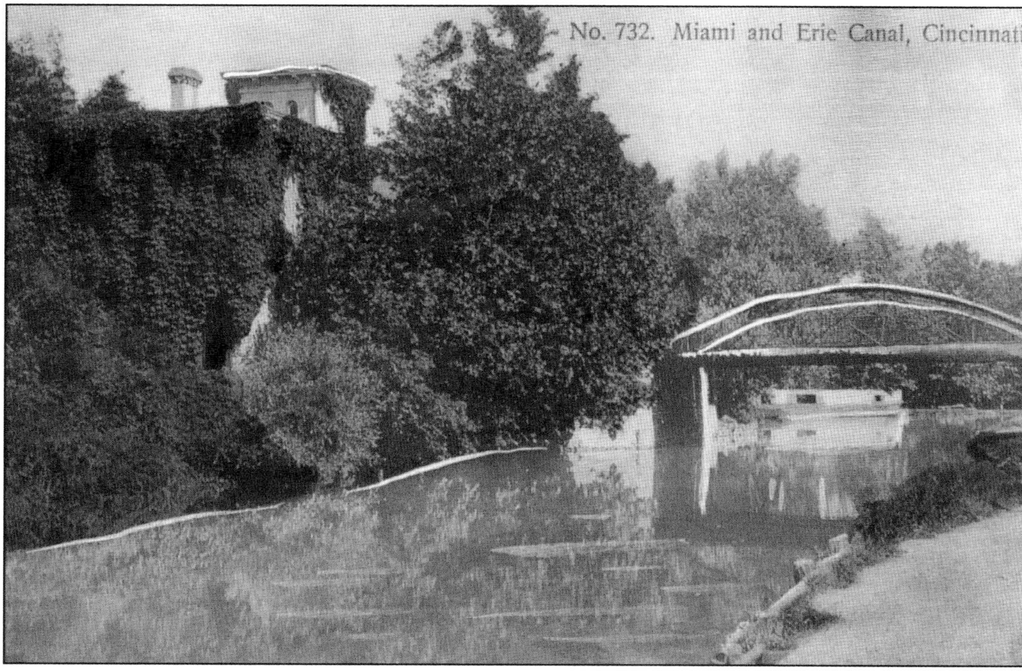

In 1884, the Puritan Boat Club foolishly tried running a steam launch on a cruise on the canal. Both a propeller and a smokestack fell off mid-trip, forcing one member to dive into the water to retrieve the equipment. Later, a tossed cigar blew into the awning, causing the unlucky vessel to erupt into flames. (From the Collection of the Public Library of Cincinnati and Hamilton County.)

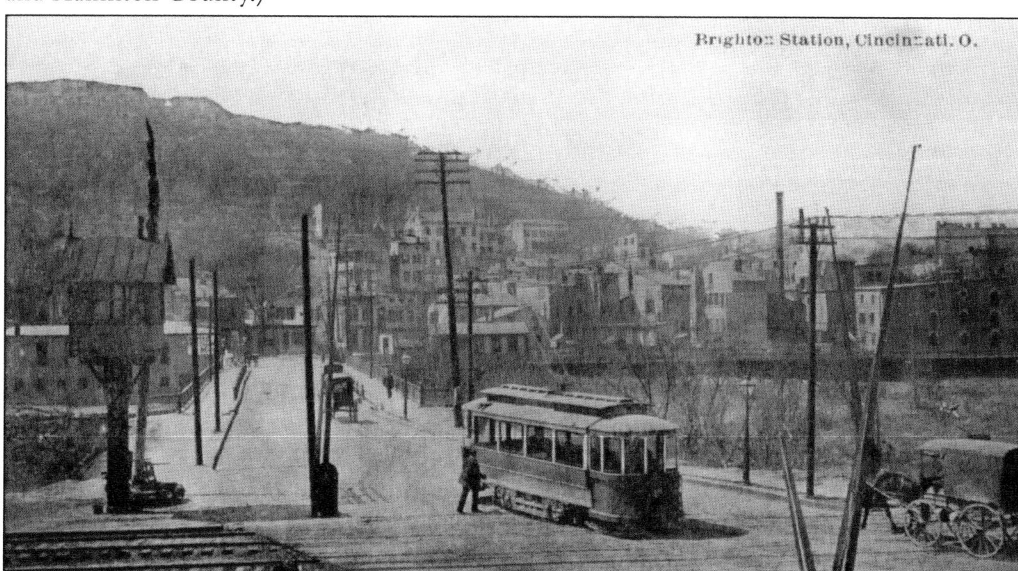

This was the area that put the "pork" in "Porkopolis." Max Mosler once described the neighborhood of Brighton as "the undisputed industrial "bee-hive" of the great Queen City of the West." Four streetcar lines intersected in this area, which was dominated by the stockyards and the Miami-Erie Canal. (From the Collection of the Public Library of Cincinnati and Hamilton County.)

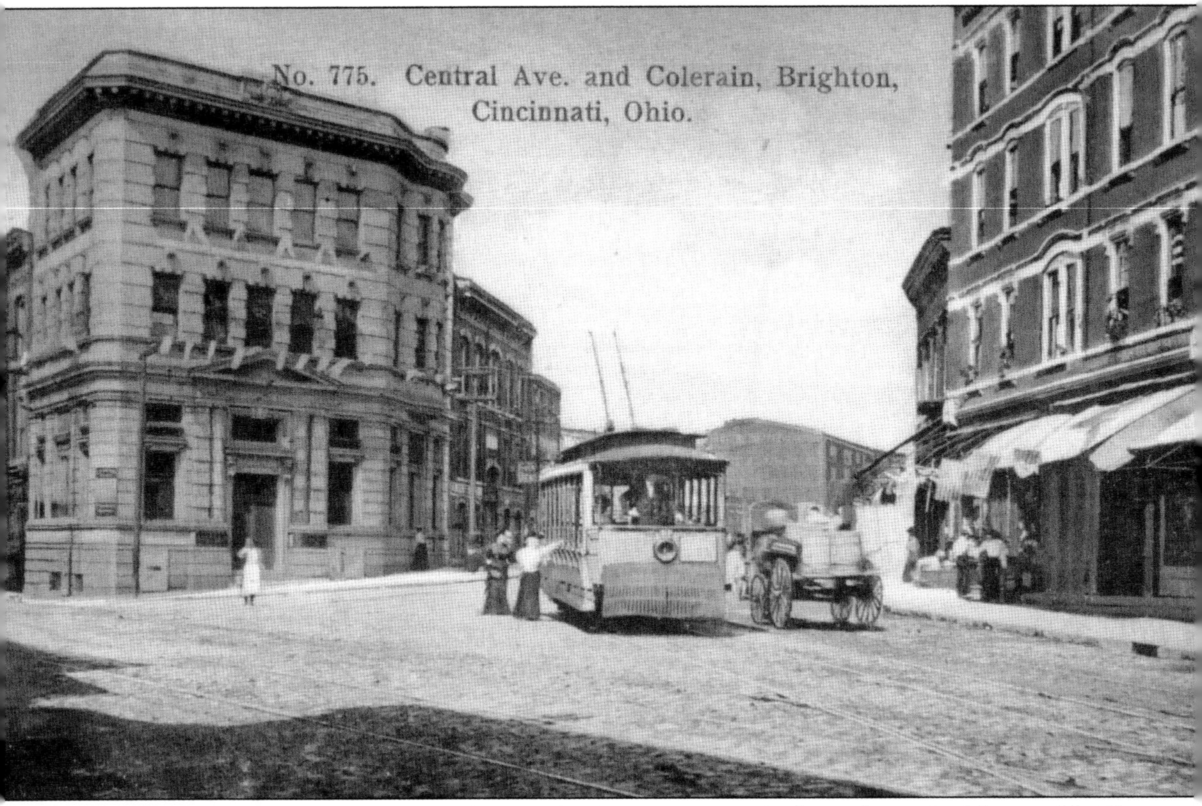

In the 1820s, religious zealot William Miller began to preach about the end of the world. His followers, known as Millerites, erected a large wooden platform at Seventh and John Streets in the West End. They referred to it as their tabernacle. In 1844, Miller announced that on October 22, the world would end and a fiery chariot would come to pick up the faithful. Some followers sold all of their possessions in anticipation of the event. One mechanic sold his $50 set of tools for a mere $3. On the appointed day, shops were closed, one with a sign on the door stating, "Gone to meet the Lord." Dressed in white robes, the followers proceeded to a hill overlooking this Brighton intersection, where they sang and prayed as they waited for Gabriel's horn. As the hours passed, the hymns became less enthusiastic. Finally, when it was apparent that this was not the date of the Second Coming, the people wandered away to try to restart their lives. (From the Collection of the Public Library of Cincinnati and Hamilton County.)

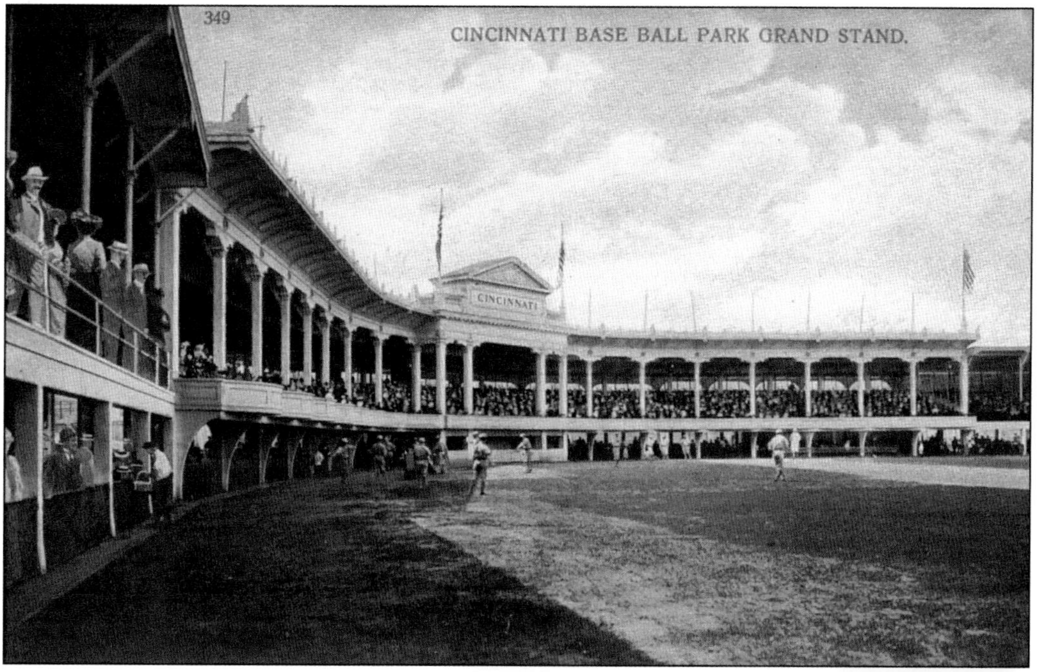

Prior to the construction of Redland (later Crosley) Field, League Park, formerly an abandoned West End brickyard, was the home of the nation's first professional baseball team, the Cincinnati Red Stockings. Fire destroyed the stands in 1900, when the team was owned by August Hermann. The price of beer at the time was 12 for $1. (From the Collection of the Public Library of Cincinnati and Hamilton County.)

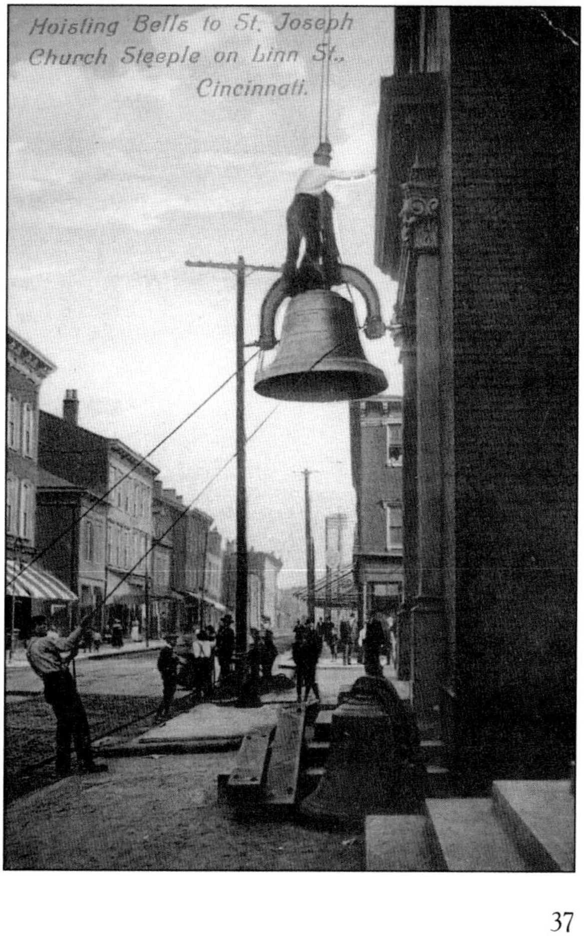

The most endearing landmarks in most communities are churches. Since the 18th century, Cincinnatians have lived their lives to the sound of church bells. Here, a young workman takes a thrilling, albeit dangerous, ride to the steeple of the old St. Joseph Church in the West End. (From the Collection of the Public Library of Cincinnati and Hamilton County.)

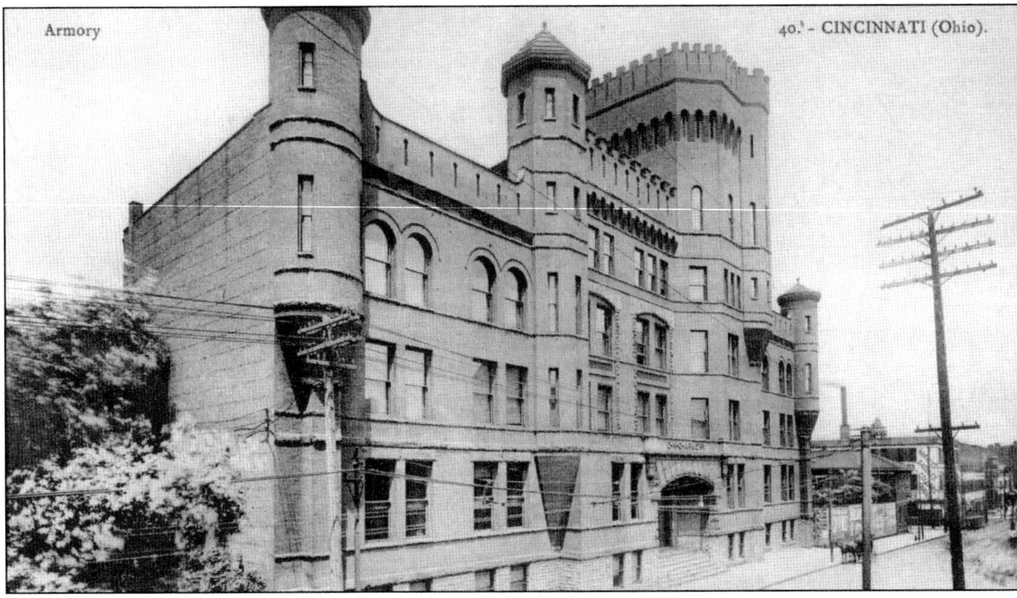

This majestic 1886 Hannaford building housed the National Guard Armory in the West End and was so magnificent that the name of the street was changed to Armory after the Spanish-American War. The building also served as a location for numerous dances and other events. It was closed in 1960 and later demolished. (From the Collection of the Public Library of Cincinnati and Hamilton County.)

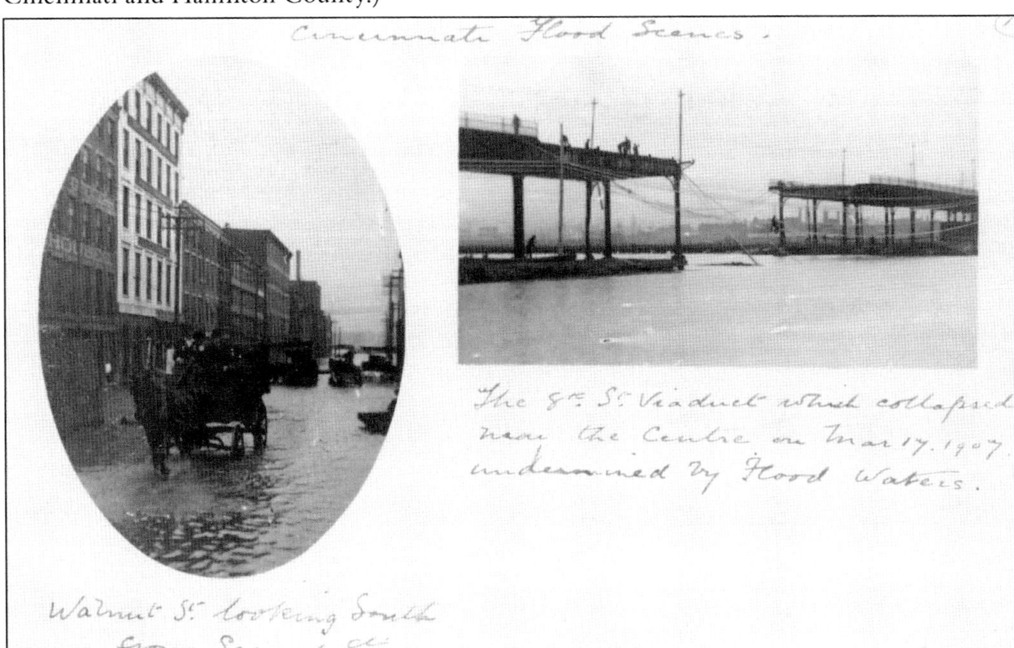

Describing the 1907 Cincinnati flood, witness John Bateman said, "I noticed the conduct of the earth, which looked as though it had cramps." Preceded by a geyser that broke through the pavement, 120 feet of this old landmark roadway collapsed into the floodwater below. Luckily, only a streetcar and two wagons were on the viaduct at the time, all stopped safely. (From the Collection of the Public Library of Cincinnati and Hamilton County.)

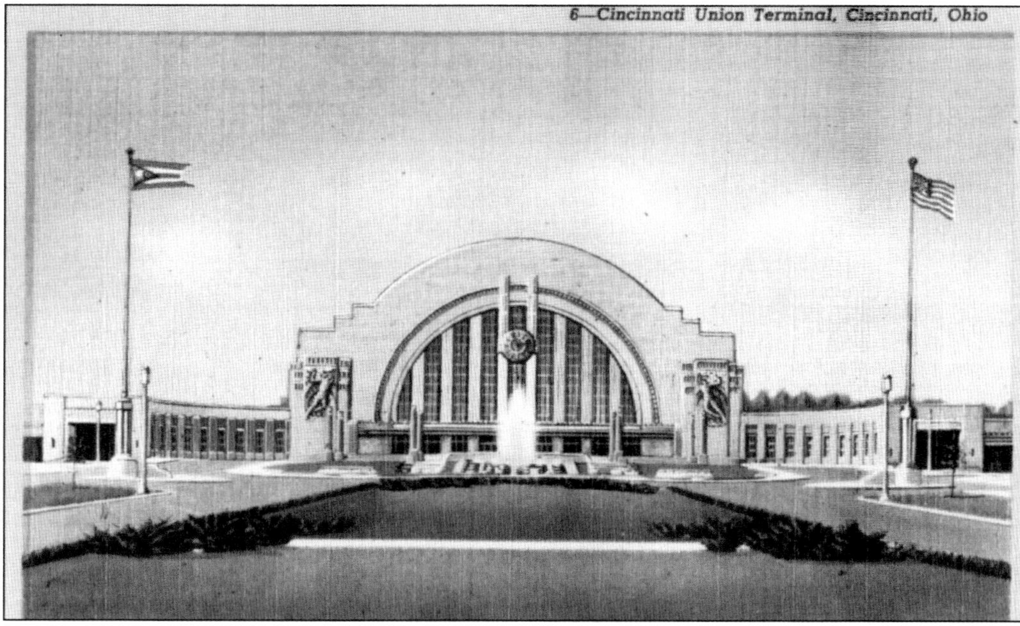

In 1933, seven railroads moved their stations to one structure, Union Terminal, in the West End. The building, designed by Alfred Fellheimer and Stewart Wagner, is a masterpiece of the Art Deco style. The building now houses the Cincinnati Museum Center, featuring three major museums, a theater, the Cincinnati Historical Society and Library, as well as special traveling exhibits. (Courtesy of the Kenton County Public Library, Covington, Kentucky.)

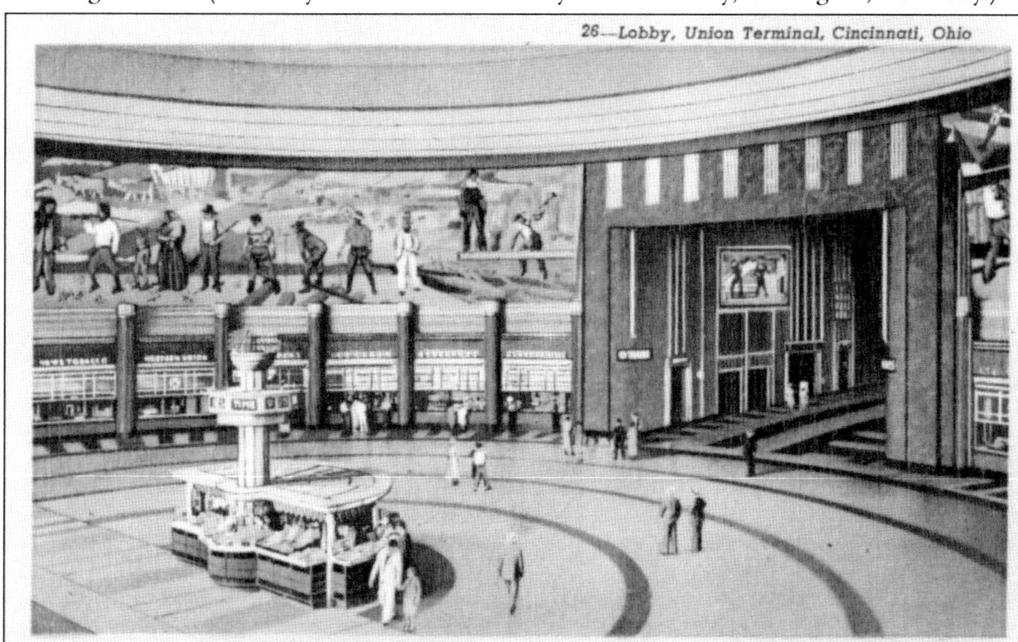

Among the most magnificent features of the Union Terminal are the majestic murals by Winold Reiss. In 1974, when the future of the building was uncertain due to the decline of passenger railroads, some of these murals were moved to the Cincinnati–Northern Kentucky International Airport. (Courtesy of the Kenton County Public Library, Covington, Kentucky.)

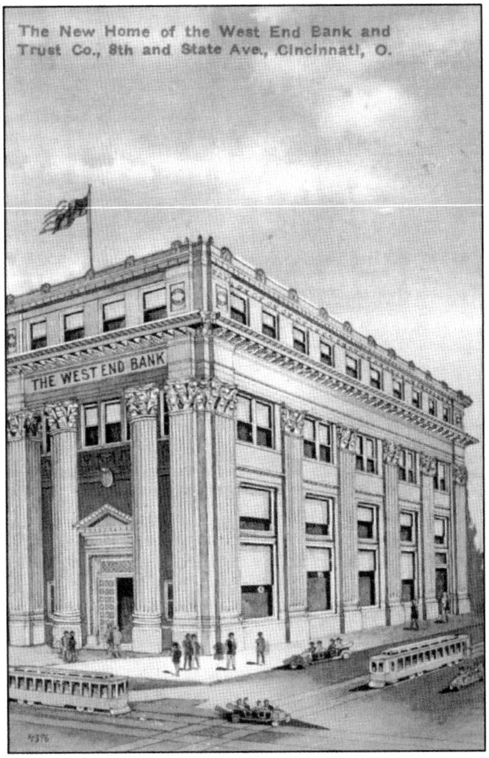

This Classical Revival structure, the West End Bank and Trust, was built in 1914. It was later a branch of the Fifth Third Bank until it closed in 1985. While the elegant building no longer functions as a bank, it still remains today as a reminder of past glories of the busy intersection of Eighth and State Streets. (From the Collection of the Public Library of Cincinnati and Hamilton County.)

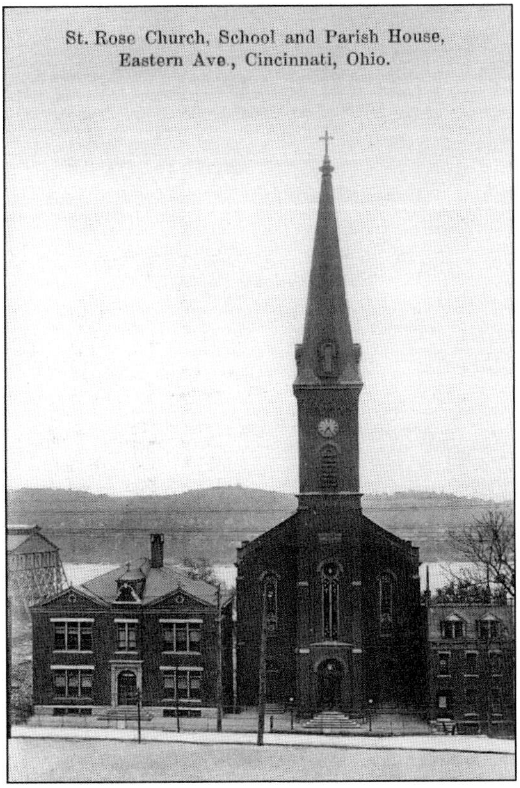

In the back parking lot of this East End church, the water levels of the many floods that have engulfed the church over the years are clearly marked on the wall. Amidst the cluster of dates, 1884 is clearly the highest. However, standing alone, 10 feet above the cluster, is the staggering mark from the 1937 flood. (From the Collection of the Public Library of Cincinnati and Hamilton County.)

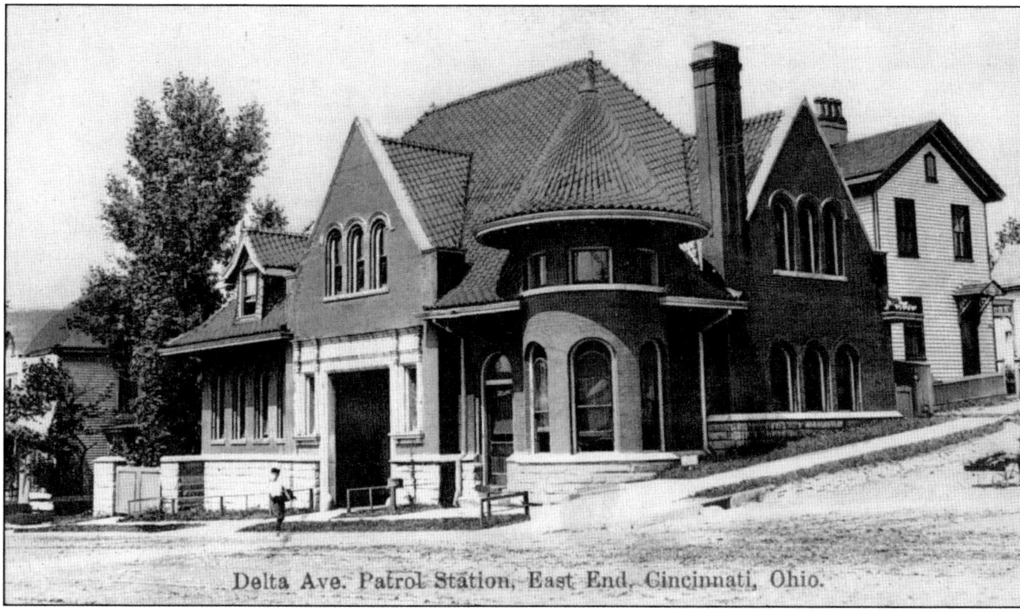

The sight of this Eastside landmark may make some people hungry. The Romanesque Revival structure at Delta Avenue and Columbia Parkway was originally Cincinnati Police Patrol House No. 6. Years later, it was purchased by entrepreneur Jeff Ruby, and in 1981, it was transformed into his popular steak house, The Precinct. (From the Collection of the Public Library of Cincinnati and Hamilton County.)

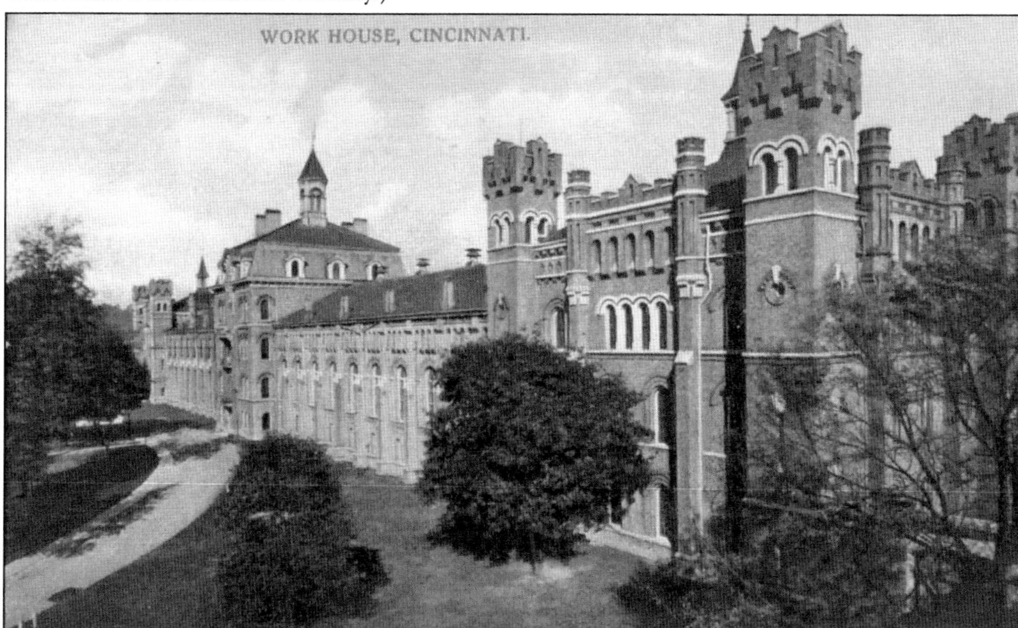

This building may look beautiful, but it is not one a person would wish to visit. The castle-like edifice, begun in 1866, is the old Cincinnati Workhouse. From 1869, thousands of prisoners were held there. Before the structure was demolished in 1991, numerous films, including Sylvester Stallone's *Lock Up*, were filmed there. (From the Collection of the Public Library of Cincinnati and Hamilton County.)

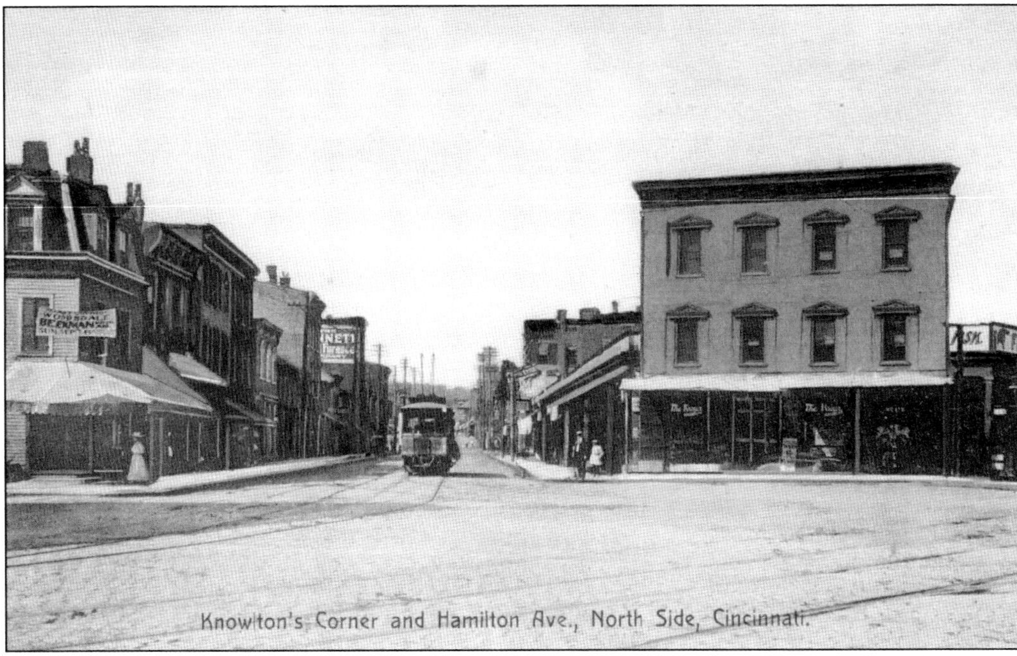

Knowlton's Corner has always been a crossroads. Native Americans had two trails that intersected at this point near the Mill Creek. By 1790, settlers had turned these trails into roads, naming them after generals Anthony Wayne and Arthur St. Clair. In 1830, Ephraim Knowlton built a store at the intersection. Later, numerous streetcar lines converged here. (From the Collection of the Public Library of Cincinnati and Hamilton County.)

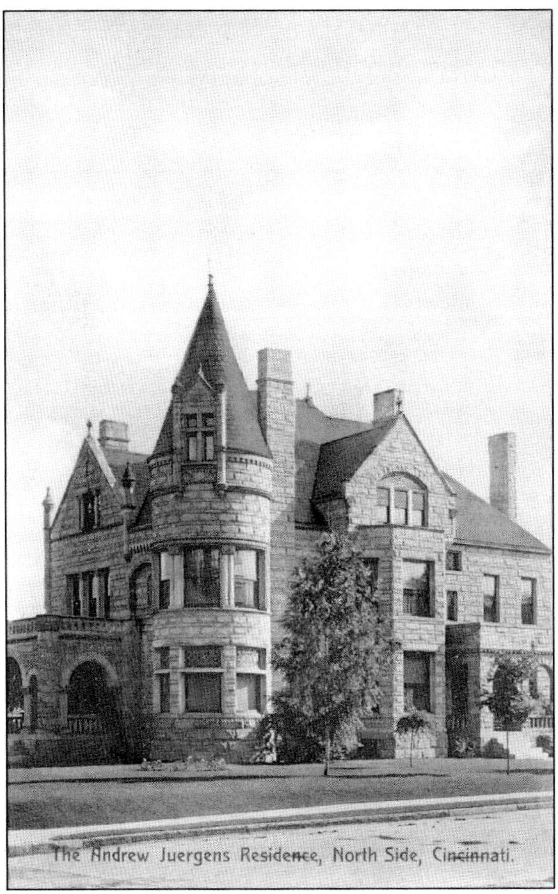

This spectacular Gothic Revival mansion at the corner of Hamilton and Bruce Avenues was the home of Andrew Jergens. After the death of his son, the mansion was torn down and converted into a playground. In 1882, Jergens cofounded what became one of the largest soap companies in the world. This intersection in Northside became known as Millionaire's Corner. (From the Collection of the Public Library of Cincinnati and Hamilton County.)

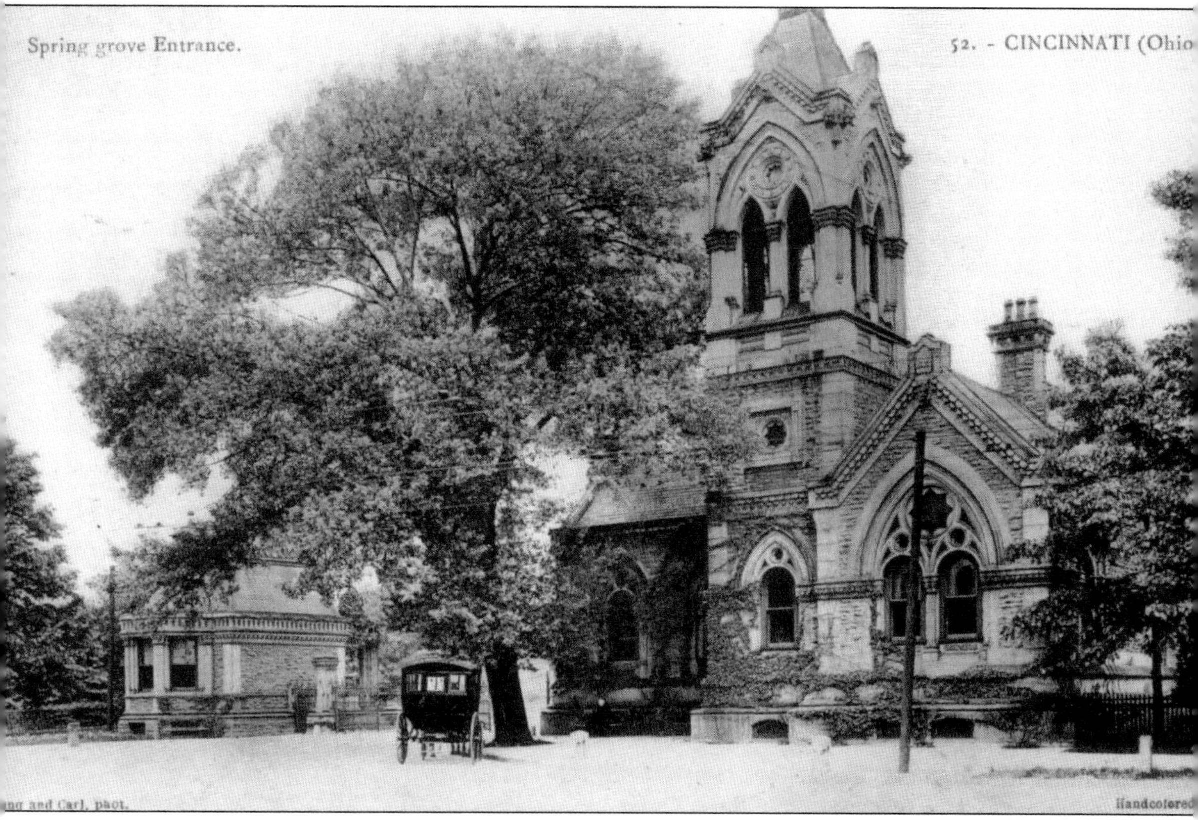

One of Cincinnati's most remarkable landmarks, Spring Grove Cemetery is among the largest in the nation and is definitely one of the most beautiful. At one time, people had to pay an admission price to enter and walk about. Chartered in 1844 by Salmon Chase, who was later Lincoln's secretary of the treasury and a chief justice, the grounds were meticulously landscaped by Adolph Strauch. There are 12 lakes and ponds amidst winding roads passing a wide array of monuments. History abounds, as there are 40 Union generals buried here, including Joseph Hooker, the warrior-poet William Lytle, and Confederate brevet general Philip Luckett. One can also see the resting places of Alphonso Taft, William Procter, James Gamble, and many others. On the gate building seen here, there is a brass plaque showing the height of the water in the 1937 flood. (From the Collection of the Public Library of Cincinnati and Hamilton County.)

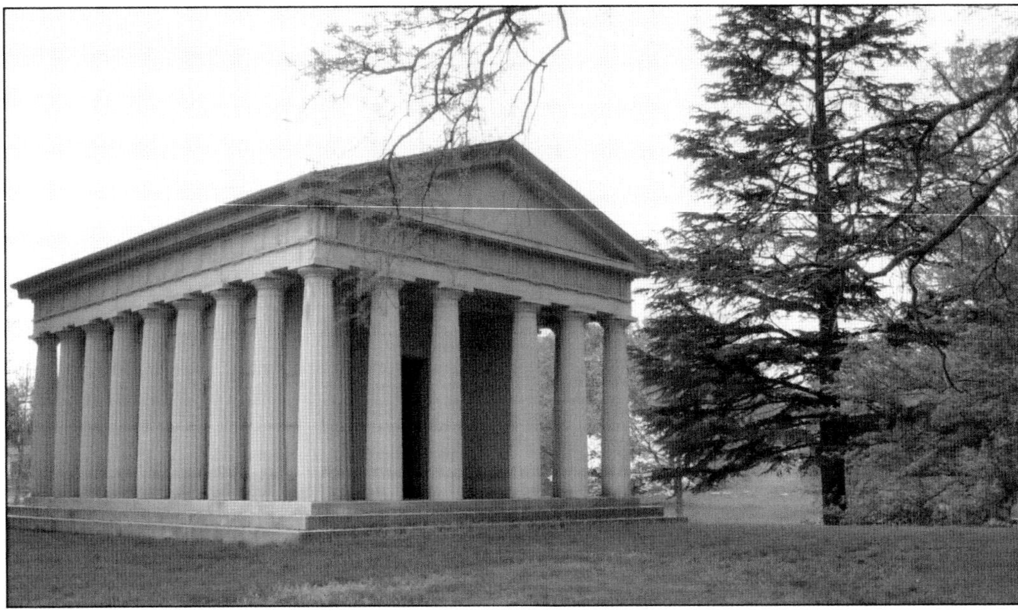

Almost every weekend of the year, bridal parties have their photographs taken in front of this ornate mausoleum based on the Parthenon. This is the resting place of Charles Fleischmann, a Hungarian immigrant and businessman, who founded the famous Fleischmann Yeast Company in 1868 with James Gaff. Fleischmann's son, Julius, was later elected mayor of Cincinnati. (Photograph by Jordan Rolfes.)

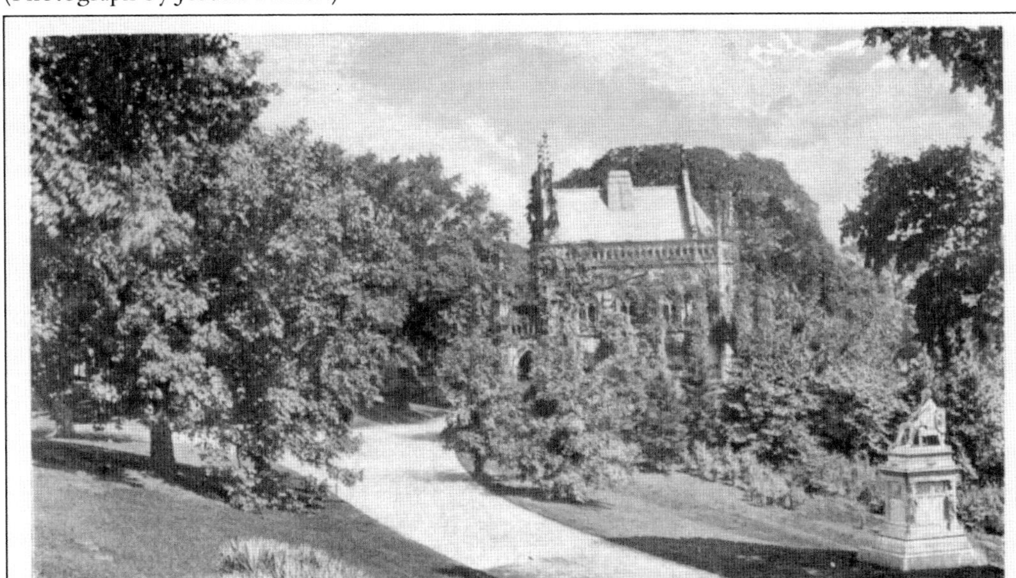

In 1869, architect James Keys Wilson, who also designed the Isaac Wise Temple, created this Gothic Revival mausoleum for Edmund Dexter, complete with flying buttresses. This is undoubtedly one of the most photographed spots in Spring Grove. Dexter was a 19th-century whiskey baron whose brother, Julius Dexter, was a state senator. The cost of the mausoleum was $100,000, a massive sum at the time. (From the Collection of the Public Library of Cincinnati and Hamilton County.)

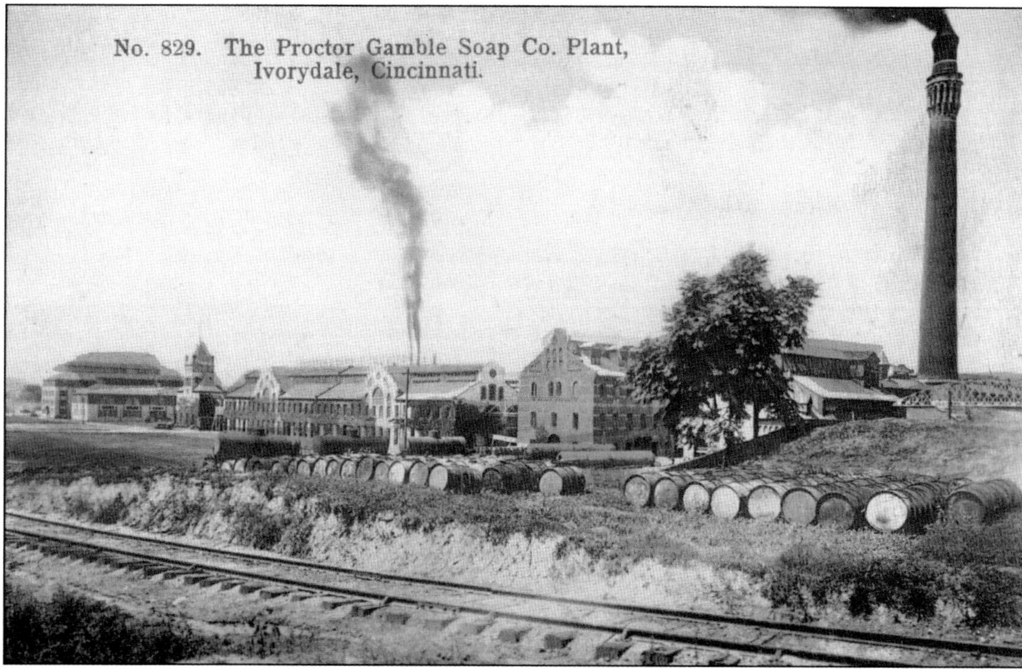

One cannot discuss Cincinnati without mentioning Procter & Gamble. In 1837, two brothers-in-law, William Procter and James Gamble, began a candle-making business at Sixth and Main Streets. They soon outgrew their modest beginnings and built a factory in the West End. In 1884, that factory burned down. They expanded again, this time to what is now known as Ivorydale. (From the Collection of the Public Library of Cincinnati and Hamilton County.)

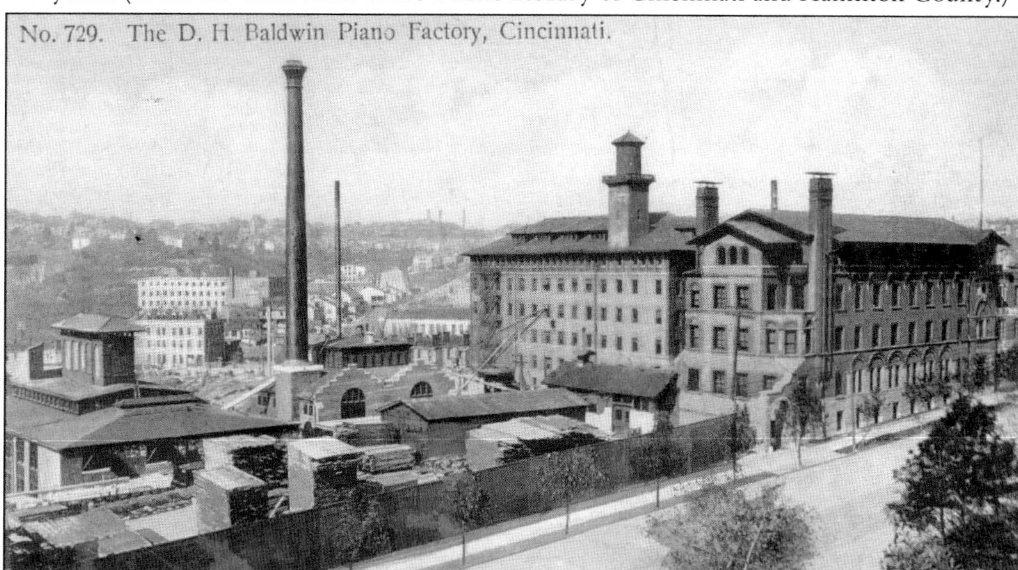

Two great keyboard manufacturers, Wurlitzer and Baldwin, began in Cincinnati in the 1800s. Dwight Hamilton Baldwin started as a piano dealer in 1862. After the Civil War, he began manufacturing his own pianos. This Gilbert Avenue factory once consisted of six buildings, including laboratories to create new wood treatments and resins to produce the finest sound. (From the Collection of the Public Library of Cincinnati and Hamilton County.)

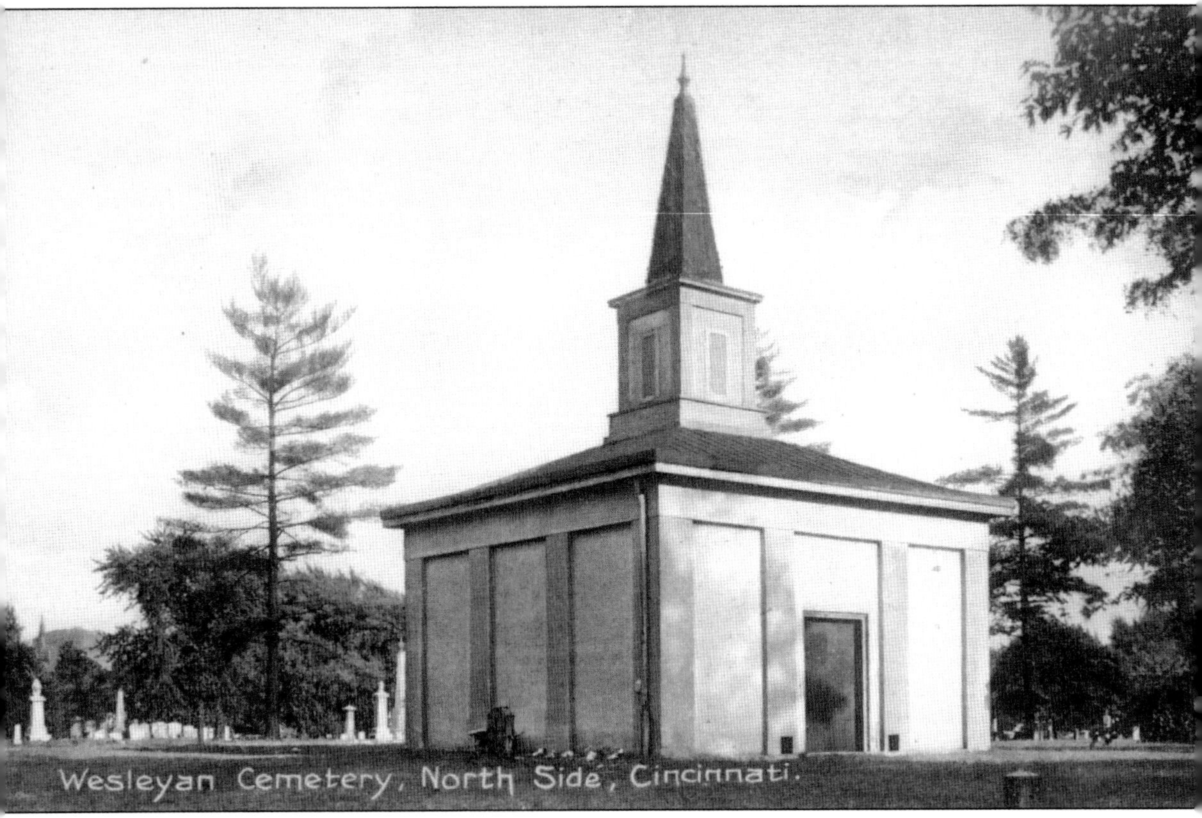

Wesleyan Cemetery on Colerain Avenue in Northside is the oldest continuous working cemetery in Hamilton County and the final resting place for veterans of the Revolutionary and Civil Wars. Among those buried here are Richard Allison, the physician general of the Army (later known as the surgeon general) from 1792 to 1796, who also established the first permanent physician's office in Cincinnati, and William Steinmetz, who received a Medal of Honor for his bravery at the Battle of Vicksburg. Thousands of families have loved ones buried in this parklike cemetery founded in 1843 by the Methodist church. Sadly, Wesleyan has been neglected for years. In 1992, investigations revealed that "Perpetual Care" funds had disappeared, graves had allegedly been resold, and human skeletal remains were discovered discarded on this once prestigious cemetery. Amidst the legal confusion, the grounds were abandoned and soon became overgrown as the fate of the cemetery was now in the hands of the courts. After a public outcry, the local government assumed care of the landscaping. Conditions at Wesleyan are now slowly improving. (From the Collection of the Public Library of Cincinnati and Hamilton County.)

Three

Riding the Inclines to the Summits

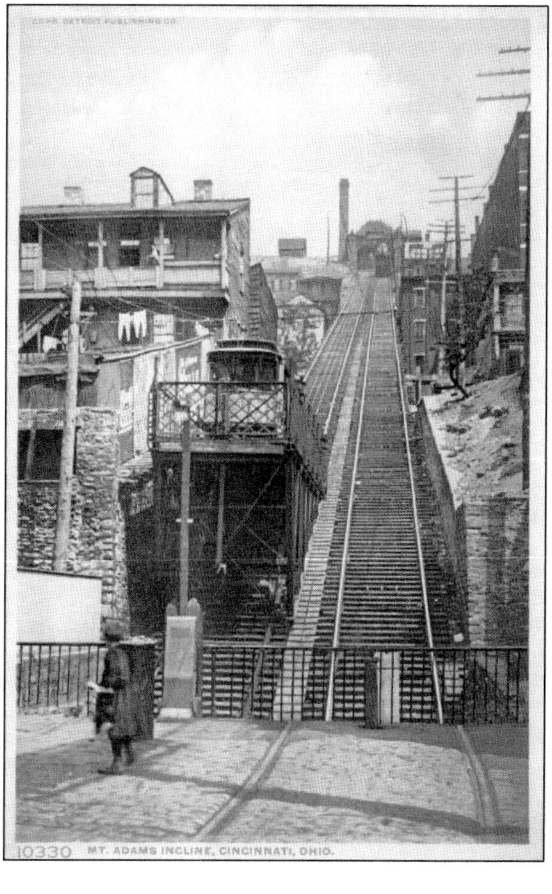

On May 12, 1872, the Over-the-Rhine area was crammed with 60,000 people, all ready to take the 60-second ride up Mount Auburn in the newfangled Incline. The machine changed the city forever, as people were able to escape the smoke and congestion of the basin and move to the summits. Only four years later, people could ride this incline to Mount Adams. (From the Collection of the Public Library of Cincinnati and Hamilton County.)

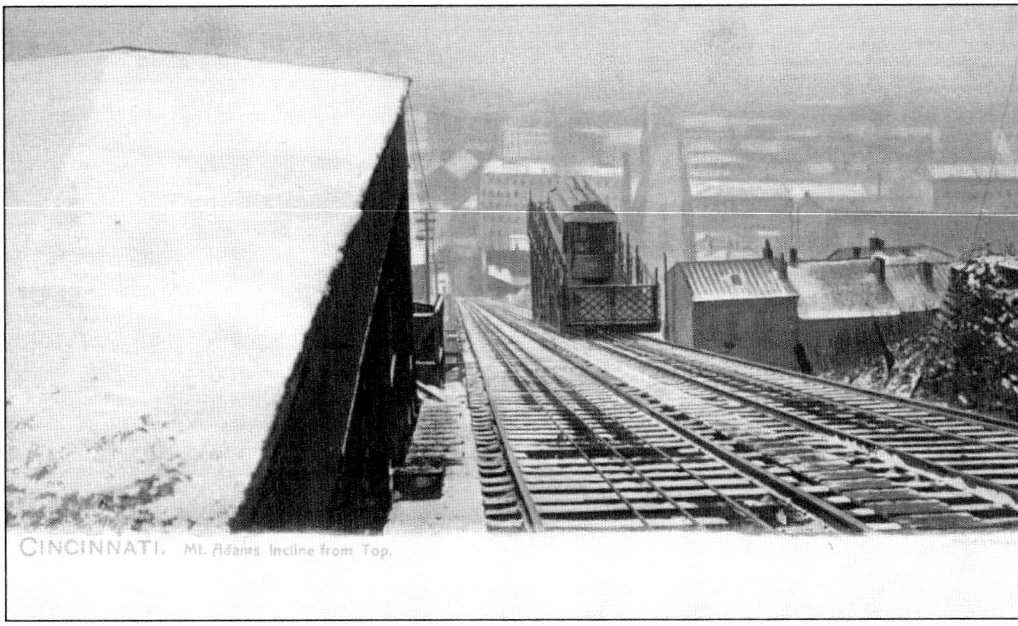

At the summit of each incline, a restaurant offered a breathtaking view of the great city below. This is the view enjoyed by patrons of the Highland House, at the top of the Mount Adams Incline. Built in 1875, Highland House was one of the most popular incline resorts. (From the Collection of the Public Library of Cincinnati and Hamilton County.)

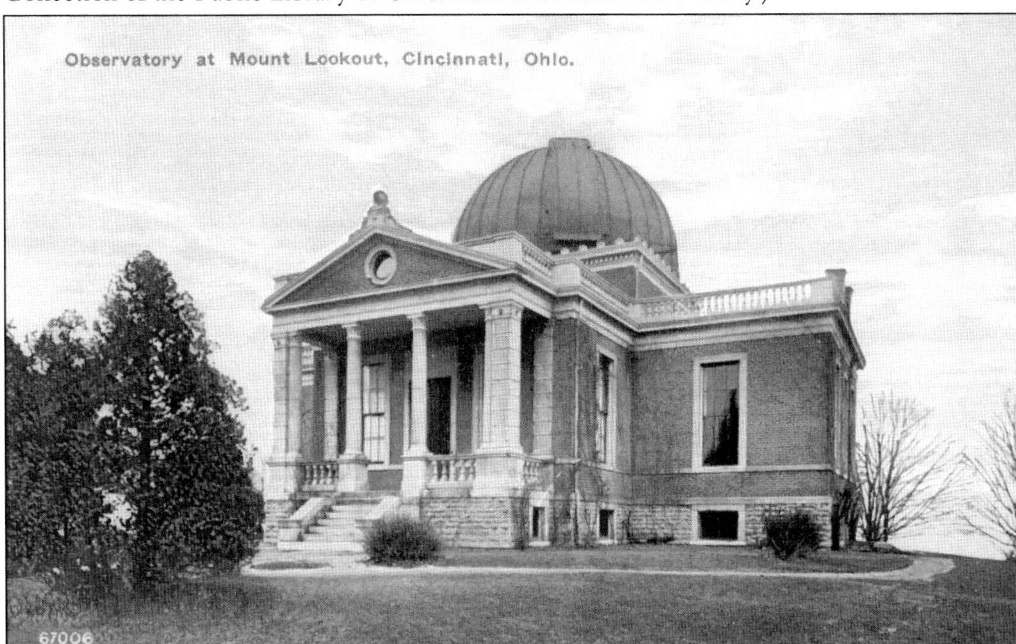

In 1843, John Quincy Adams gave a speech dedicating the almost completed observatory on Mount Ida, which was later named Mount Adams. The observatory was the brainchild of Ormsby Mitchel, who died in the Civil War. When it was finally completed in 1873, the air was too dirty to see anything, so the facility was moved to Mount Lookout. (From the Collection of the Public Library of Cincinnati and Hamilton County.)

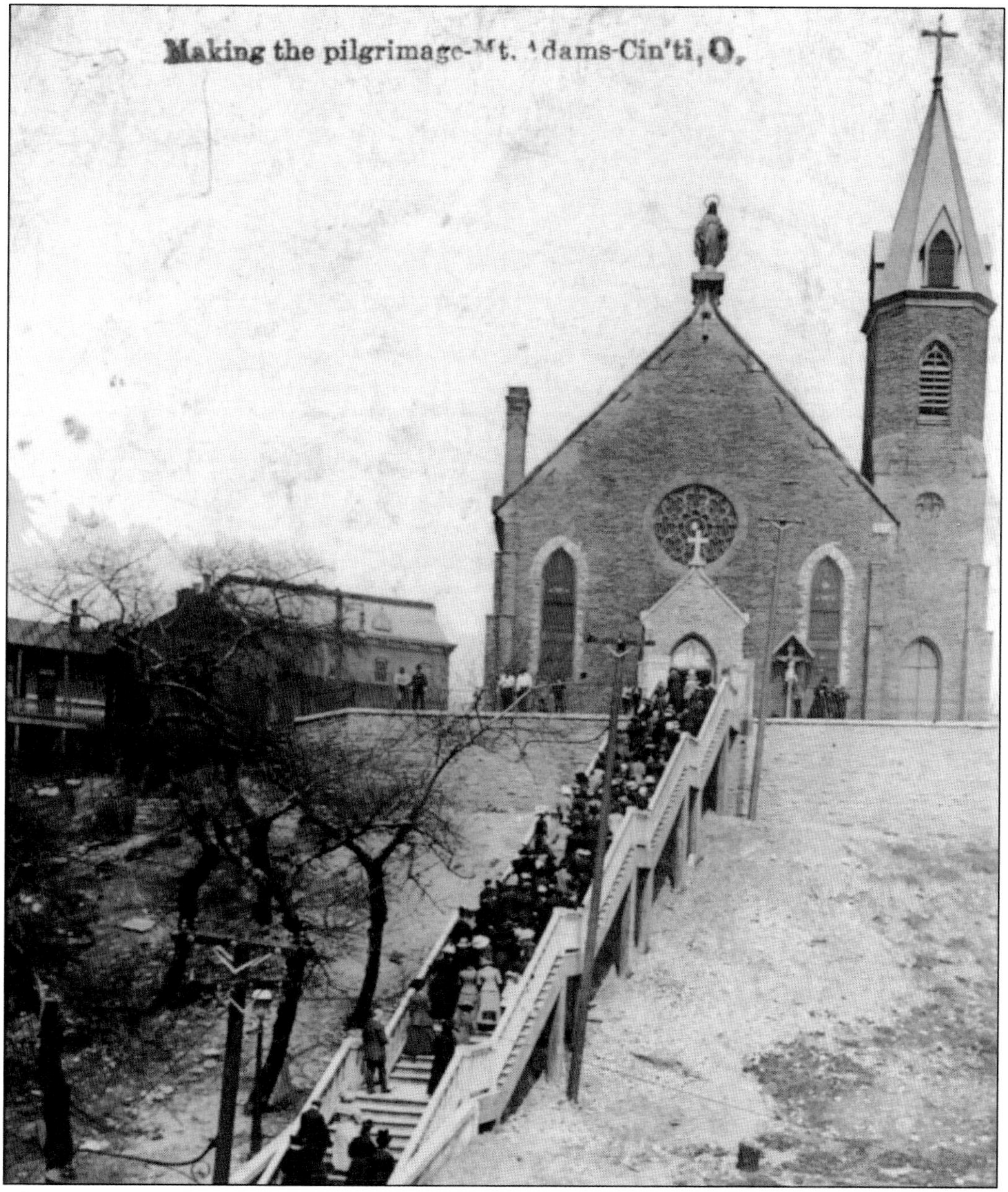

The statue of Mary stands watch over the city below, a reassuring landmark visible from the entire basin area. The famous Immaculata Church in Mount Adams was the result of a prayer made by Archbishop John Baptist Purcell. When caught in a storm at sea, he promised to build a church at the highest point in Cincinnati. A curious and beautiful tradition has grown from this Gothic Revival church: since 1860 on Good Friday, Christians of all denominations have come together to "pray the steps" leading up to the church. Once at the top, it is customary to kiss the crucifix by the entrance to the church. The cross that stands there now is a replacement of the original. Over the decades, the steps have had to be replaced several times due to the wear of the annual army of pilgrims. This ritual of faith has continued uninterrupted for 150 years, with many families passing on the tradition from generation to generation. (From the Collection of the Public Library of Cincinnati and Hamilton County.)

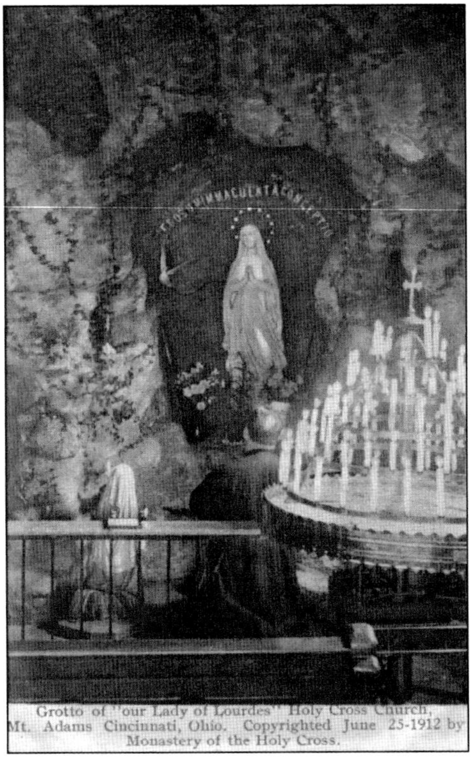

The final stop for Good Friday pilgrims was at the nearby Holy Cross Monastery, the original site of the observatory, where, rather than studying the heavens, one would pray to heaven. Here, pilgrims descended into a catacomb to venerate the relics of a Roman martyr. The monastery closed in 1977, and the structure is now an office building. (From the Collection of the Public Library of Cincinnati and Hamilton County.)

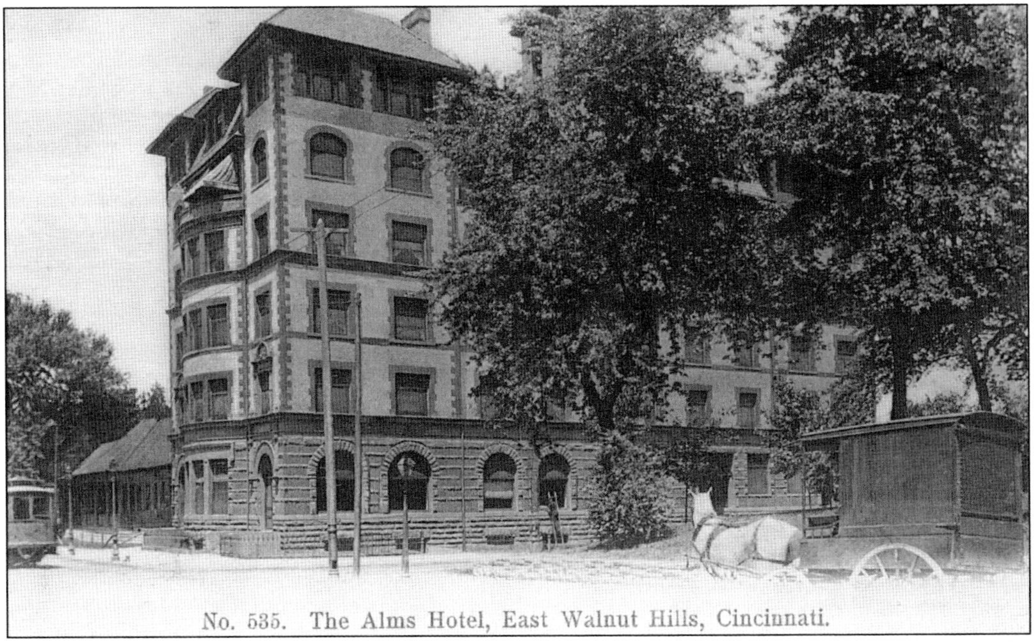

It was from this Walnut Hills hotel, the Hotel Alms, that Imogene Remus began the fateful journey that ended in her murder in Eden Park. The lodging was opened in 1891 by Frederick Alms, whose own house was right across the street (behind the wagon in this postcard). Radio stations WKRC and later WAIF were once located in the building. (From the Collection of the Public Library of Cincinnati and Hamilton County.)

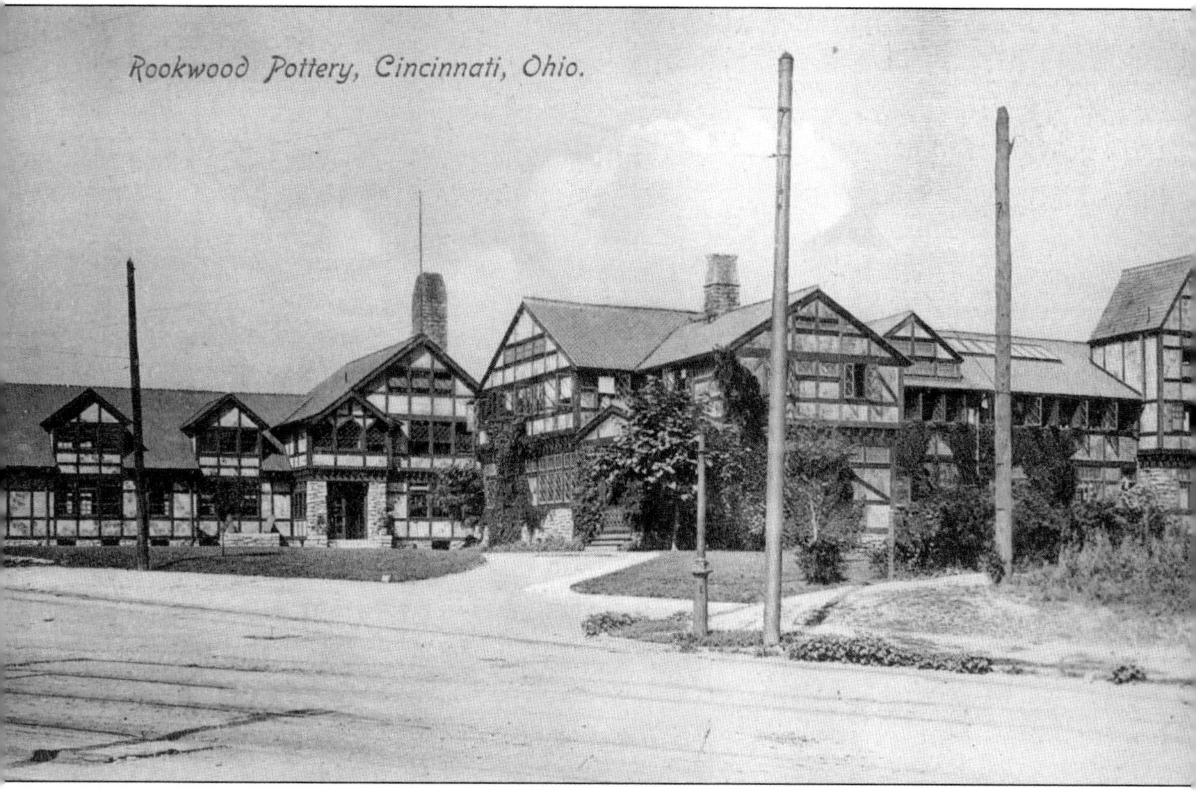

An angry young woman, a misplaced letter, and an exasperated father all helped to create one of Cincinnati's most beloved landmarks. In 1877, the Pottery Club was formed and Maria Longworth, the daughter of Joseph Longworth, was invited to join. However, the letter never arrived. In anger, she determined that she would make her own pottery. Despite the fact that her wealthy father said he could easily afford to buy any pottery she wanted, she insisted on making her own. Joseph Longworth first purchased an old schoolhouse on Eastern Avenue for her ceramics and later moved the operation to an abandoned fireworks factory on Celestial Street in Mount Adams. Soon, masterpieces in pottery were being created here. Known as the Rookwood, it soon became a thriving business, creating stunning works of art. The artists engaged here included the celebrated painter Henry Farny and Japanese artist Katoro Shirayamadani. The pottery closed in 1960, and the building is now a popular restaurant commanding a magnificent view of the city below. (From the Collection of the Public Library of Cincinnati and Hamilton County.)

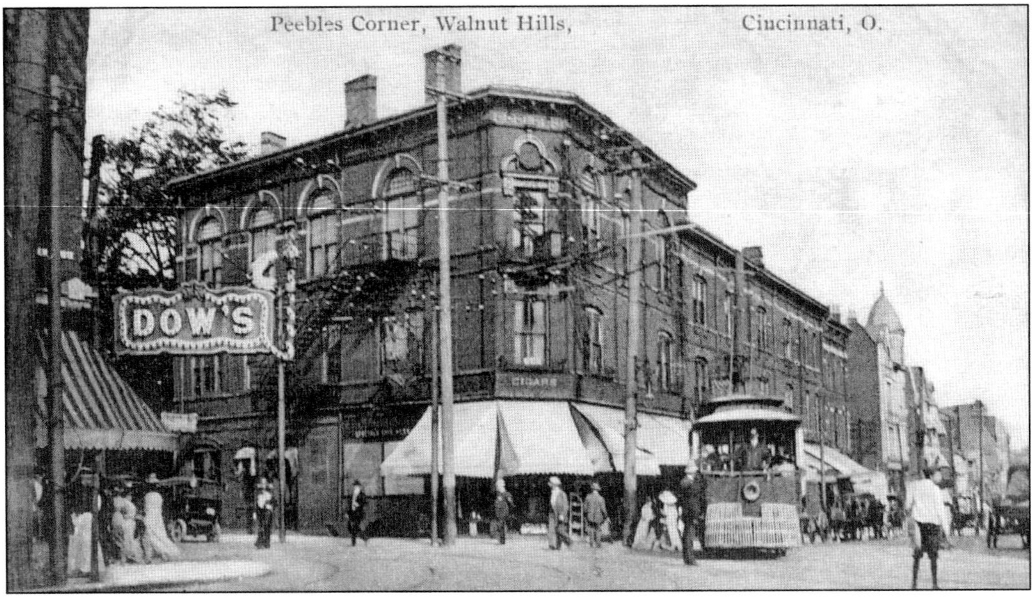

Looking at Peebles Corner today, one can scarcely imagine how prosperous the area once was. Named after the grocery owned by Joseph Peebles, it was one of the city's busiest intersections. Founded in 1883, the store served customers from as far away as Tennessee. The Peebles shrewdly used cigars to bribe streetcar conductors to call out "Peebles Corner." (From the Collection of the Public Library of Cincinnati and Hamilton County.)

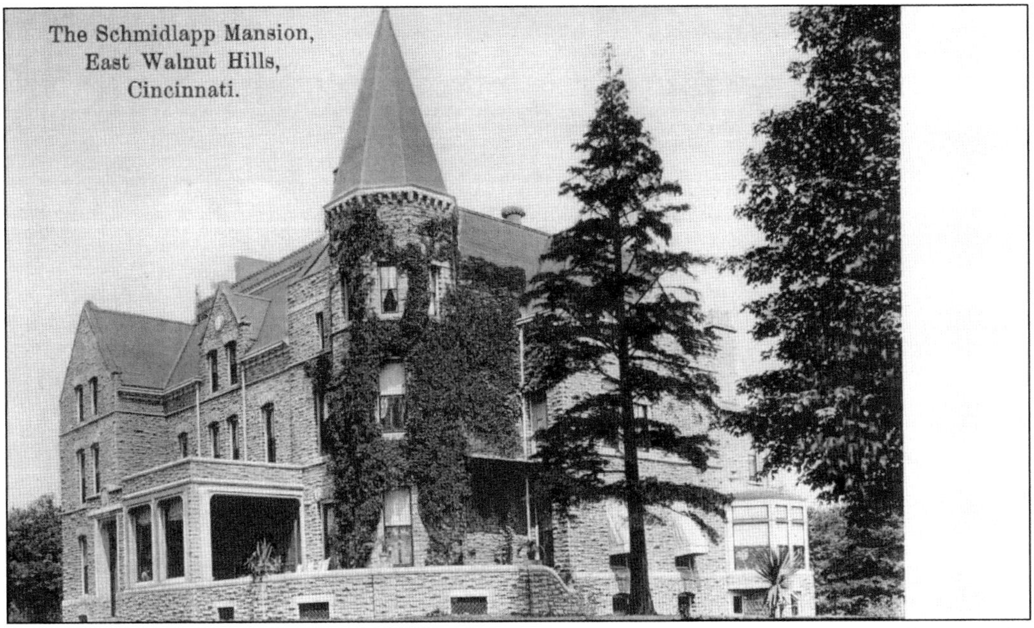

This East Walnut Hills mansion once belonged to Jacob Schmidlapp, a pioneer in housing for the poor. Disgusted by the conditions that poor African Americans lived in, he created his own early housing projects. He devised a plan he called the "Philanthropy Plus Five Percent Plan," where one day's wages purchased one week's rent. Schmidlapp described his work by saying, "This is my church: here I worship God." (From the Collection of the Public Library of Cincinnati and Hamilton County.)

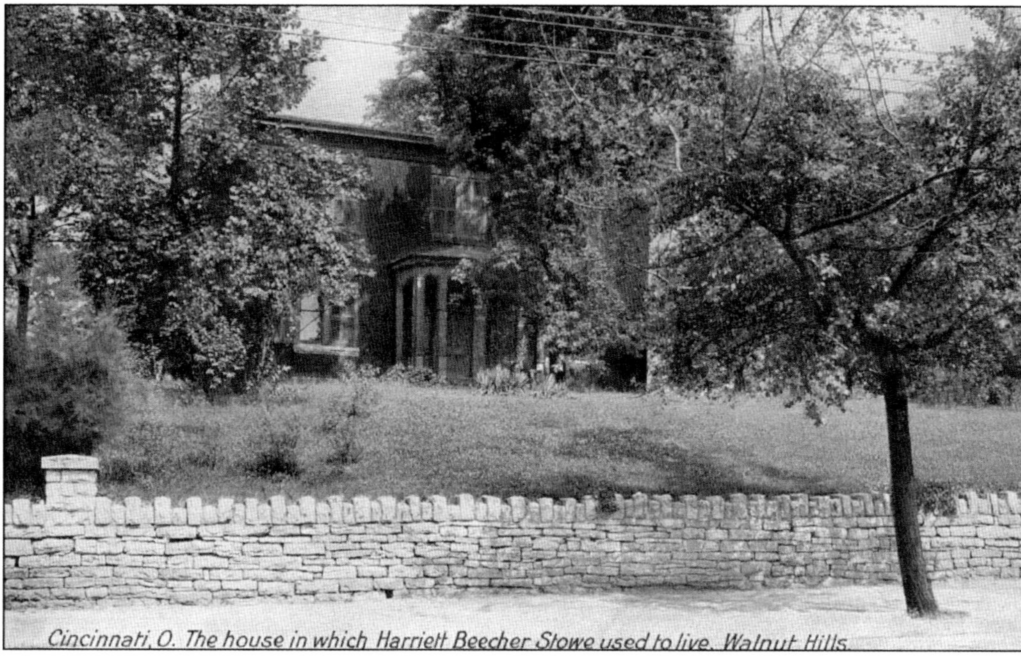

This Gilbert Avenue house was once the residence of author and abolitionist Harriet Beecher Stowe. Her family arrived in Cincinnati in 1832, where her father, Lyman Beecher, taught at Lane Seminary. While in Cincinnati, Harriet enjoyed the company of noted abolitionists before moving to Brunswick, Maine, in 1850, where she put her experiences into her classic novel *Uncle Tom's Cabin*. (From the Collection of the Public Library of Cincinnati and Hamilton County.)

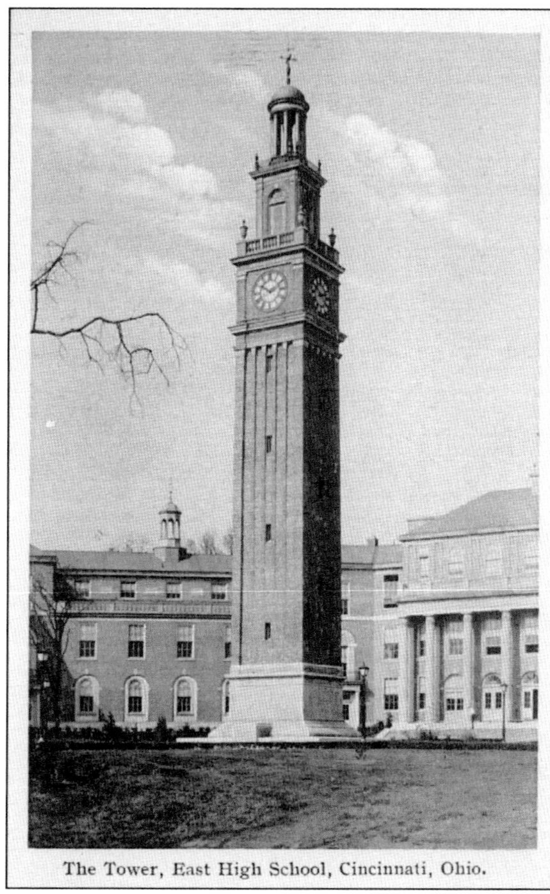

Now called Withrow High School, this public school has two distinct architectural features that make it stand out. Students cross a bridge to enter the school and can look up at a 114-foot clock tower. When the school first opened, there were no bells. Instead, a bugle sounded when it was time to change classes. (From the Collection of the Public Library of Cincinnati and Hamilton County.)

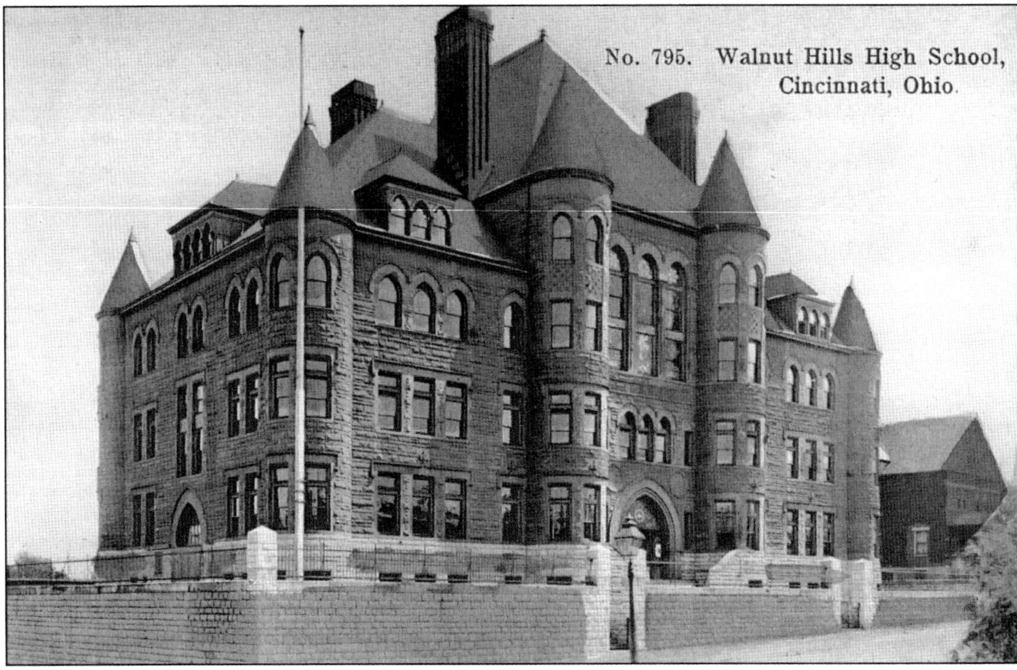

Walnut Hills, a college-preparatory public high school, has a long list of famous graduates, including famed actresses Theda Bara and Evelyn Venable, astronomer Alan Dressler, and conductor James Levine. The school probably wants to forget that Charles Manson attended, although he was only enrolled briefly and did not graduate. (From the Collection of the Public Library of Cincinnati and Hamilton County.)

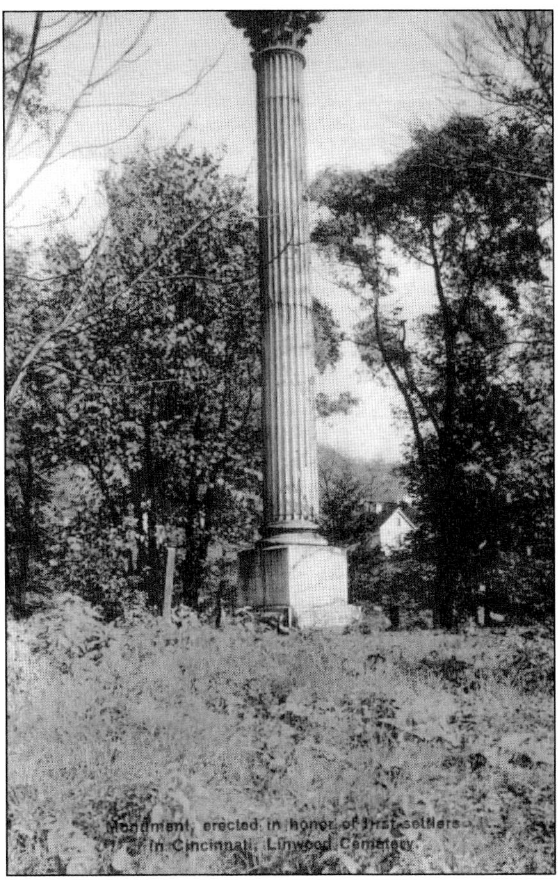

This column memorializing the first settlers in the region is a rarely visited landmark. Located on the site of the Columbia Baptist Church, the Corinthian column was taken from the old 1856 post office, which was designed by James Keys Wilson, who also designed the Plum Street Temple, the Dexter mausoleum, and the Rookwood Pottery building. (From the Collection of the Public Library of Cincinnati and Hamilton County.)

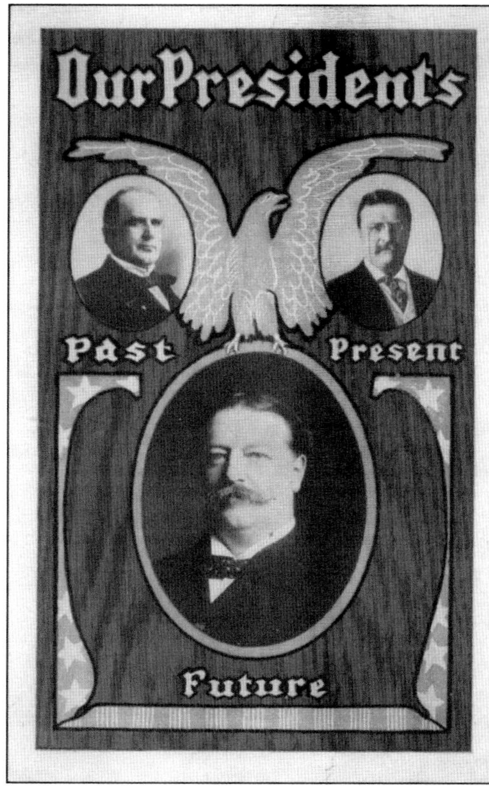

A small museum on Auburn Avenue displays the boyhood home of William Howard Taft. Taft worked as a reporter, a lawyer, and later as a revenue collector, a position he resigned because he did not want to be shackled by patronage. Encouraged by his wife, Helen, he served in the first Roosevelt administration and was later elected president and was later appointed chief justice of the US Supreme Court. (From the Collection of the Public Library of Cincinnati and Hamilton County.)

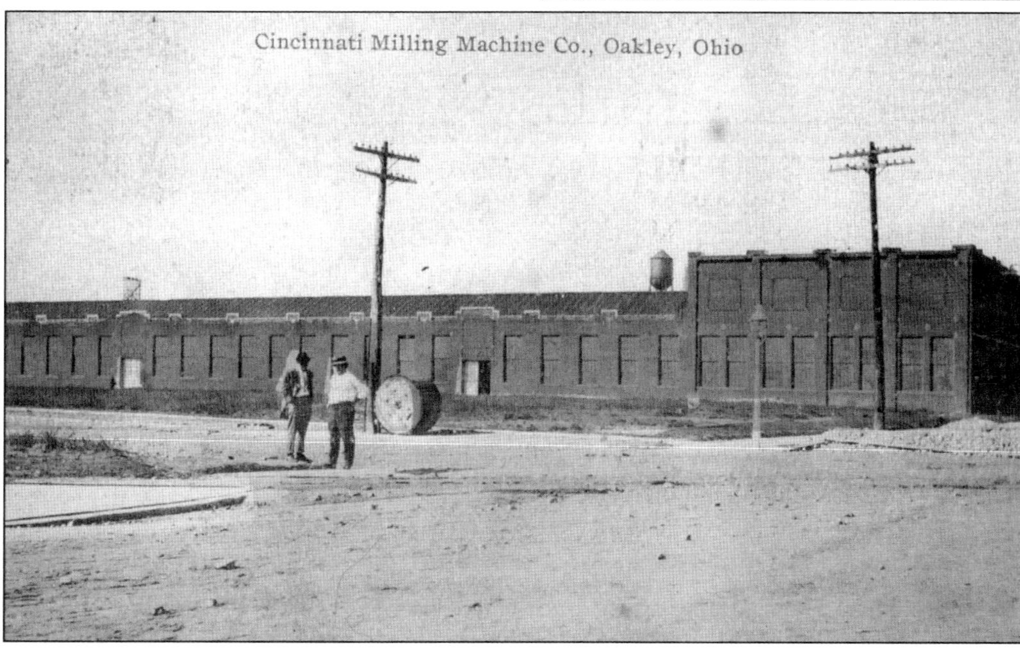

Cincinnati was famous for its machine tool industry, led by "The Mill," Cincinnati Milacron Company. Begun in 1884 as the Cincinnati Screw and Tap Company, the firm existed for more than a century. The old landmark was recently razed to make way for retail development. (From the Collection of the Public Library of Cincinnati and Hamilton County.)

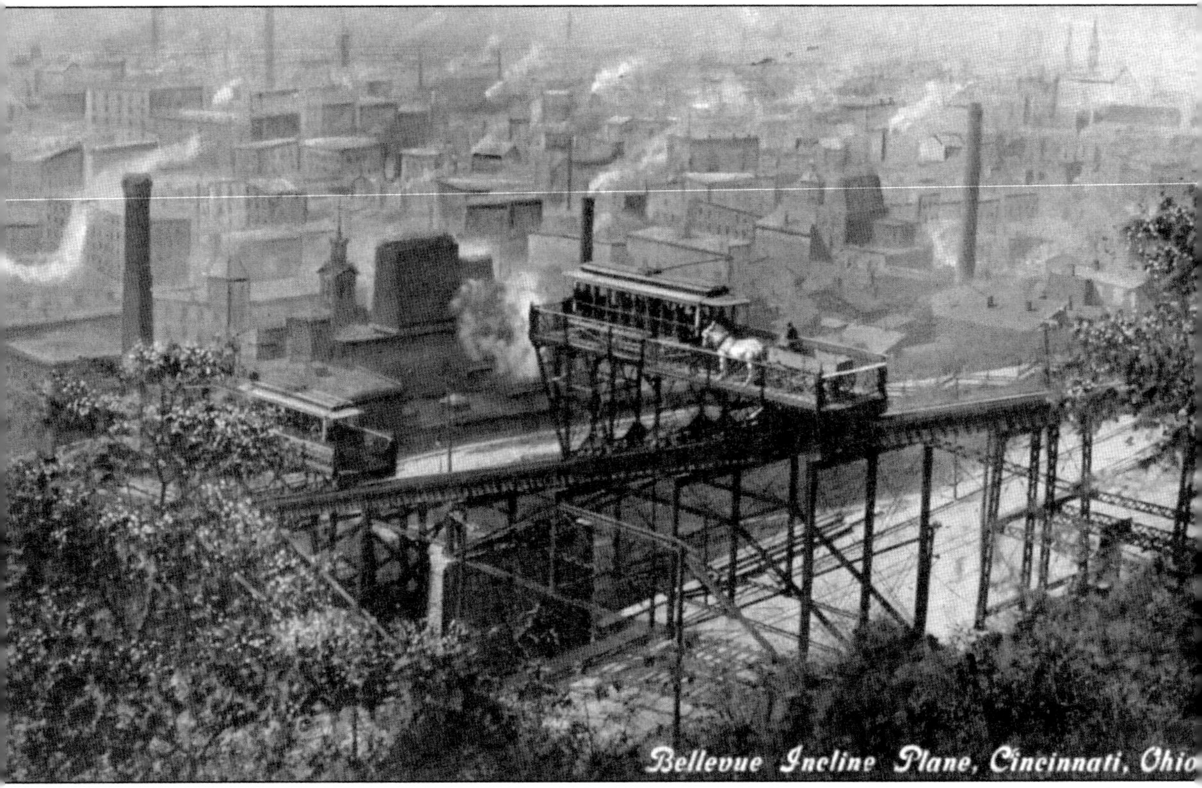

Travelers going north had their choice of three inclines—the Fairview on McMicken Street; the Mount Auburn on Main Street, which ended at the Lookout House; and this one, the Bellevue, at the end of Elm Street. These patrons are likely riding up to the opulent Bellevue House. On October 15, 1872, the unthinkable happened. In the morning, operating engineer Charles Goble noticed that the machinery was running strangely. Rather than closing the incline until proper repairs could be made, he "fixed" it by simply putting more oil in the mechanism. This worked, but only for a short time. At noon, as seven passengers ascended, to his horror, the machinery continued to turn. Although he tried desperately to stop the motor, the cable snapped, sending the car hurling back down the steep hill. Crashing at the bottom, the car flew across the street and into a grocery store. Three people died on the scene, three died later, and three more were seriously injured. The incline was temporarily closed, rebuilt, and then reopened. (From the Collection of the Public Library of Cincinnati and Hamilton County.)

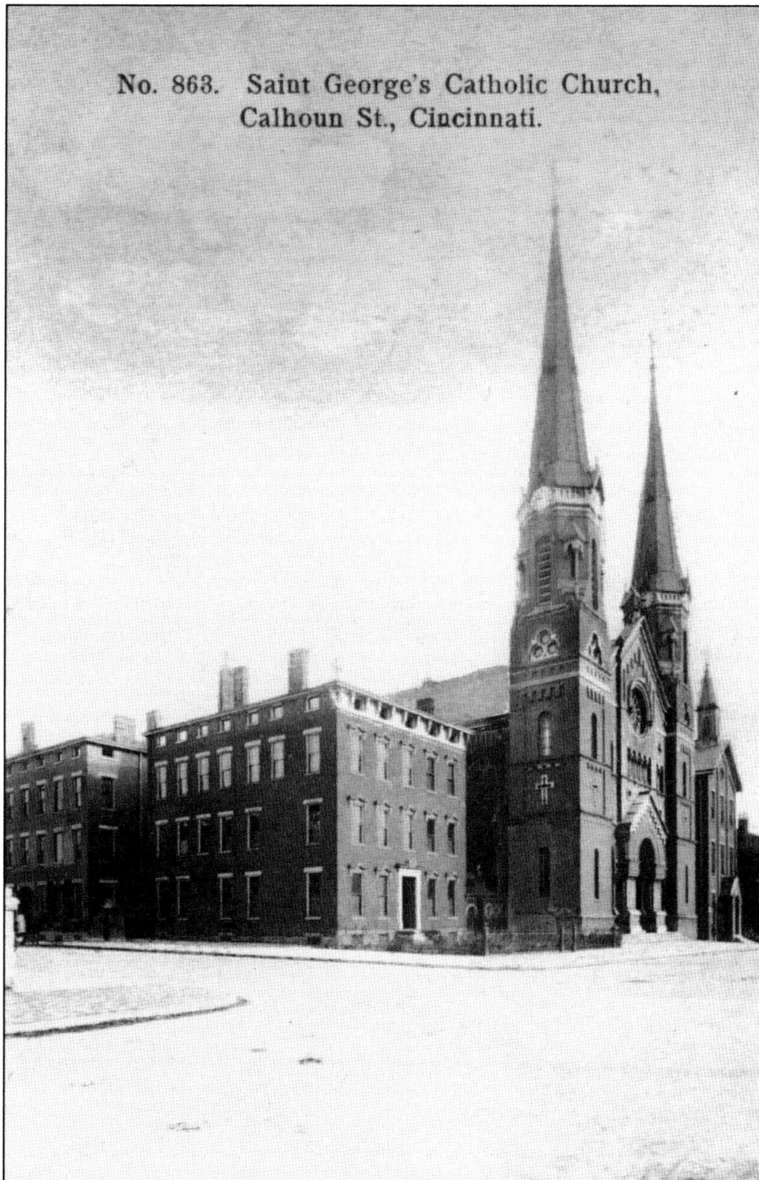

One single lightbulb left too close to combustible material forever changed the skyline of Cincinnati. Standing proud on the Clifton Hill with its two spires pointing to heaven, St. George's Catholic Church in Clifton is shown in numerous old photographs of the Cincinnati skyline. It was closed as a Catholic church, and in 1994, the historic building was purchased by the Christian Ministries Center. Eventually, it no longer functioned as a church but was often rented out for meetings or weddings. On February 1, 2008, a three-alarm fire destroyed the twin steeples. Firemen could not save the spires because of their massive bells. Fearing that the bells would collapse on the firemen or their equipment, the order was given to pull back and save the building itself. People could only look on in horror as the twin spires of this majestic church, so long a landmark of old Cincinnati, were destroyed. The church stands today with two stubs where the proud steeples once stood. (From the Collection of the Public Library of Cincinnati and Hamilton County.)

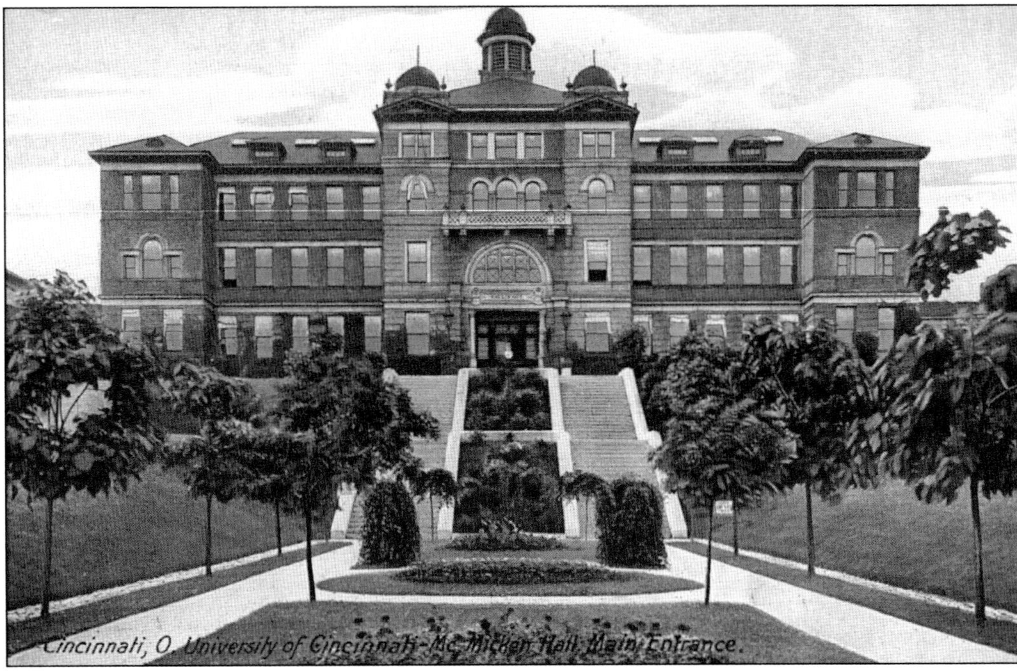

Visitors to the University of Cincinnati's McMicken Hall will notice two stone lions, Mic and Mac, by the front steps. Around the time of finals, the rear ends of the lions will show lipstick from being kissed because a campus superstition states that kissing the lion's rump will bring good exam grades. (From the Collection of the Public Library of Cincinnati and Hamilton County.)

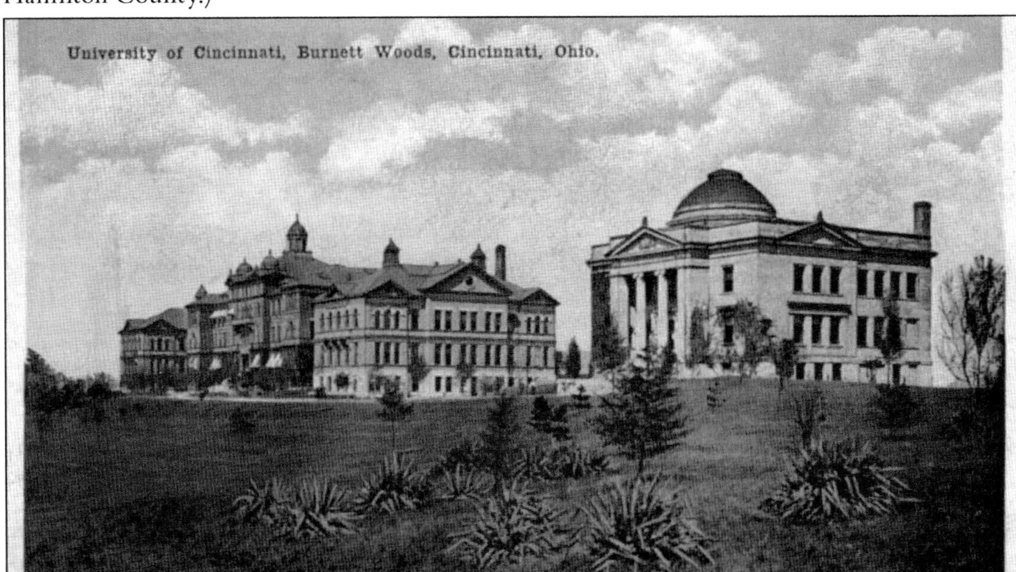

Despite this serene postcard scene, the relationship between the University of Cincinnati and its next-door neighbor, Burnet Woods, has not always been harmonious. Several times, the university has attempted to annex parkland, and students often use the woods as a parking lot. Ironically, Jacob Burnet owned much of the land that is now UC. (From the Collection of the Public Library of Cincinnati and Hamilton County.)

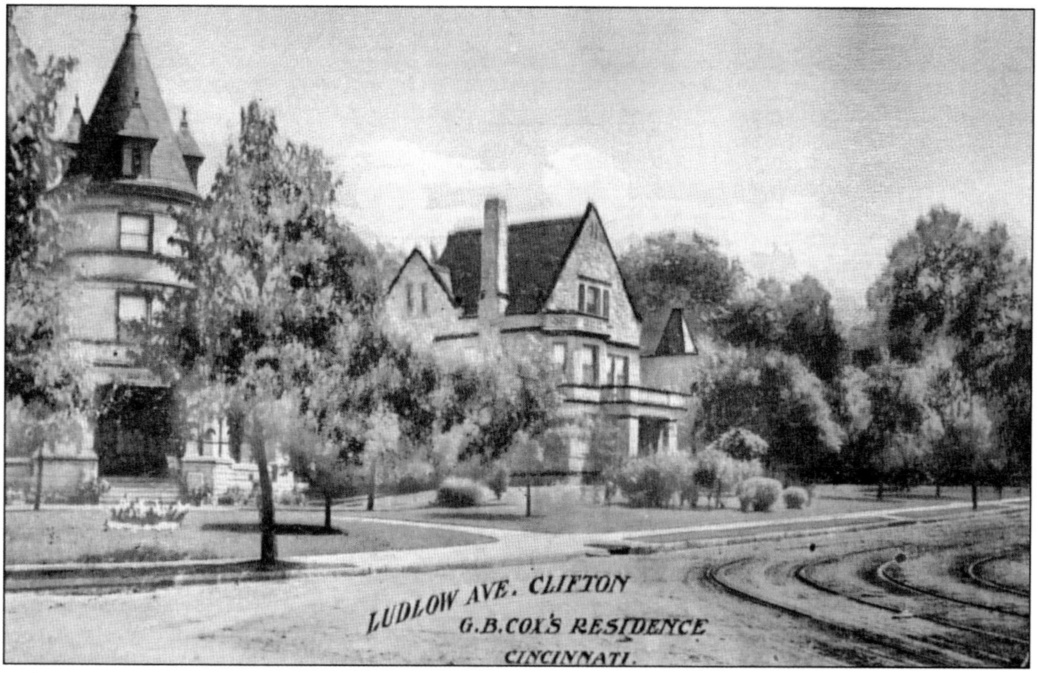

When George "Boss" Cox managed an amateur baseball team, its motto was "Win, tie, or fight." Cox carried this philosophy into city politics, rising to become one of the most powerful city bosses in the nation. In 1894, he too made the so-called wealthy pilgrimage up the hill away from the basin to this elegant house in Clifton built by Samuel Hannaford. (From the Collection of the Public Library of Cincinnati and Hamilton County.)

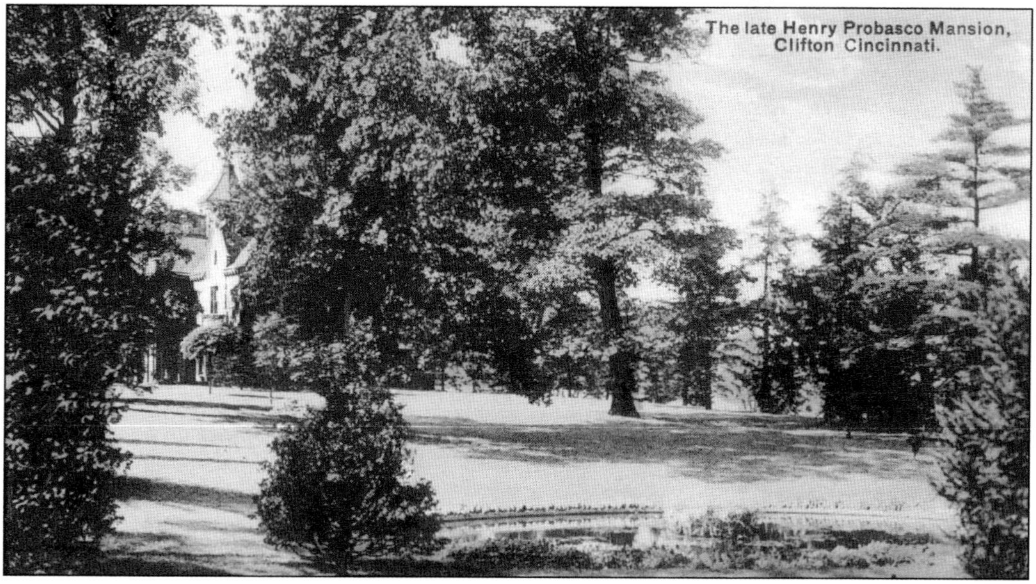

The man who gave the gift of Fountain Square to the city, Henry Probasco, also created one of the great millionaire "castles" in Cincinnati. Located in Clifton Heights, the Probasco mansion was an early attempt to combine sandstone with the more common limestone. Inside, murals were created by the artist Francis Pedretti, who also painted the city hall murals. (From the Collection of the Public Library of Cincinnati and Hamilton County.)

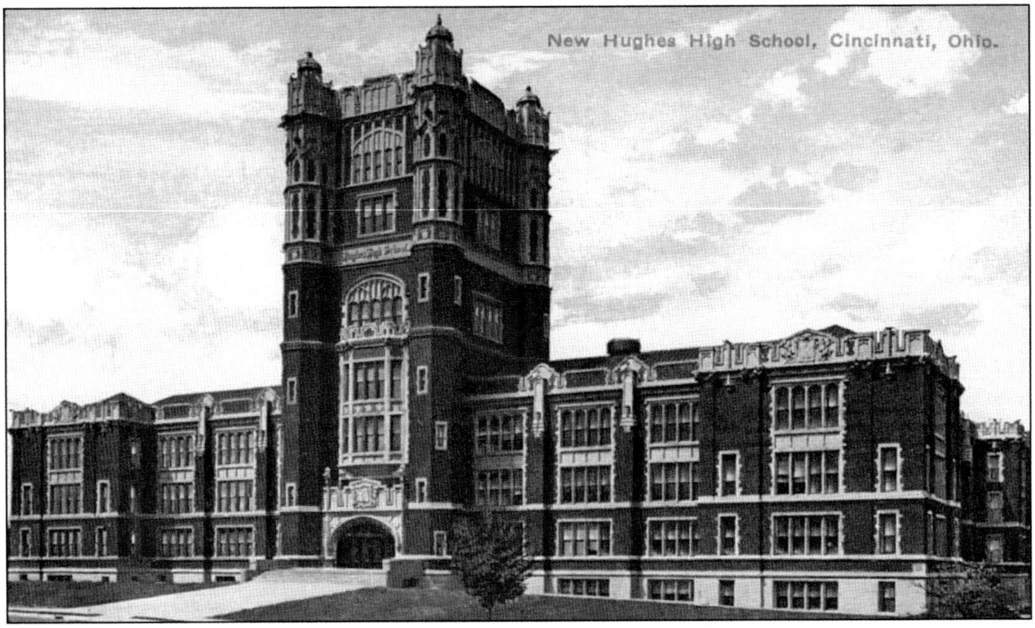

Cobbler Thomas Hughes had his business right next to tanner William Woodward's enterprise. Both men founded high schools. Architect Walter Stevens added some rather unique features to Hughes High School, including the numerous gargoyles students look up to see upon entering the school. (From the Collection of the Public Library of Cincinnati and Hamilton County.)

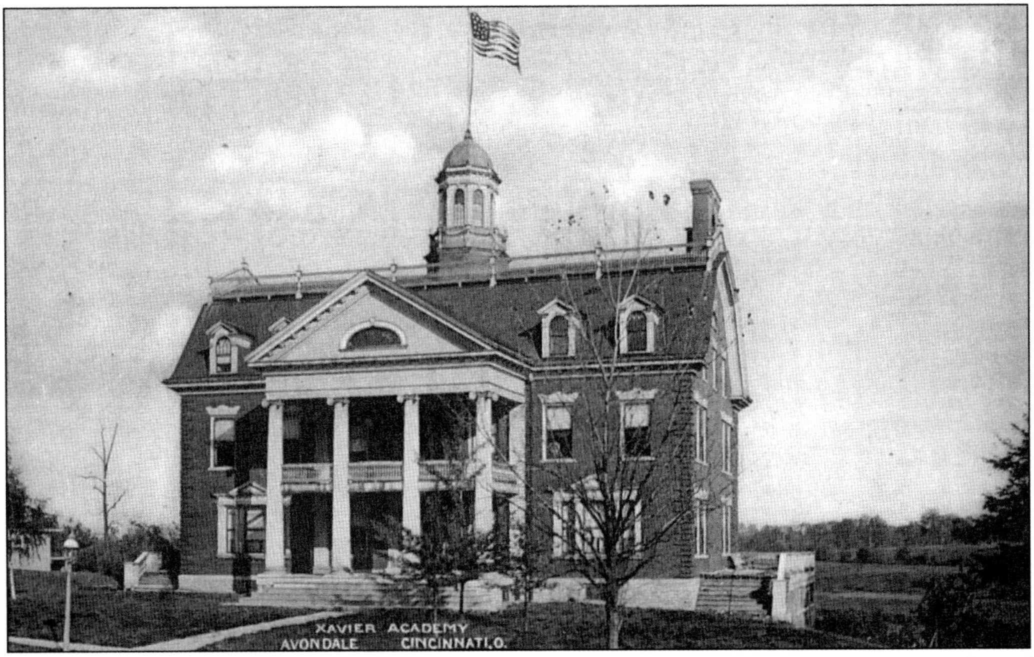

Xavier University began in 1831 as the College of the Athenaeum. Located at Seventh and Sycamore Streets, it was the first Catholic college in the Northwest Territory. It outgrew its original location, and in 1906, the institution moved to Lincoln and Gilbert Avenues in Walnut Hills. In 1912, it was relocated to this three-story building in Avondale. (From the Collection of the Public Library of Cincinnati and Hamilton County.)

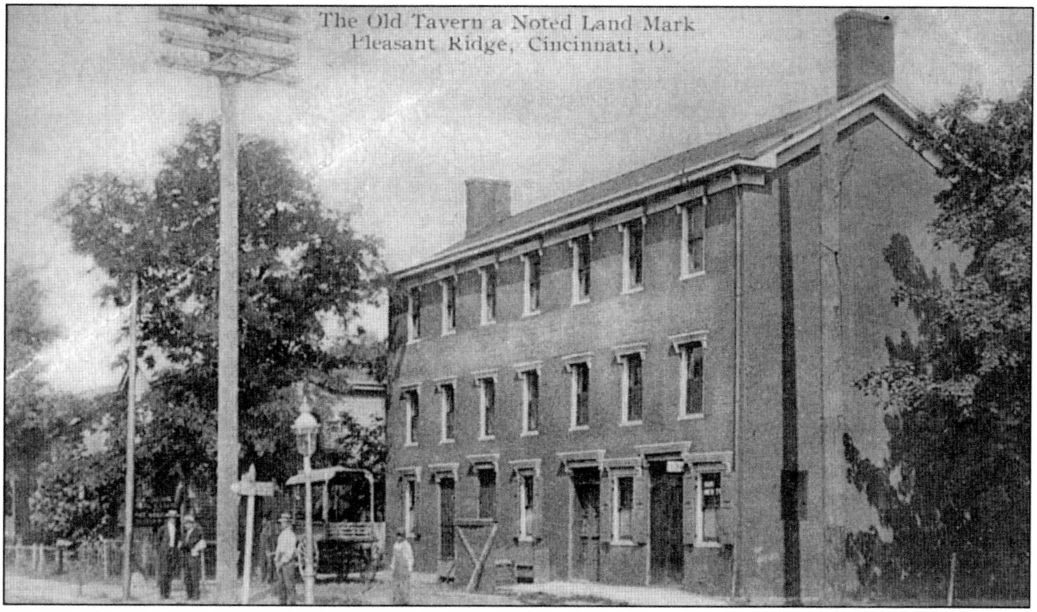

Many outlying suburbs were originally farm areas with taverns and hotels for travelers. One of these was Pleasant Ridge, a small community named after a cemetery. Stagecoaches on their way to Lebanon would stop here. After making their way up the hill, the drivers would stop to change horses, while the innkeeper would "water" the passengers. (From the Collection of the Public Library of Cincinnati and Hamilton County.)

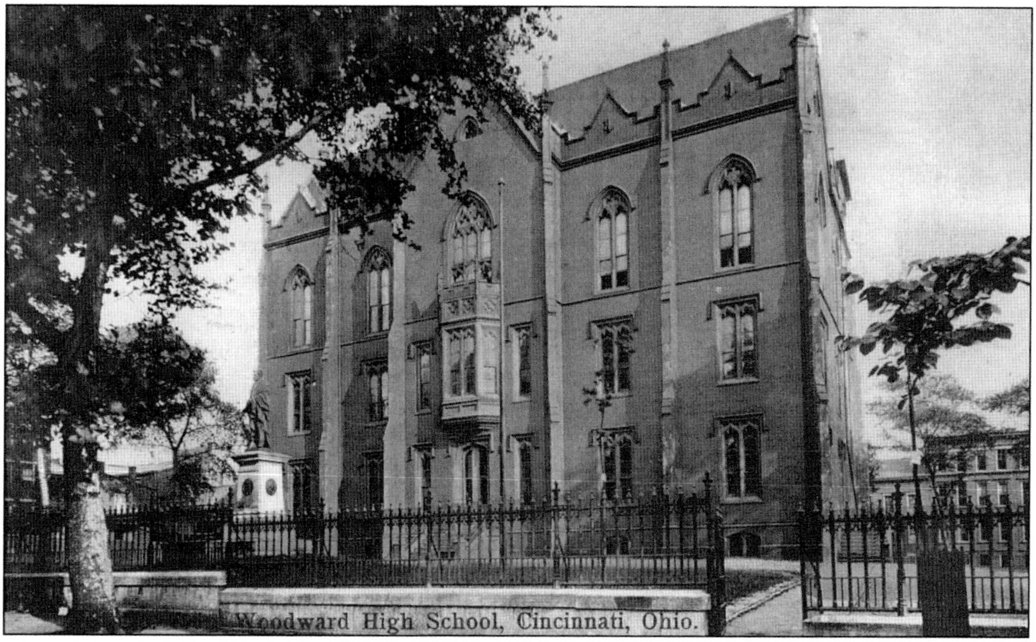

This free school began on land donated by William Woodward in 1831. It was originally at Thirteenth and Sycamore Streets, on the site of what was once Levi Coffin's home and a major station along the Underground Railroad. William McGuffey of McGuffey's Readers fame taught here. William Howard Taft was one of the graduates. (From the Collection of the Public Library of Cincinnati and Hamilton County.)

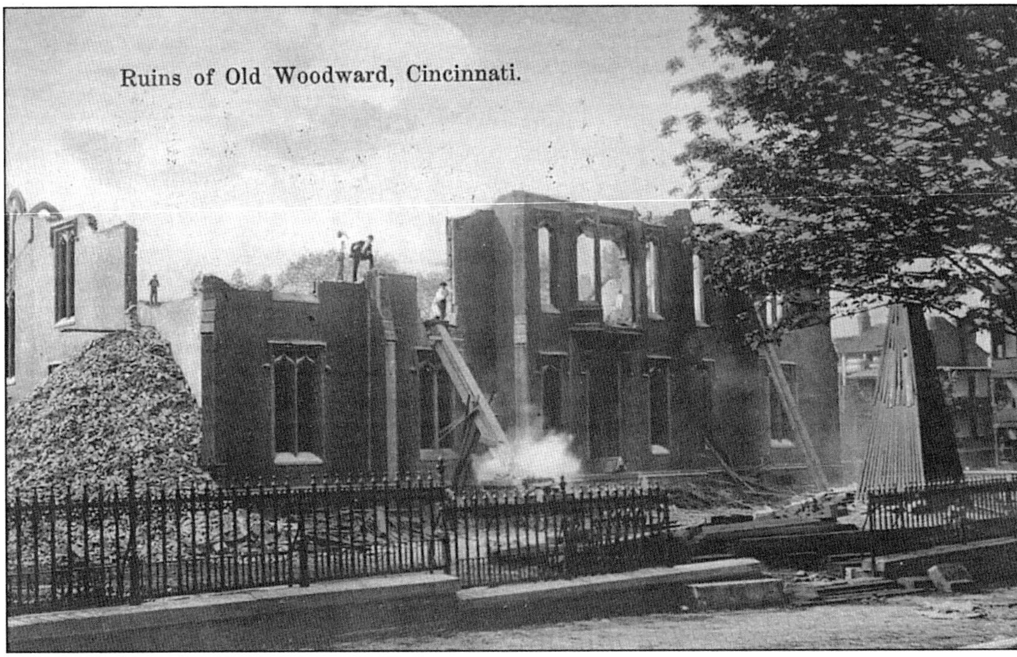

Woodward High School has undergone numerous renovations in its nearly two centuries of service, including this one in 1907. Alumnus William Howard Taft inaugurated the new building. The school is now located in Bond Hill. (From the Collection of the Public Library of Cincinnati and Hamilton County.)

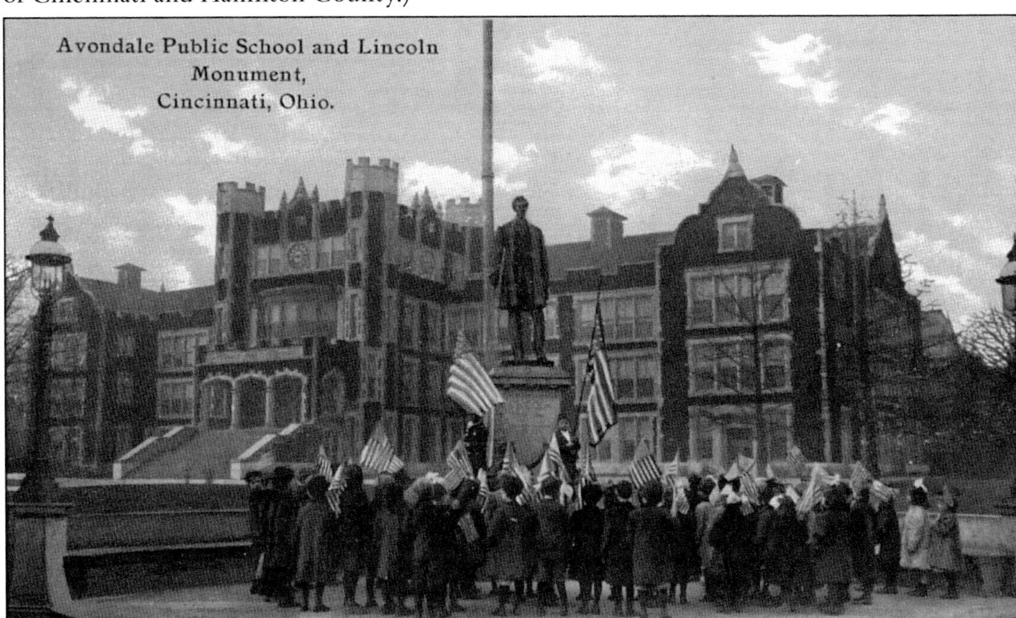

This statue of Lincoln at the corner of Rockdale and Reading is actually a copy of a statue honoring veterans from Illinois. In 1904, Capt. Charles Clinton of the Missouri Cavalry commissioned sculptor William Hastings to create the monument. The original is in Bunker Hill, Illinois. Captain Clinton later lived in Cincinnati and had the copy made. (From the Collection of the Public Library of Cincinnati and Hamilton County.)

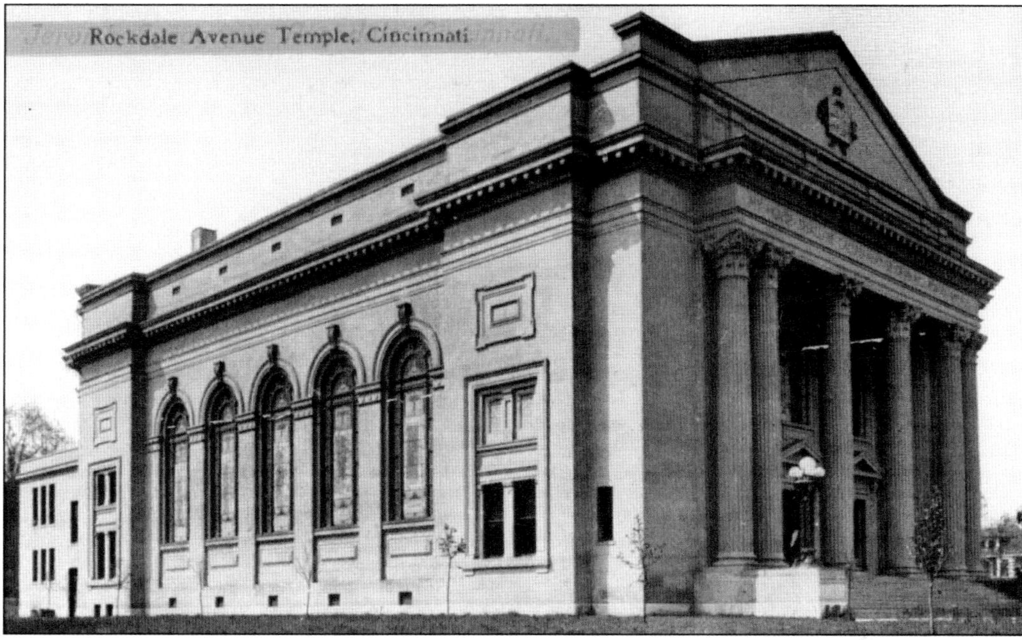

Avondale's numerous Jewish families successfully fought off an annexation attempt by Cincinnati in 1869, but they could not fight the Cox machine in 1896. This magnificent temple on Reading Road and Harvey Avenue was designed by Rudolph Tietig and William H. Lee. After it was looted in riots in 1969, it was closed. The land is now a vacant lot—another lost treasure. (From the Collection of the Public Library of Cincinnati and Hamilton County.)

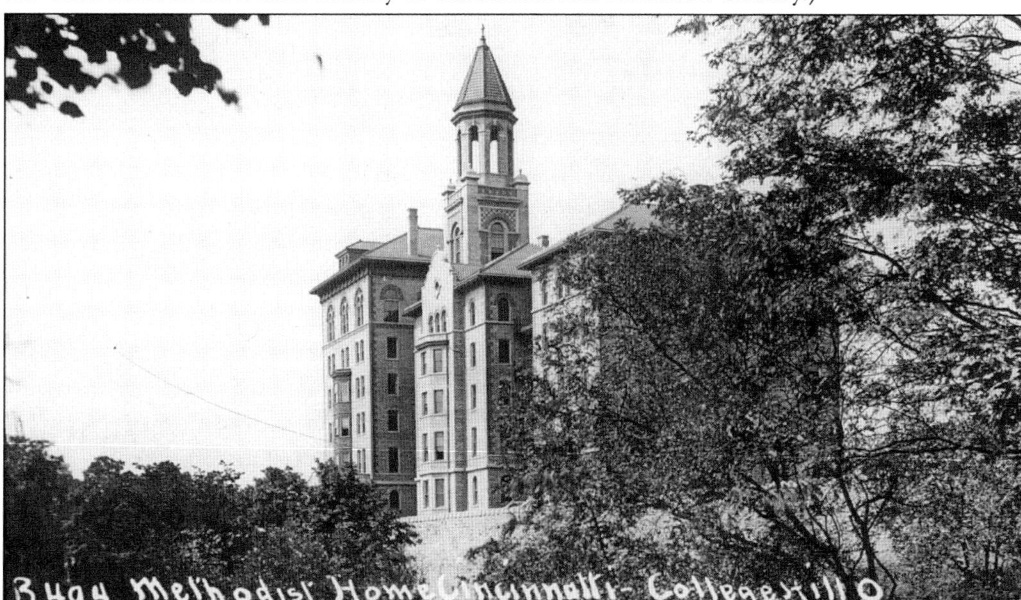

This Hannaford building commands a spectacular view of the city below. The Methodist Home for the Aged is usually referred to as the Twin Towers. It was originally located in a former hotel in Yellow Springs. That building burned down in 1902, prompting the construction of this grand edifice in College Hill. (From the Collection of the Public Library of Cincinnati and Hamilton County.)

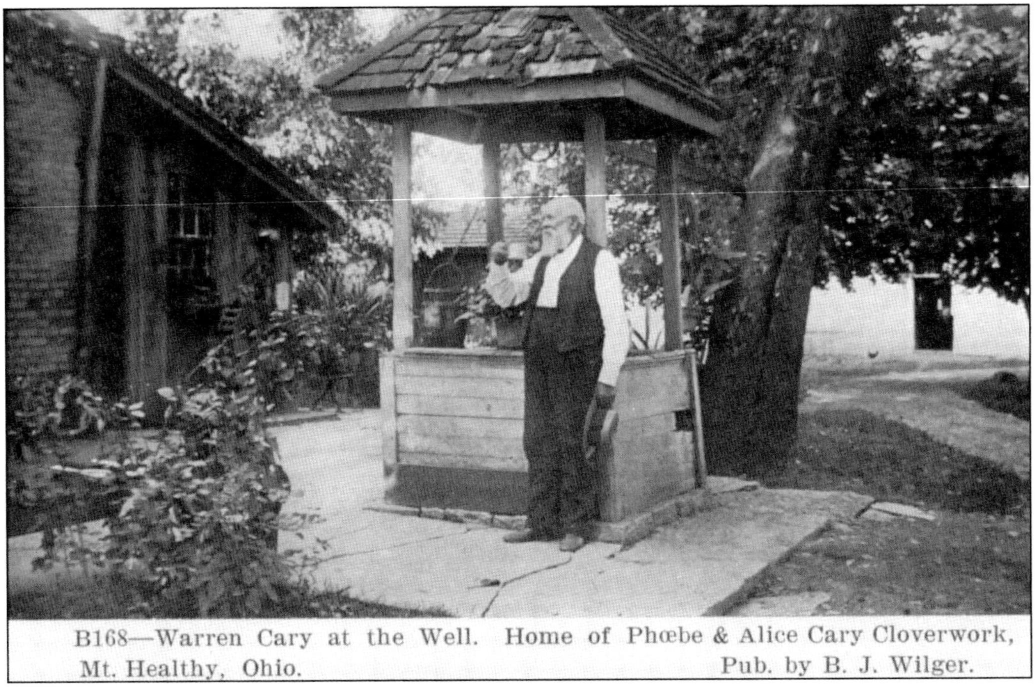

Robert Cary did not want his daughters, Alice and Phoebe, wasting their time writing poetry. Both, however, became renowned poets in the mid-1800s. Even Edgar Allan Poe is said to have admired their work. The Cary homestead, Clovernook Farm, has been preserved as a small museum in North College Hill. This 1908 image shows the sisters' younger brother Warren at the house. (From the Collection of the Public Library of Cincinnati and Hamilton County.)

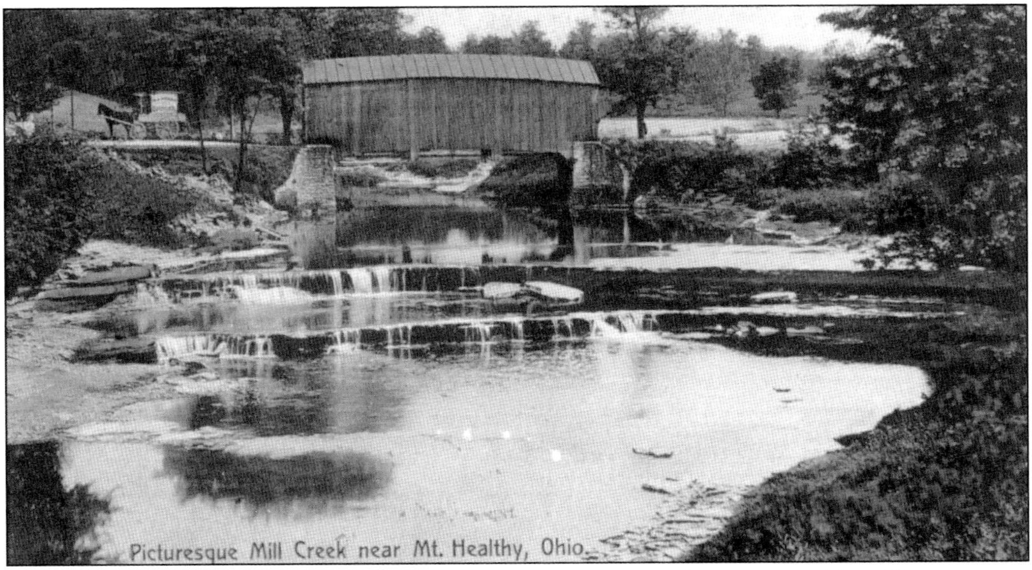

This romantic covered bridge still stands in the suburban city of Mount Healthy. The town was originally named Mount Pleasant, but the name was changed after the area was used as a refuge during the horrific 1850 cholera epidemic. It was certainly "healthy" for many escaped slaves, as two major stations along the Underground Railroad were located nearby on Hamilton Avenue. (From the Collection of the Public Library of Cincinnati and Hamilton County.)

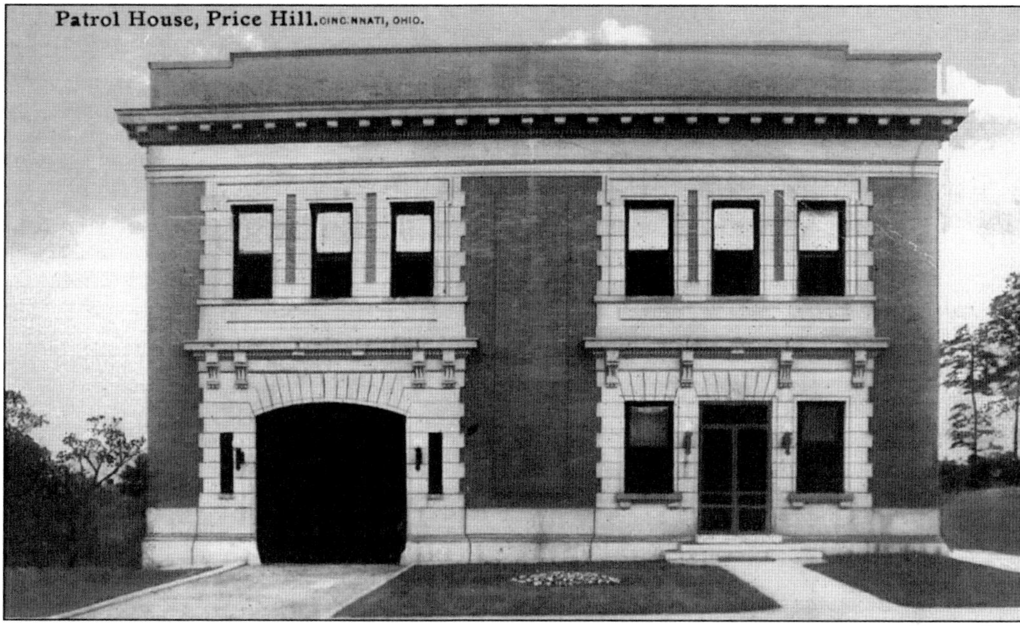

The Price Hill incline made the western hillside area, with its clean air, accessible for new residents. In 1902, the Cox machine annexed the quiet village of Warsaw into the ever-growing Cincinnati. Five years later, the District Three Police Station (pictured) was built on Warsaw Avenue. (From the Collection of the Public Library of Cincinnati and Hamilton County.)

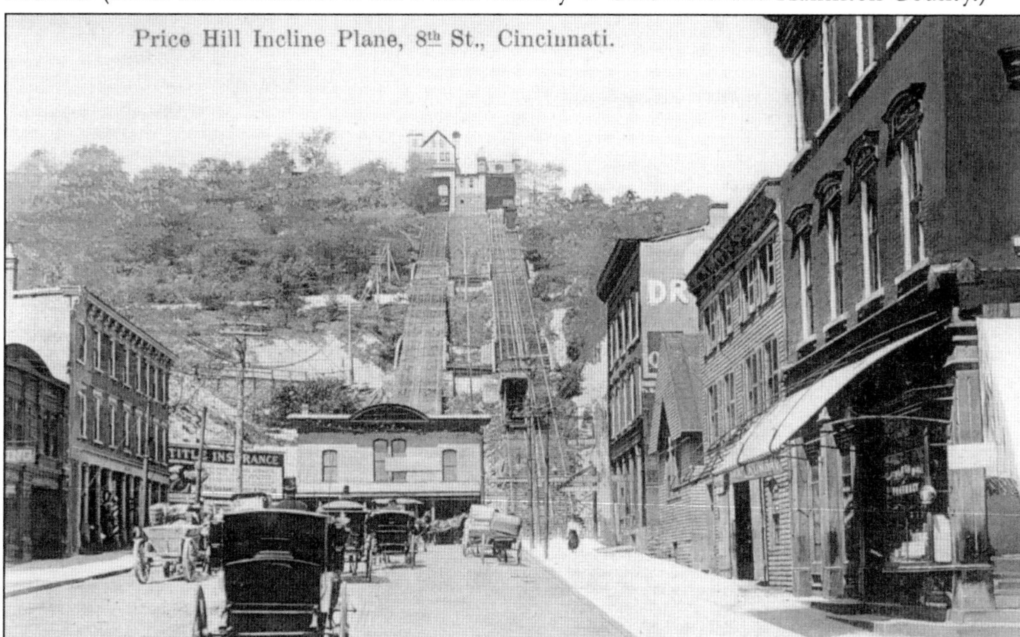

All inclines except the Fairview featured restaurants at the summit. When William Price built this double-tracked incline to scale Price Hill, he cleverly forbade alcohol sales at the top. This made for a more family-friendly environment, giving the area the nickname Buttermilk Hill. Saloons at the bottom displayed signs enticing travelers with such warnings as "Last chance." (From the Collection of the Public Library of Cincinnati and Hamilton County.)

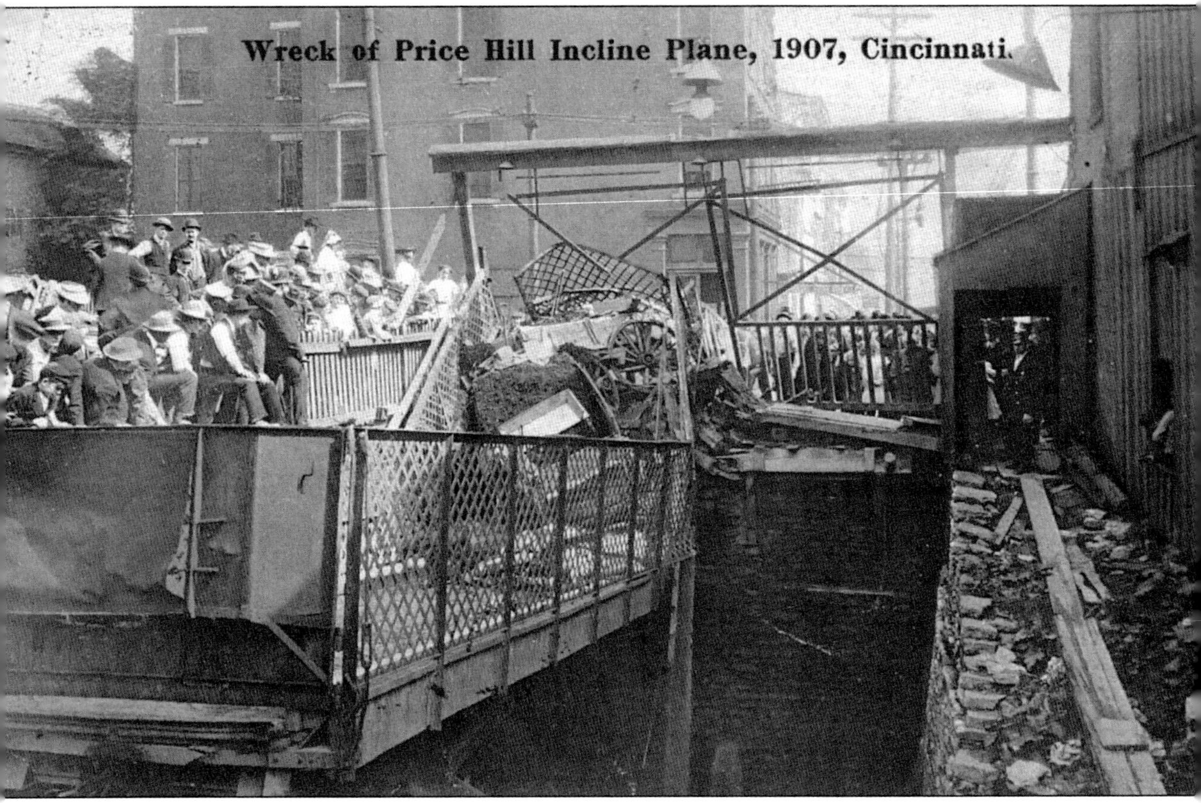

Potential tragedy was transformed into comedy in 1906 when the cable pulling the car up the Price Hill Incline suddenly snapped a mere six feet from the summit. Fearing another tragedy such as the one that occurred on the Bellevue Incline in 1872, cartman Joe Strossel looked about desperately for a soft place to land. With only seconds to make his decision, he had no choice but to leap into his cargo—a load of manure. When the car crashed at the bottom, Strossel and his freight spilled out into Eighth and State Streets. He was understandably shaken up, utterly filthy, but more or less unhurt. Men poured out of saloons and took Strossel inside for their own special "first aid." He was cleaned up and given free drinks and a new derby. Later, it was speculated that the cause of the near fatal accident was animal urine that had fallen on the cable over the years, slowly disintegrating it. (From the Collection of the Public Library of Cincinnati and Hamilton County.)

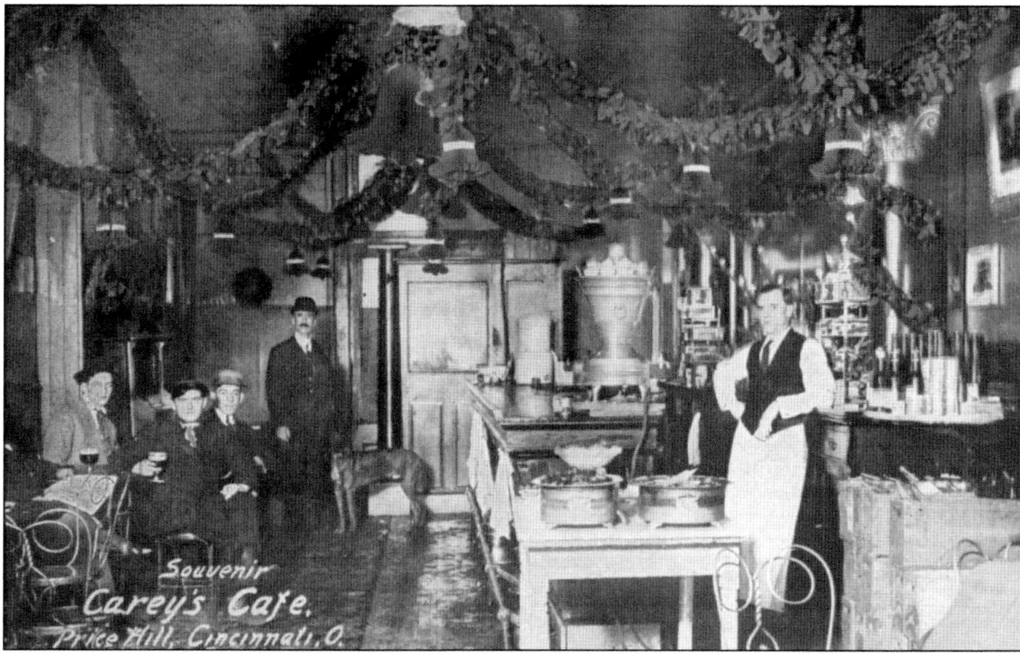

This Price Hill landmark, the old Carey's Café on Glenway Avenue, was right next to the site of another Cincinnati landmark: the very first Skyline Chili, which opened in 1949. (From the Collection of the Public Library of Cincinnati and Hamilton County.)

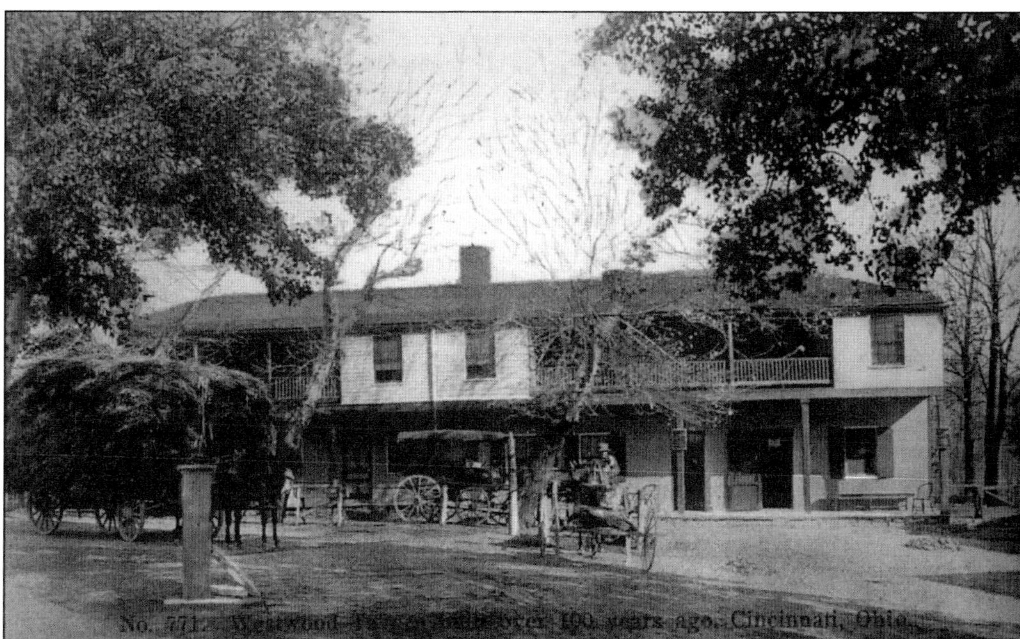

The area of Westwood was so remote that in 1874 some wealthy residents, including James Gamble and Michael Werk, organized a narrow-gauge railroad to connect the area to the city. From the beginning, the venture was a failure, ceasing operation in 1941. (From the Collection of the Public Library of Cincinnati and Hamilton County.)

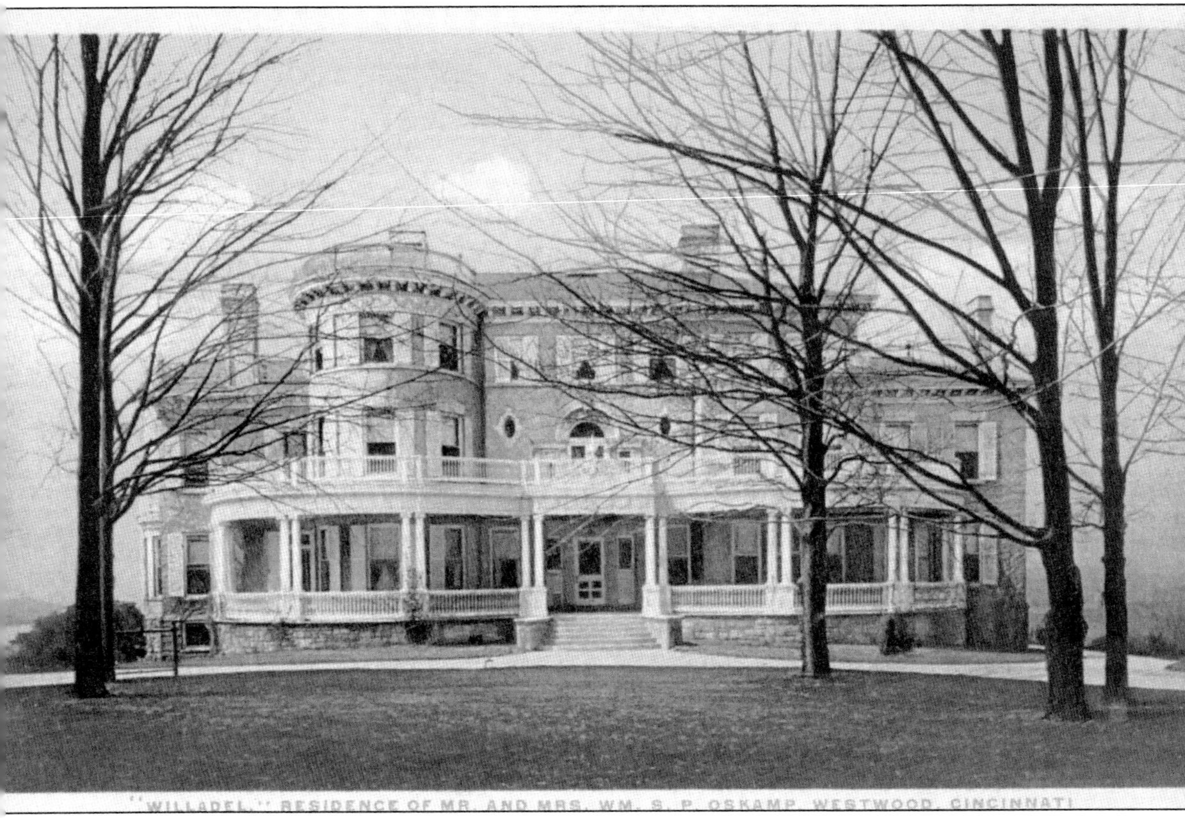

This elegant Harrison Avenue mansion, Willadel, combined the names William and Adele. Adele, the daughter of Thomas Werk, married jeweler William Oskamp, and they built the home in the 1890s. In 1887, William had formed a partnership with Charles Nolting to create the Oskamp Nolting Jewelry Company, located at Seventh and Race Streets. The architect of Willadel, William Franklin, also designed the Pogue mansion. In its prime, the Willadel estate comprised 19 acres and contained a lake. It was the scene of many society events throughout the years. Oskamp died in 1933, and the estate eventually became the Baptist Home for the Aged in 1946. As it was filled with priceless art, it was a beautiful setting for the residents, but it presented some curious dilemmas for the new owners—the Baptists had to contend with a baroque mural featuring the Roman wine god Bacchus looking down on them as they prayed in their chapel. (From the Collection of the Public Library of Cincinnati and Hamilton County.)

Four
A Day in the Park

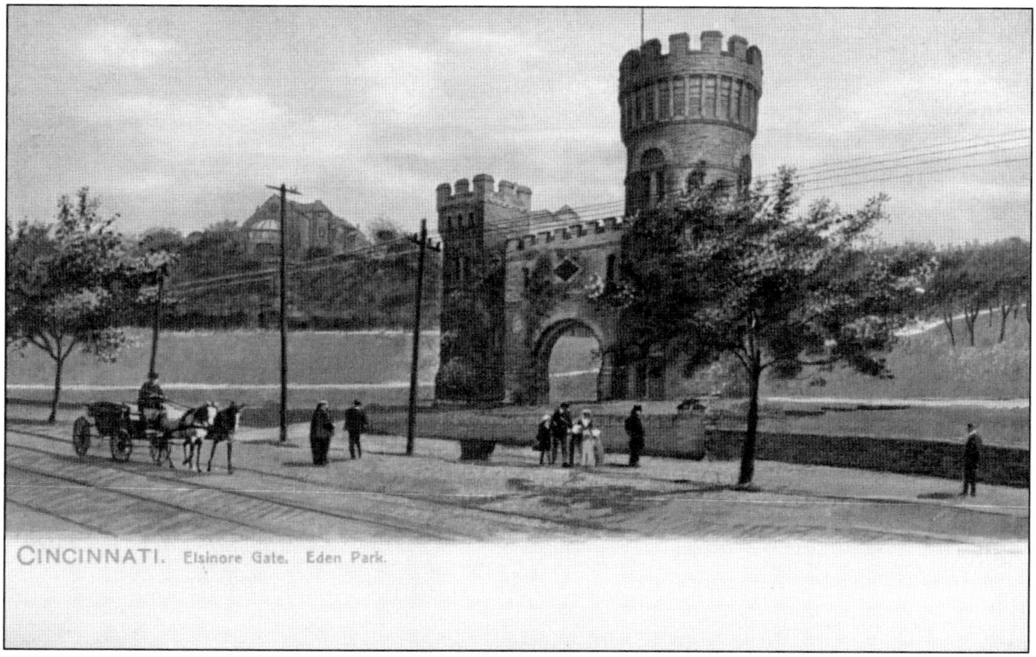

In 1883, Shakespearean actor James Murdoch returned to his hometown of Cincinnati to perform *Hamlet*. By coincidence, at the same time, the Water Works was preparing to build a structure to control water flow. The set for the play features the majestic Elsinore (Kronborg) Castle. Murdoch persuaded architect Samuel Hannaford to construct this Shakespearean tower for the machinery. (From the Collection of the Public Library of Cincinnati and Hamilton County.)

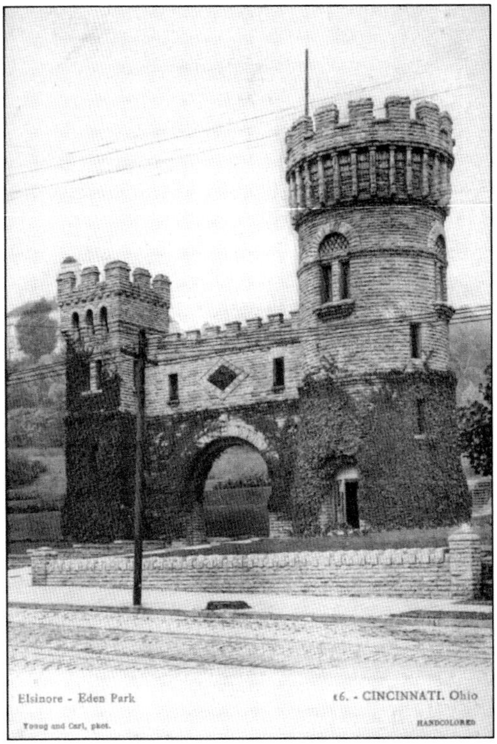

On June 12, 1949, three boys climbed a rope to get into the Elsinore Tower, quickly learning that there was no way out. One boy fell 15 feet and then called for help. After being trapped for four hours, the explorers were at long last rescued. (From the Collection of the Public Library of Cincinnati and Hamilton County.)

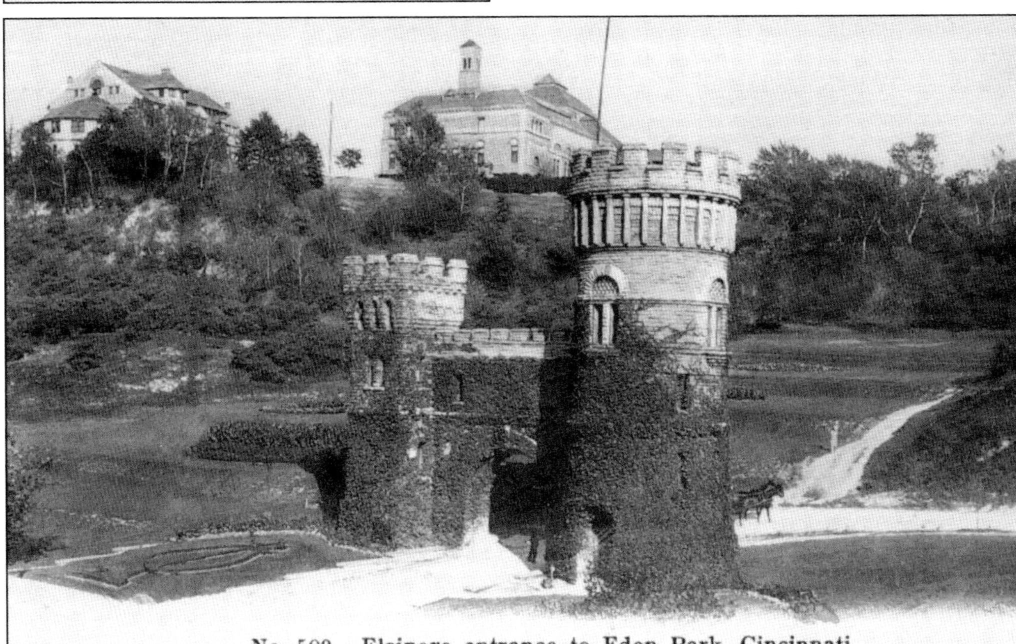

This land was once used by Nicholas Longworth to grow Catawba grapes to make his famous champagne. When blight destroyed his grape business, he donated the land to the city to become the modern Eden Park. The park's designer, Adolph Strauch, also landscaped the picturesque Spring Grove Cemetery. (From the Collection of the Public Library of Cincinnati and Hamilton County.)

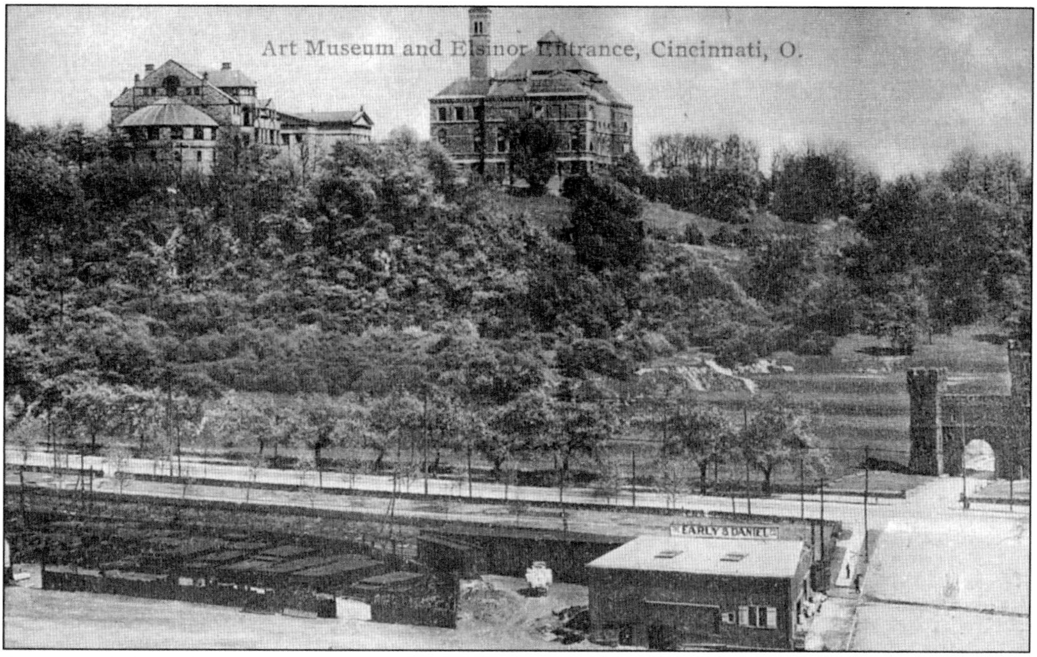

On top of the hill above Elsinore Castle are the Cincinnati Art Museum and Art Academy of Cincinnati. The first art museum in Cincinnati was established in 1828, followed by another in 1854. Both eventually closed. The Women's Art Museum Association established the current museum. The memorial plaque outside of the museum is a who's who of Cincinnati in the Gilded Age. (From the Collection of the Public Library of Cincinnati and Hamilton County.)

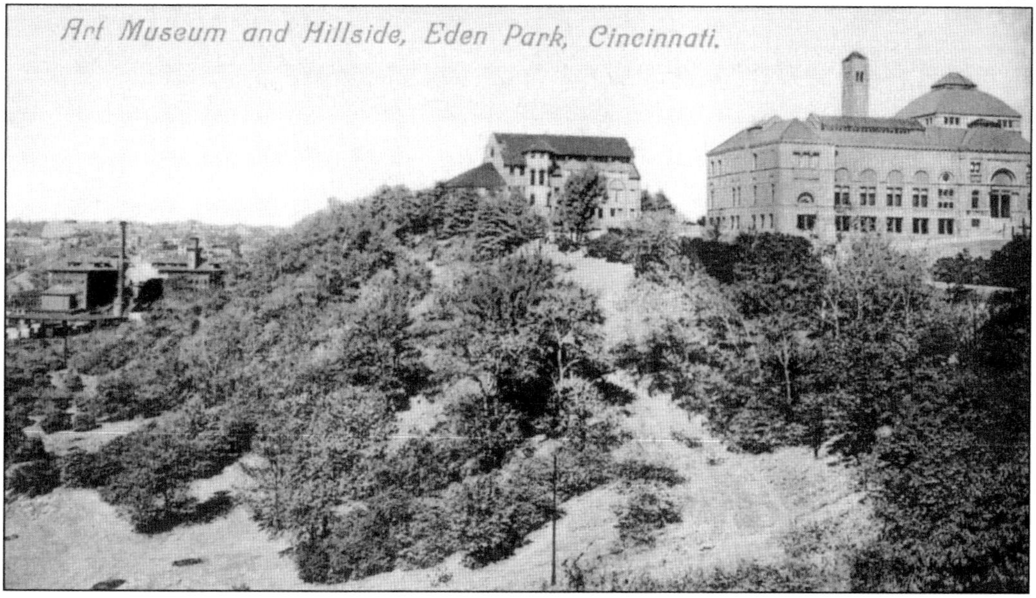

When the Art Museum and Art Academy revived the old costumed event tradition of the Beaux Arts Ball, a number of curators undoubtedly held their breath. Such events were ended in the 1940s for fear of liability and damage. Some attendees came dressed nearly as naked as Eve, and too many inebriated patrons slid down the banisters. (From the Collection of the Public Library of Cincinnati and Hamilton County.)

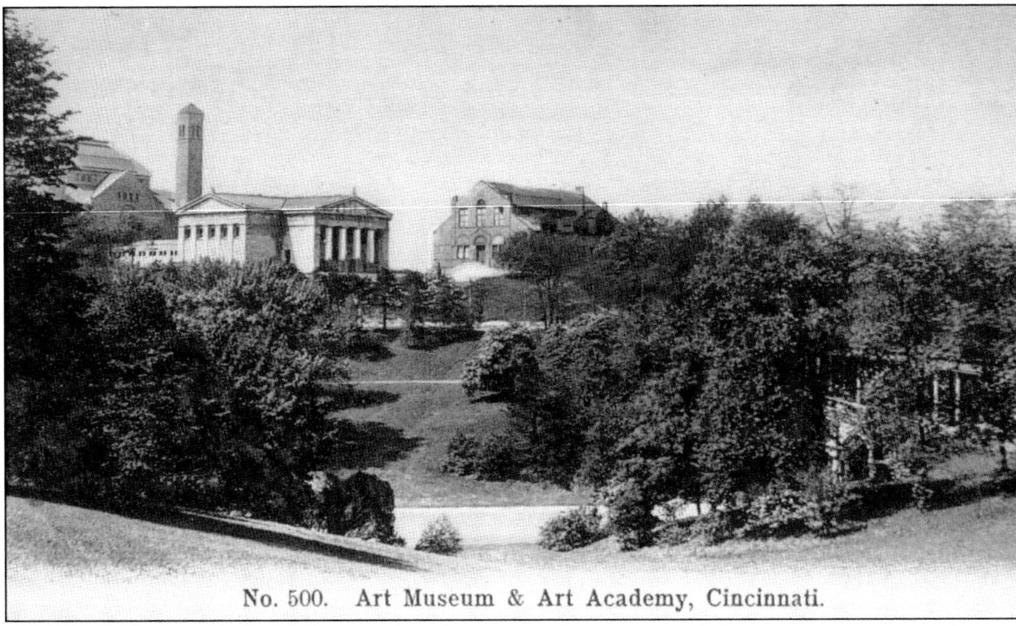

The Art Academy has had a number of distinguished graduates, including the inventor of the comic strip, Richard Felton Outcalt, a newspaper artist and graduate from what was then the McMicken School of Design. In 1888, Outcalt met Thomas Edison at a Cincinnati Exposition. From this, Outcalt eventually created *Hogan's Alley* with the memorable character the Yellow Kid. (From the Collection of the Public Library of Cincinnati and Hamilton County.)

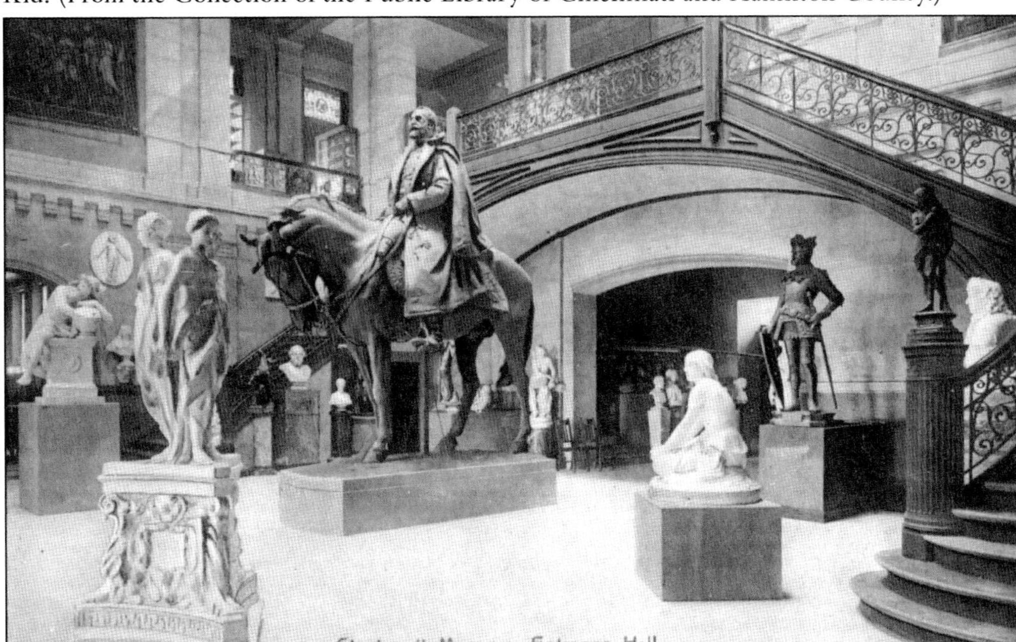

The Art Museum has many ghost stories. A Civil War soldier has reportedly been seen walking through the galleries, a seven-foot monk has appeared in a Spanish chapel, an unearthly mist has been seen over a mummy case, and a clock with no working interior parts sometimes chimes. (From the Collection of the Public Library of Cincinnati and Hamilton County.)

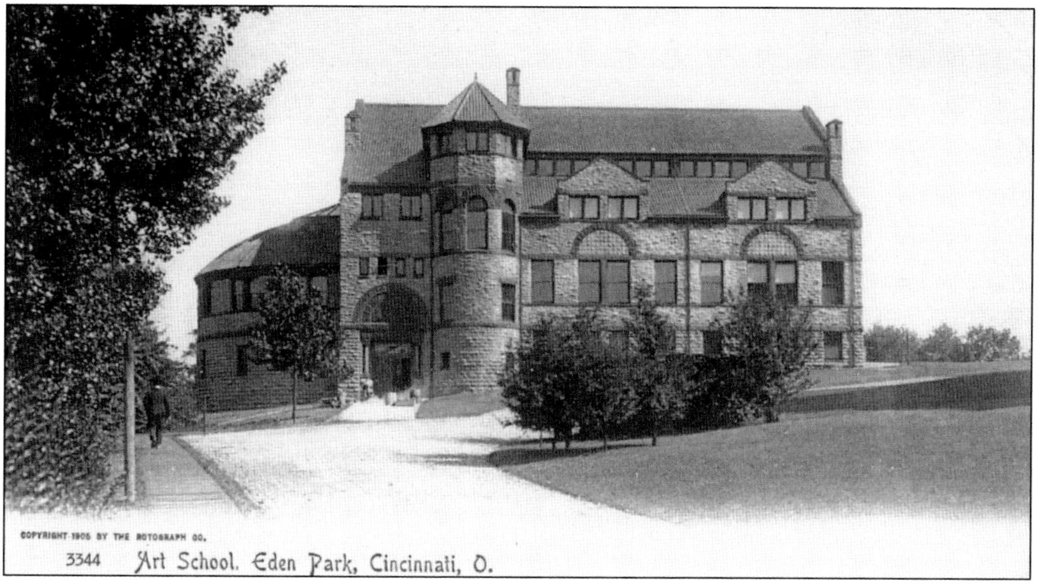

In addition to the ghostly stories related on the previous page is a moving tale of love surviving the grave. In 1909, artist Frank Duveneck was made director of the Art Academy. In 1888, his wife Elizabeth had died in Paris and was buried in Florence. A mold of her sarcophagus is on display in the Art Museum next door. A misty female figure has reportedly been seen rising from the effigy and vanishing. Her husband's paintings are displayed nearby. (From the Collection of the Public Library of Cincinnati and Hamilton County.)

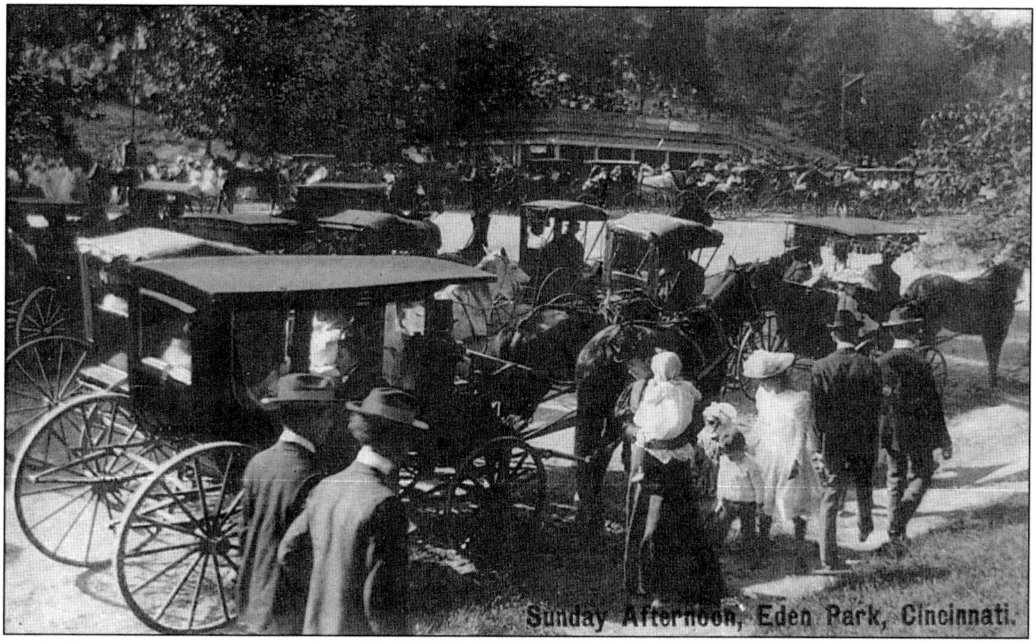

Nicholas Longworth called his vineyard a "Garden of Eden." When the park first opened, few people without the luxury of a carriage could enjoy it because of its steep hillside. By the 1870s, with the opening of the Mount Adams Incline, thousands of people escaped the smoke and heat of the city to enjoy some time in Eden. (From the Collection of the Public Library of Cincinnati and Hamilton County.)

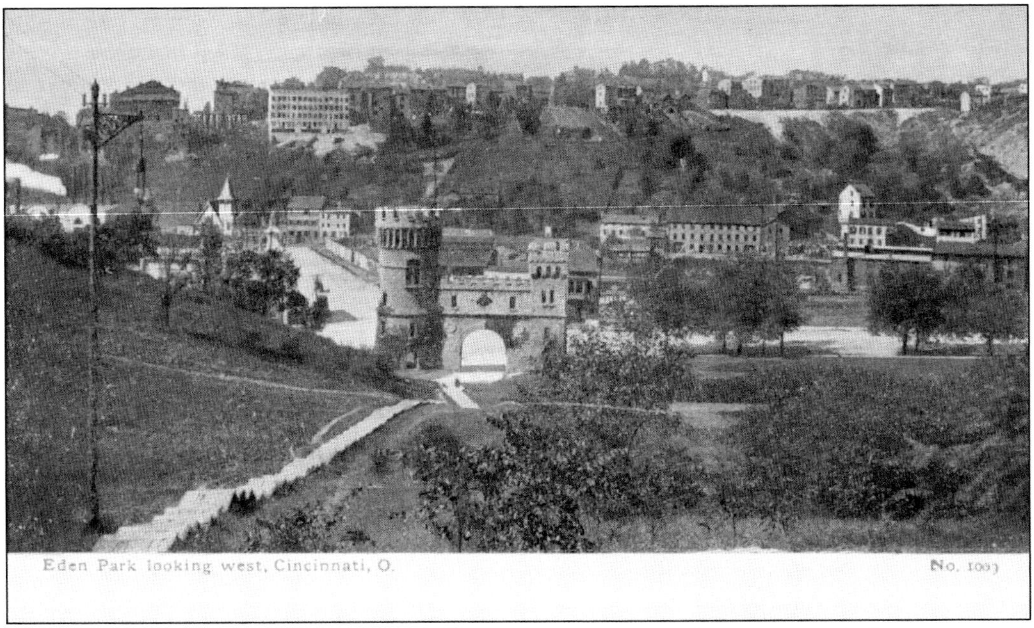

There would probably not be an Eden Park today were it not for water. Nicholas Longworth tried unsuccessfully to sell the land to the city when his grape crops failed, but it was the water department that convinced city hall that the property could be used as a reservoir for the city's water supply, saving money in the process. (From the Collection of the Public Library of Cincinnati and Hamilton County.)

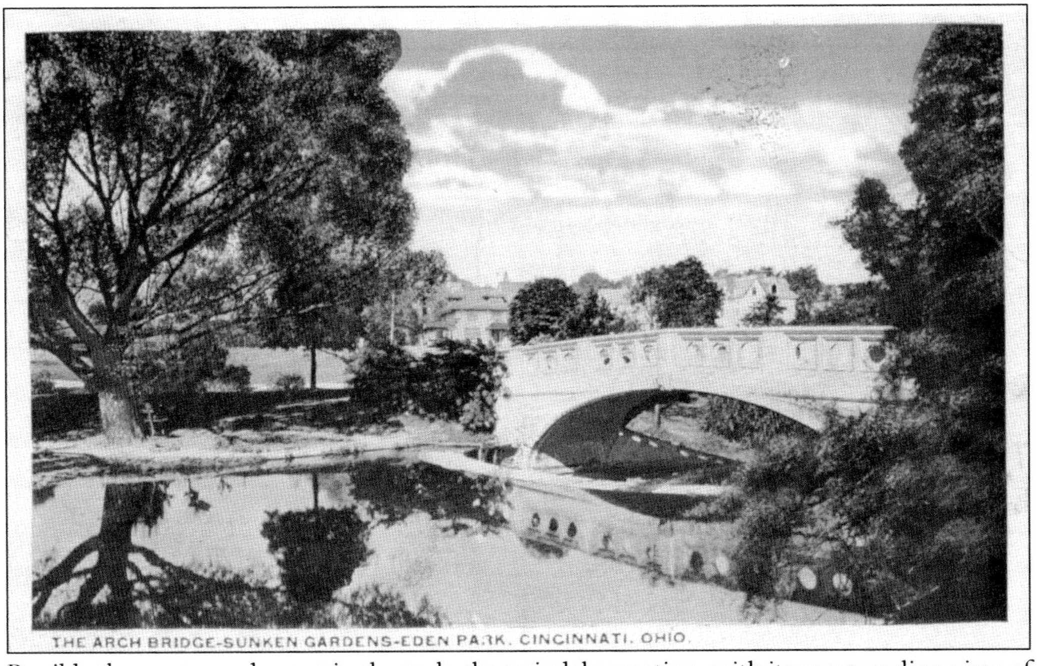

Possibly the most popular spot in the park, the twin lakes section, with its commanding view of the Ohio River and northern Kentucky, was developed in 1891. This area is actually the site of the quarry from which the limestone was excavated to construct the retaining wall of the nearby reservoir. (From the Collection of the Public Library of Cincinnati and Hamilton County.)

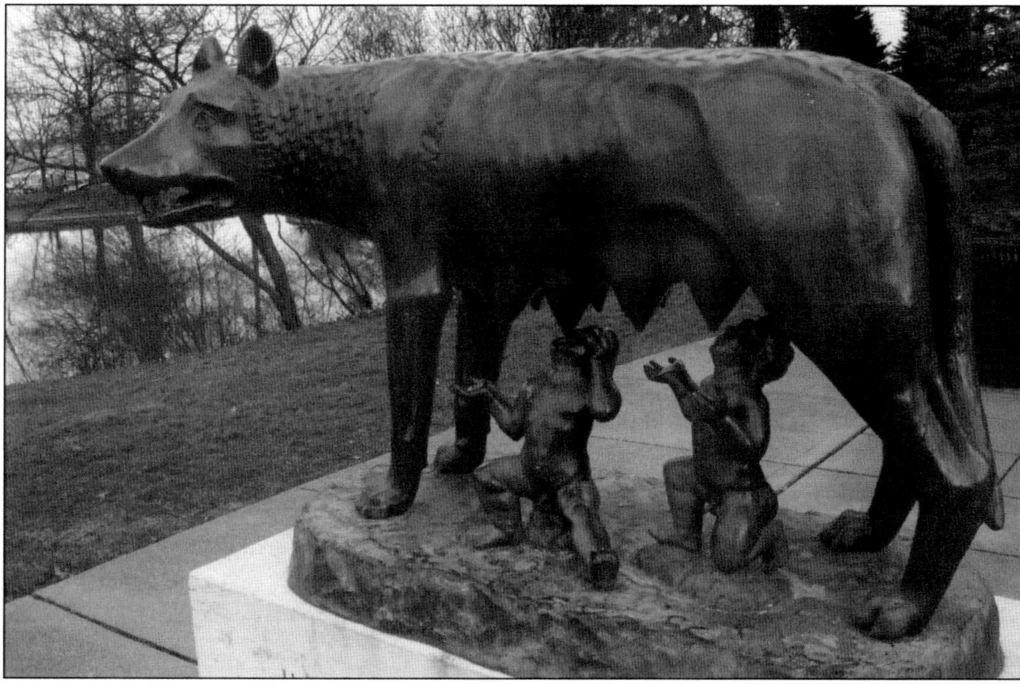

During an earthquake in 1931, a replica of the famous statue depicting a she-wolf nursing Romulus and Remus was being dedicated. It was a gift from the Italian dictator Benito Mussolini. During World War II, some irate citizens announced they were going to sneak in and blow it up. Thankfully, they did not, and the statue stands today, its Fascist origins forgotten. (Photograph by Jordan Rolfes.)

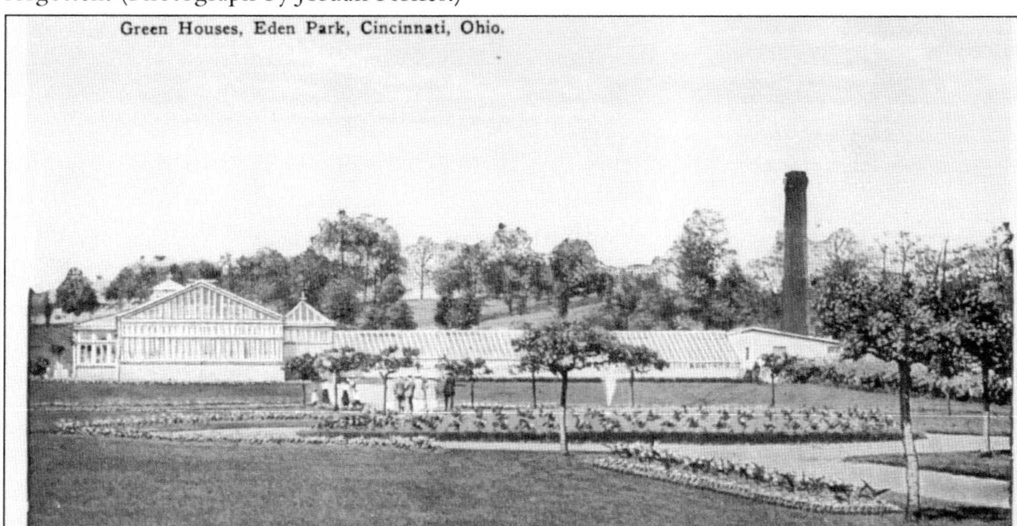

Greenhouses have been located in Eden Park since the 1880s. This earlier institution was replaced in 1933 by the Krohn Conservatory. Today, the Krohn features numerous plants on display—from cacti to orchids—as well as Western-Southern's Christmas manger scene and a popular butterfly show. A 2006 temporary exhibit displayed such rarities as the corpse flower, which smells like rotting meat. (From the Collection of the Public Library of Cincinnati and Hamilton County.)

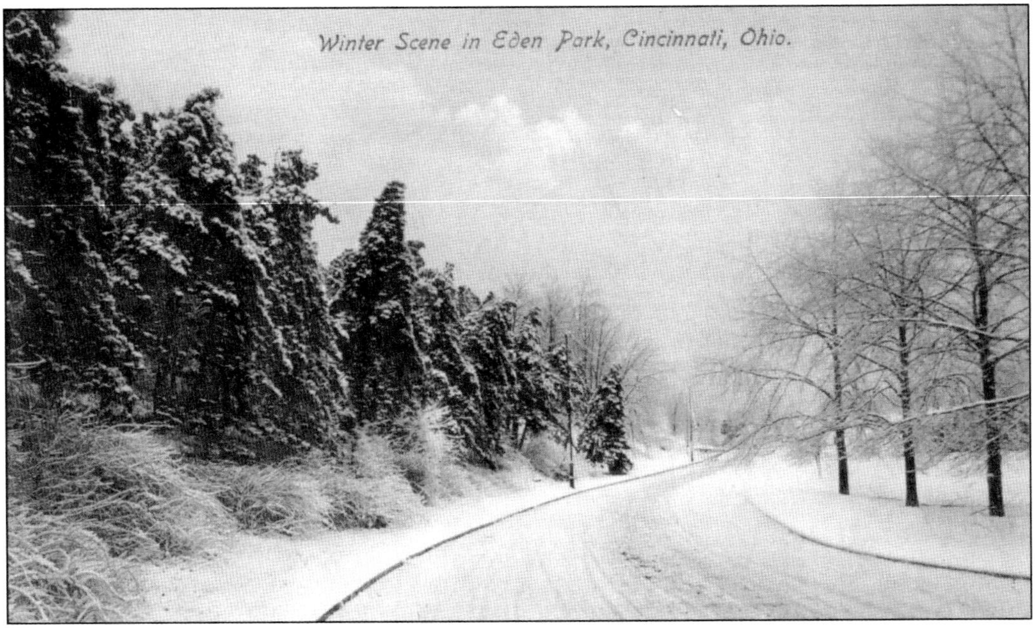

While Eden Park is beautiful in all seasons, it is especially majestic in the winter, with Mirror Lake a favorite spot for ice-skating. The roads, however, with their many curves and steep grades on the sides, can be a bit challenging. (From the Collection of the Public Library of Cincinnati and Hamilton County.)

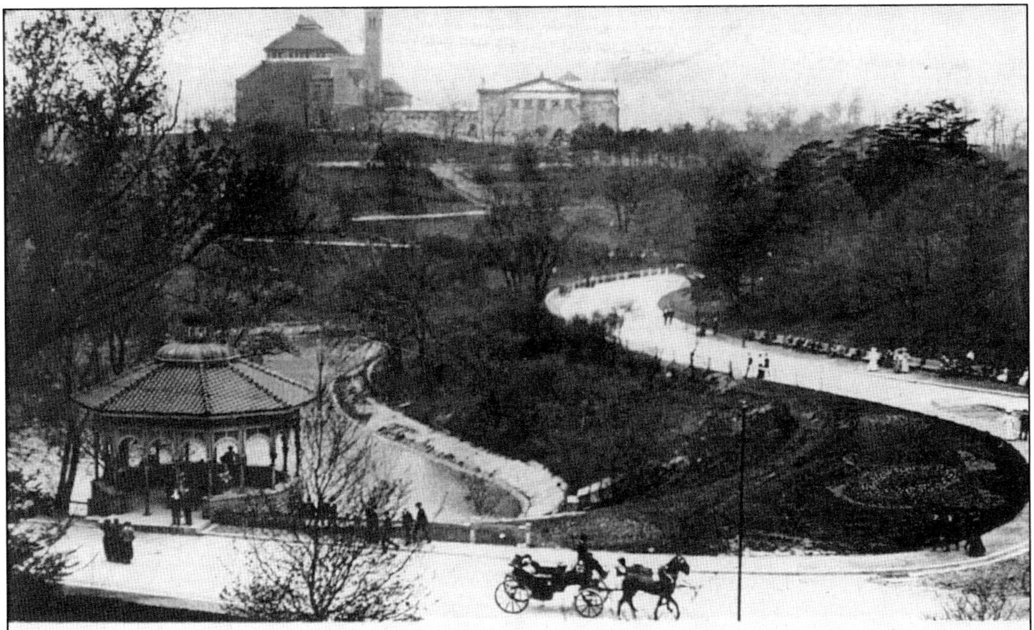

The massive reservoir underneath Mirror Lake was an answer the growing city's water needs. Few people realize while jogging about in spring or ice-skating on Mirror Lake near the gazebo in winter that they are actually on the roof of the reservoir. (From the Collection of the Public Library of Cincinnati and Hamilton County.)

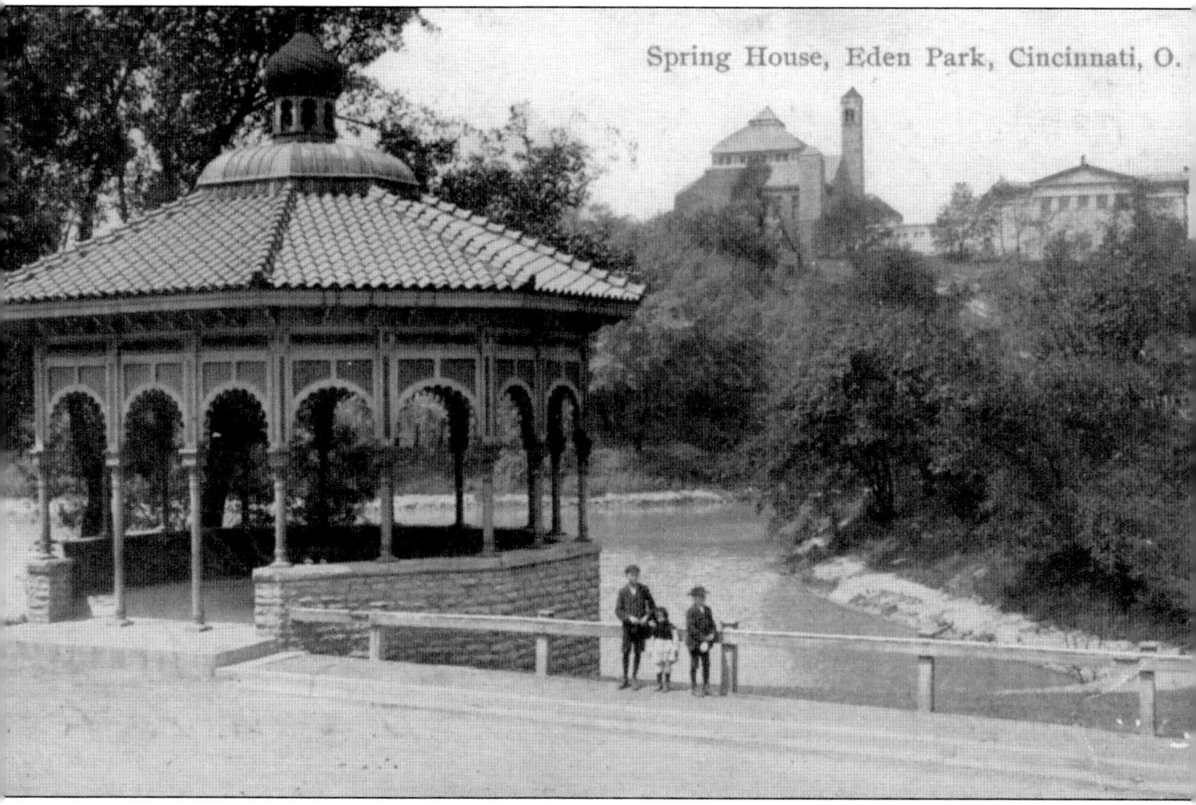

This Moorish gazebo has an incredible story behind it. The edifice is said to be haunted by the ghost of Imogene Remus, the unfaithful wife of the famous gangster George Remus. Remus ran a massive bootlegging empire from the Gehrum farm along Queen City Avenue. At his 1922 New Year's Eve party, he gave away diamond necklaces and new automobiles to his guests as party favors. After he was sent to prison, Imogene ran off with the federal agent who had convicted him. In 1927, on the way to finalize his divorce, the enraged bootlegger chased down Imogene's cab and shot her to death at this gazebo. As a lawyer, Remus believed he could win his trial, so he defended himself. His opponent was Charles Taft, the son of former president William Howard Taft. Going against the legal giant, Remus won the case. He went on to live peacefully in Covington, Kentucky. Imogene's ghost is said to still haunt the gazebo. (From the Collection of the Public Library of Cincinnati and Hamilton County.)

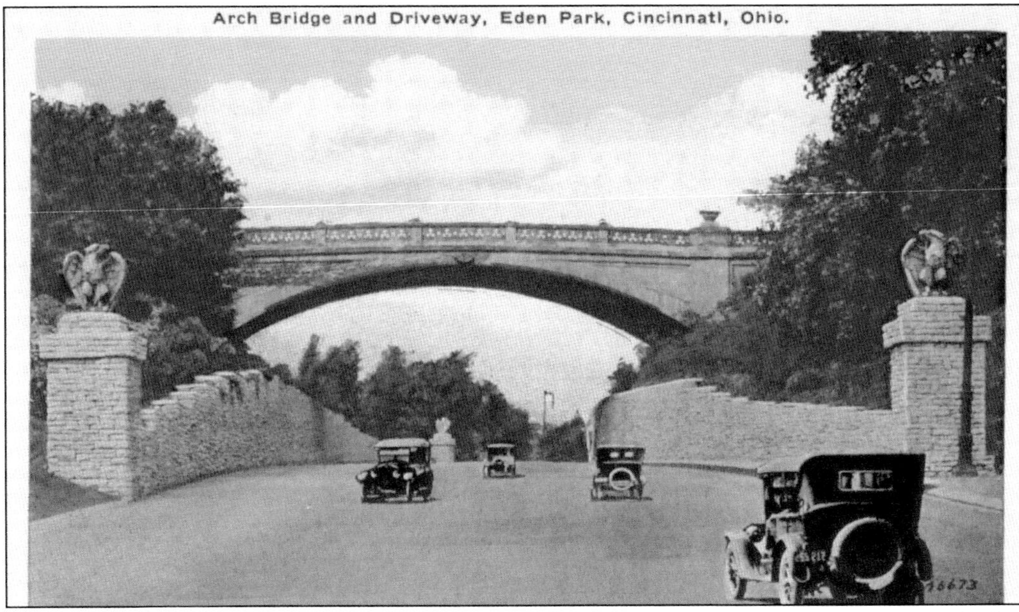

One of the most scenic spots in Eden Park is the Melan Arch Bridge, a stone structure flanked by patriotic eagles. The majestic birds were not carved for the bridge, they were actually part of the huge Gothic Revival Chamber of Commerce Building downtown and were rescued after the building was destroyed by fire in 1911. (From the Collection of the Public Library of Cincinnati and Hamilton County.)

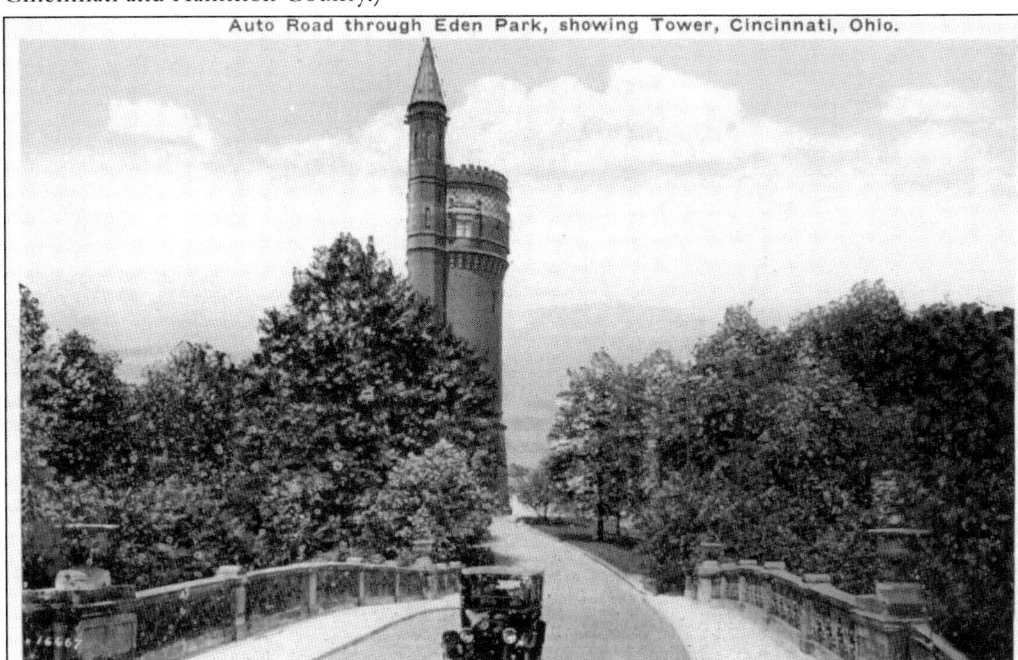

Samuel Hannaford, who designed many of the landmarks of the Queen City, designed not one but two medieval towers in Eden Park. Besides the Elsinore Castle on Gilbert Avenue, he also created this water tower further up in the park, complete with gargoyles. (From the Collection of the Public Library of Cincinnati and Hamilton County.)

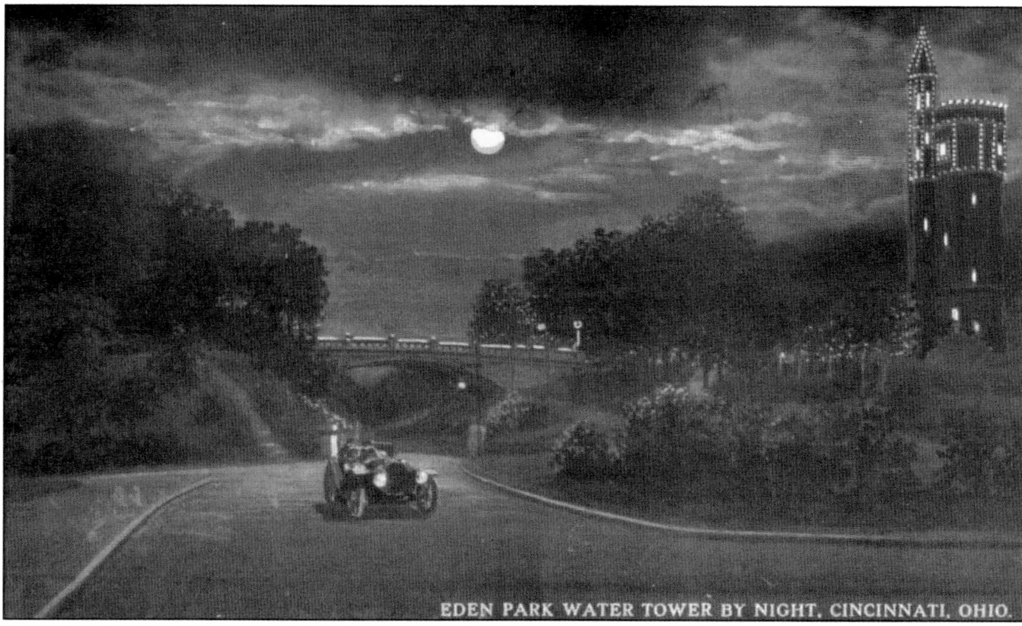

Hannaford's old water tower is even more beautiful at night. Built in 1894, the turret was originally designed as a pressure tank. However, the city was growing so fast that this tower, while attractive, was inefficient. By 1916, it was no longer used as a water tank, but it remains a charming feature in the park. (From the Collection of the Public Library of Cincinnati and Hamilton County.)

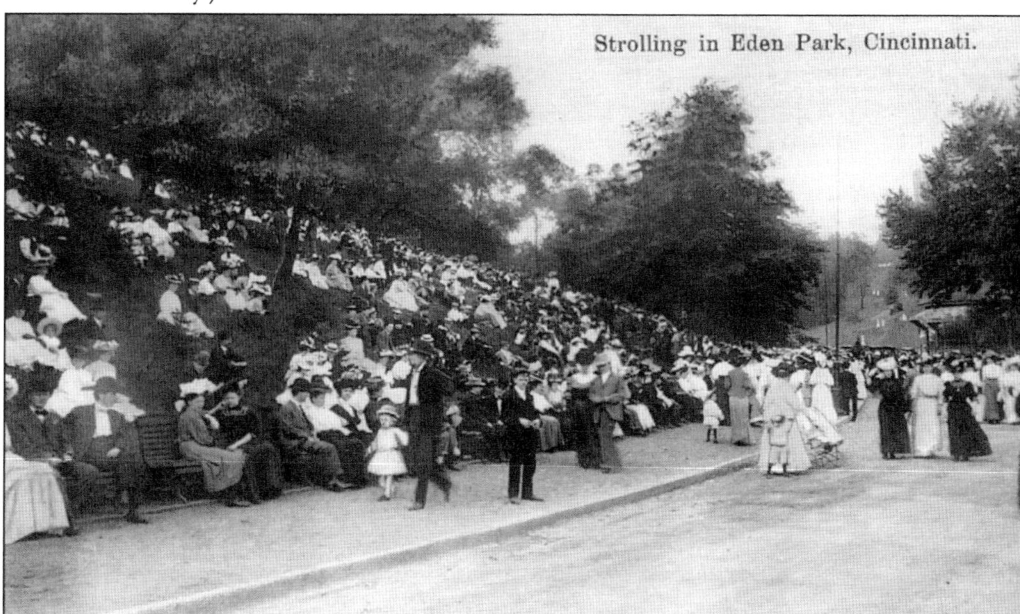

Eden Park has always been the home to the arts. These Sunday afternoon walkers are no doubt listening to a band concert. The tradition continues, as today the Playhouse in the Park offers live theater and has even created a new Cincinnati holiday tradition with its annual performance of Charles Dickens's *A Christmas Carol*. (From the Collection of the Public Library of Cincinnati and Hamilton County.)

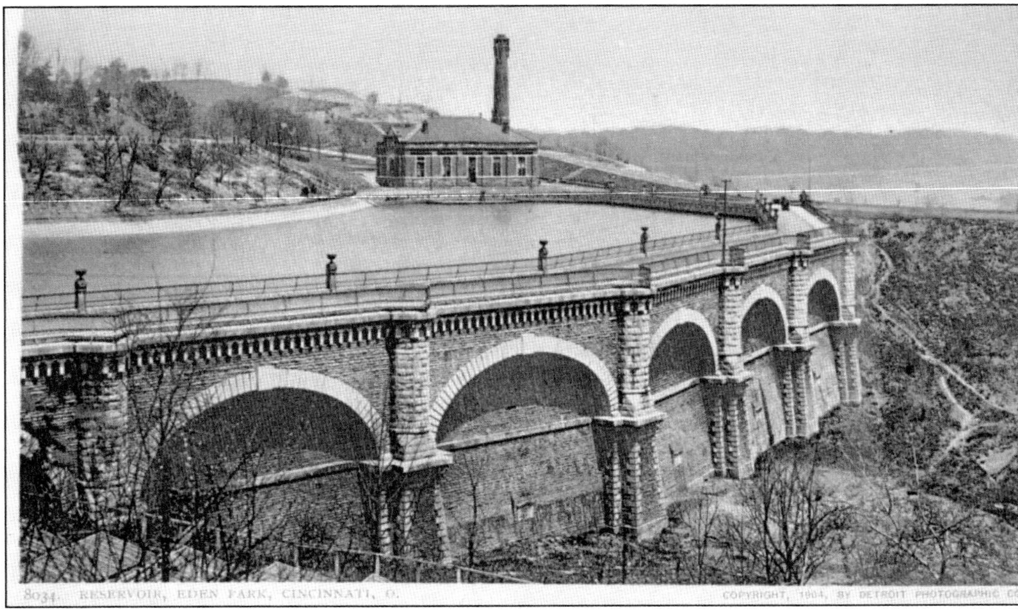

The stone walls of this old reservoir still remain, now attracting rock climbers. To the left of this card is the modern Mirror Lake. In 1998, city council was compelled to have the bottom of the lake painted an unnatural color to prevent people or animals from wandering in. The water is not chlorinated. (From the Collection of the Public Library of Cincinnati and Hamilton County.)

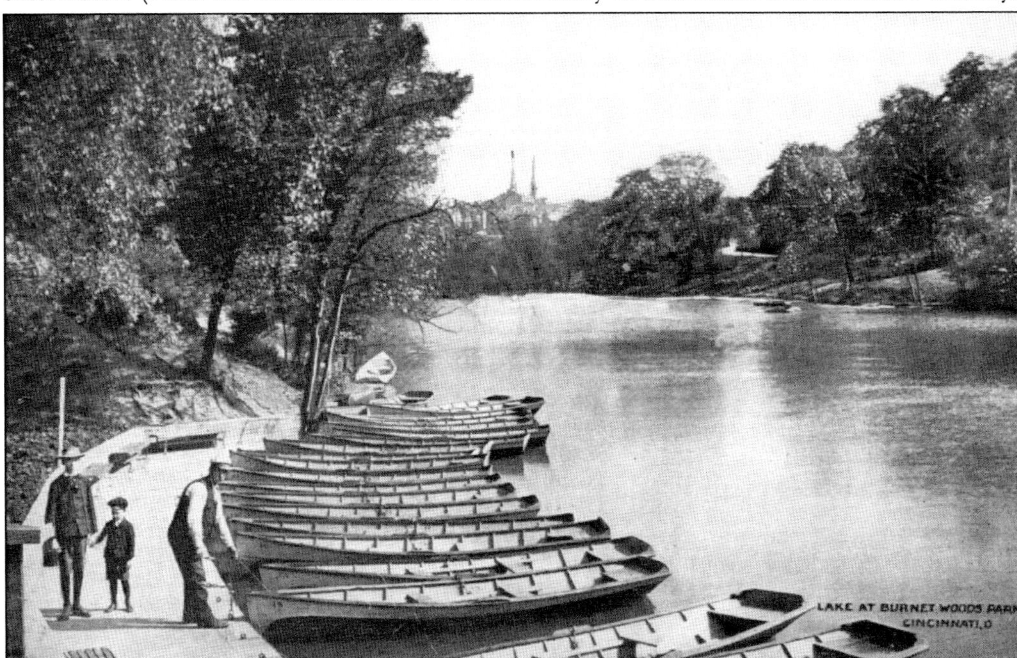

In 1936, the Works Progress Administration (WPA) constructed a much larger vessel on this lake, a replica of the HMS *Pinafore*. The WPA also constructed a Trailways Museum in Burnet Woods. However, people became irate in 1937 when the old 1874 Shelter House was torn down. Many romances had begun there, and many lovers' initials had been carved into nearby trees. (From the Collection of the Public Library of Cincinnati and Hamilton County.)

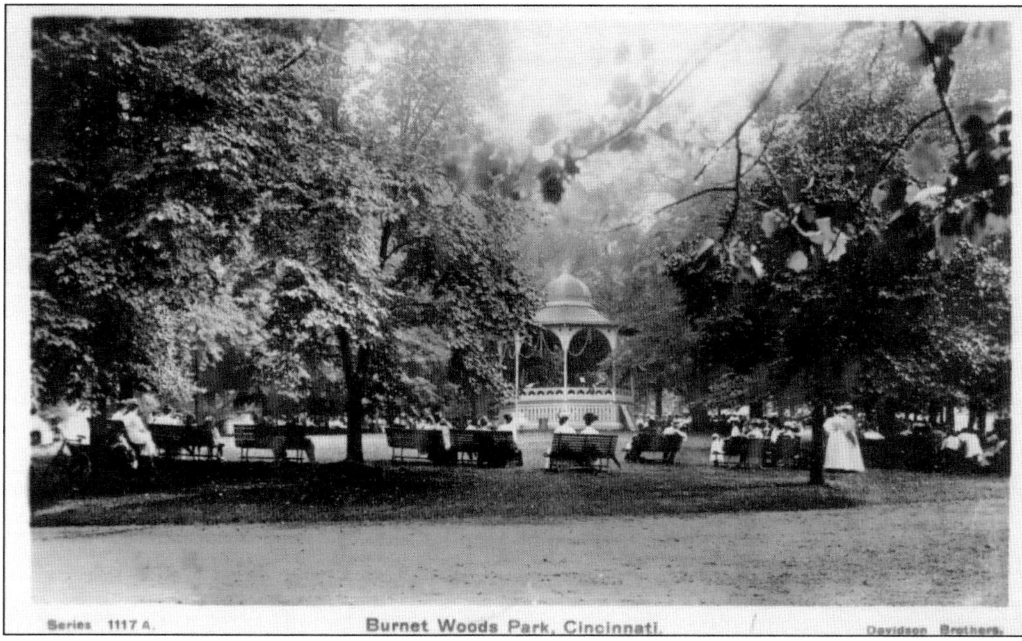

On Thursday evenings in the summer, people escaped the heat and the filthy air and flocked to musical entertainment on this small bit of nature among the trees. The free concerts in Burnet Woods were managed by the Groesbeck Concert Fund, beginning in 1875 as a gift to the people of the city from William Groesbeck. (From the Collection of the Public Library of Cincinnati and Hamilton County.)

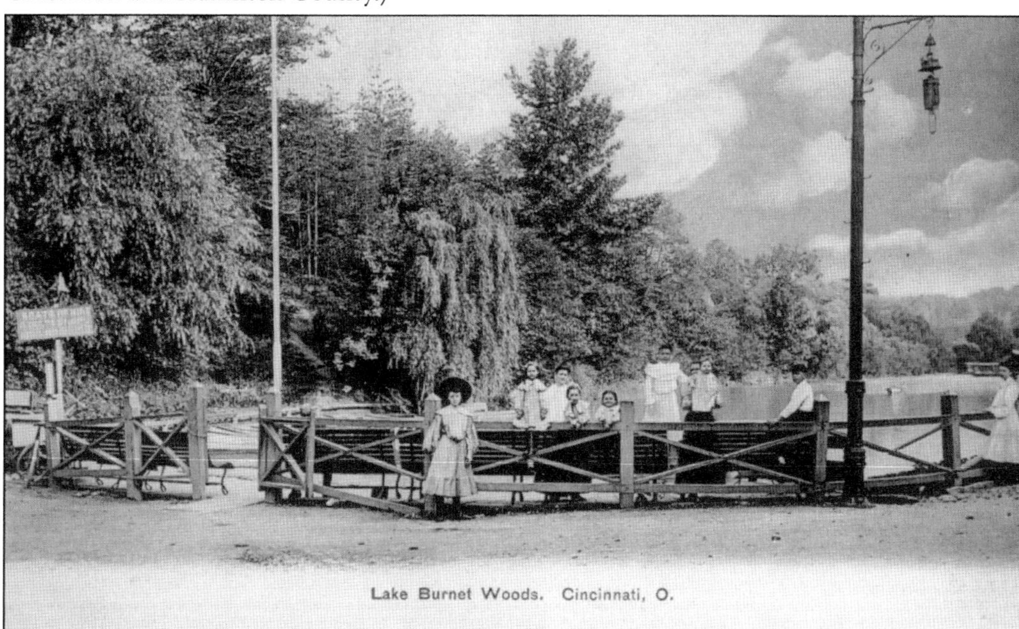

While many recreational activities still go on in Burnet Woods, golf is no longer one of them. In the 1870s, a Cincinnati alderman was walking through the park when an errant golf ball knocked his top hat off of his head. The very next day, he introduced legislation to outlaw the game in the park. (From the Collection of the Public Library of Cincinnati and Hamilton County.)

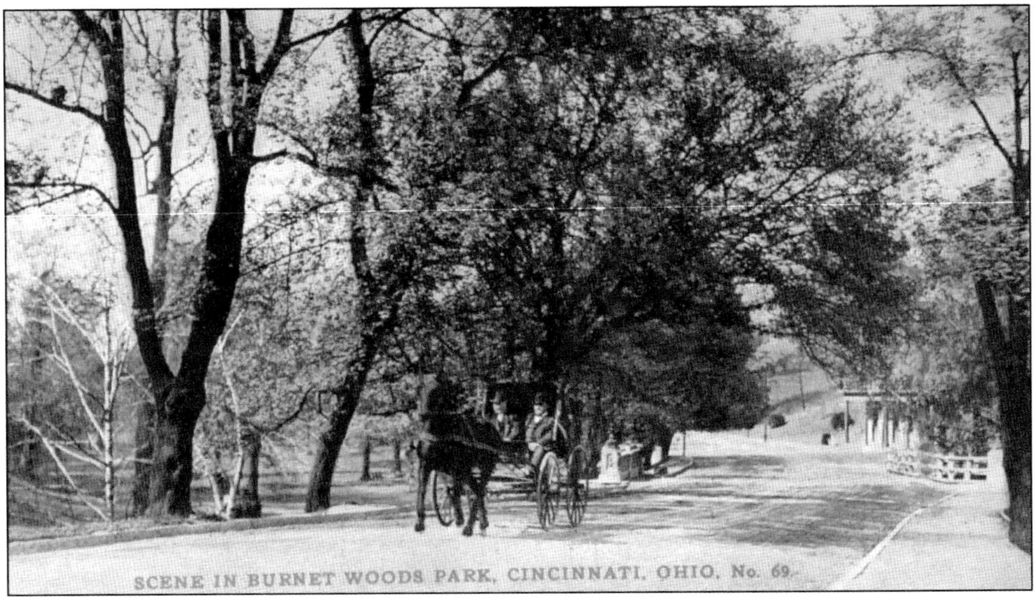

It is curious to think that at one time, Germans were not allowed to enjoy Burnet Woods. In 1918, Michael Devanney, a federal marshal, made a number of locations in the city off-limits for German nationals, including Burnet Woods, Carthage Fair, and even the old Medical College Building. He warned Germans that these regulations would be "vigorously enforced." (From the Collection of the Public Library of Cincinnati and Hamilton County.)

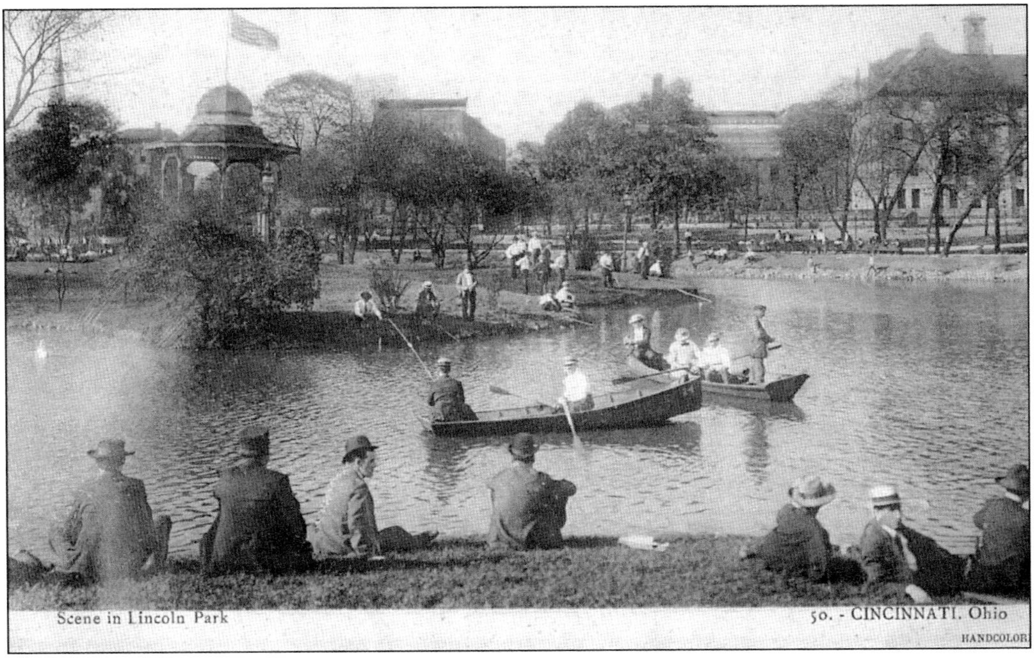

Lincoln Park, with its magnificent lake, is a lost treasure of the West End. For a penny, children could take a boat ride, and in winter, thousands skated there. The grounds were so pleasant that in the heat of summer, people actually slept here in the cool night air. The park was replaced in the 1930s by Union Terminal. (From the Collection of the Public Library of Cincinnati and Hamilton County.)

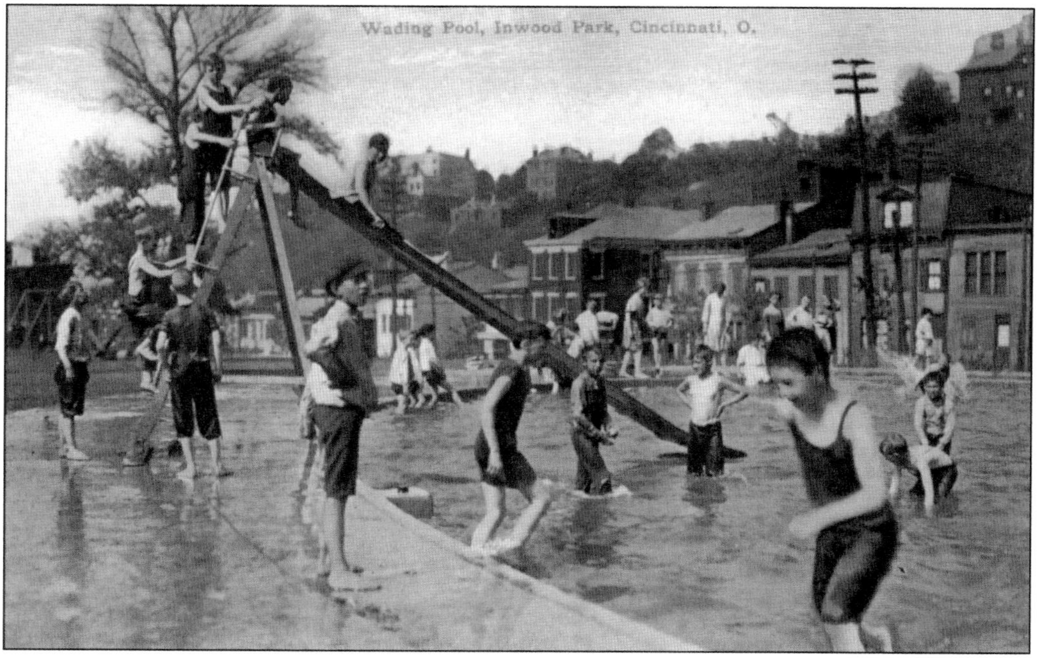

This land has changed many times over the years—from Deer Lodge to a quarry and from dump to a beautiful park. Originally the summer retreat of wealthy iron merchant George Schoenberger, the site was later a dump until it was purchased by the city in 1904. Turner parades marched here, ending at a statue of the movement's founder, Friedrich Ludwig Jahn. (From the Collection of the Public Library of Cincinnati and Hamilton County.)

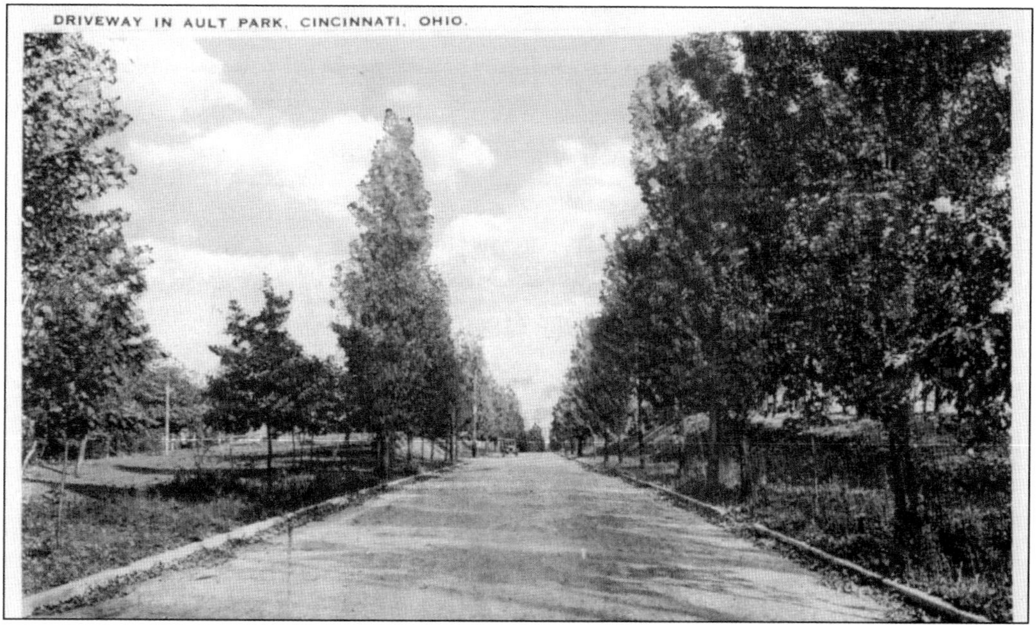

Mount Lookout's Ault Park is seen here in 1926. On land donated by Levi Addison Ault, the city created one of its most beautiful parks, with a spectacular view. Not seen here is the unique method the city used to cut the grass and trim the brush: 97 sheep. (From the Collection of the Public Library of Cincinnati and Hamilton County.)

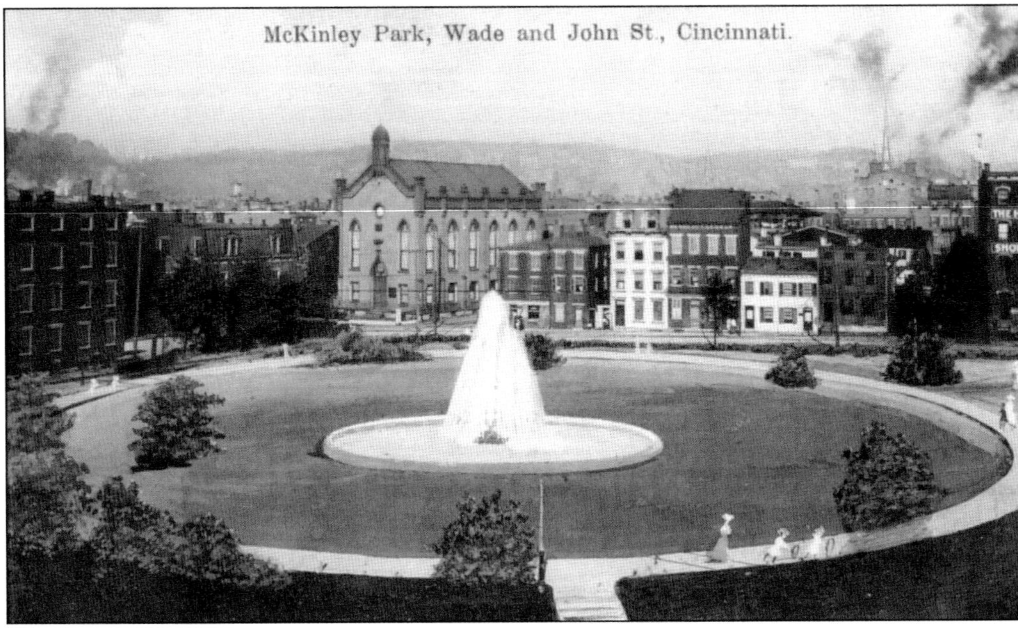

This idyllic spot is now known as Laurel Playground. Very few remember that it is located near the site of one of Cincinnati's grisliest murders. In the 1870s, journalist Lafcadio Hearn wrote at length about two killers whom he dubbed the Furnace Fiends after they incinerated their victim's body in a nearby factory. (From the Collection of the Public Library of Cincinnati and Hamilton County.)

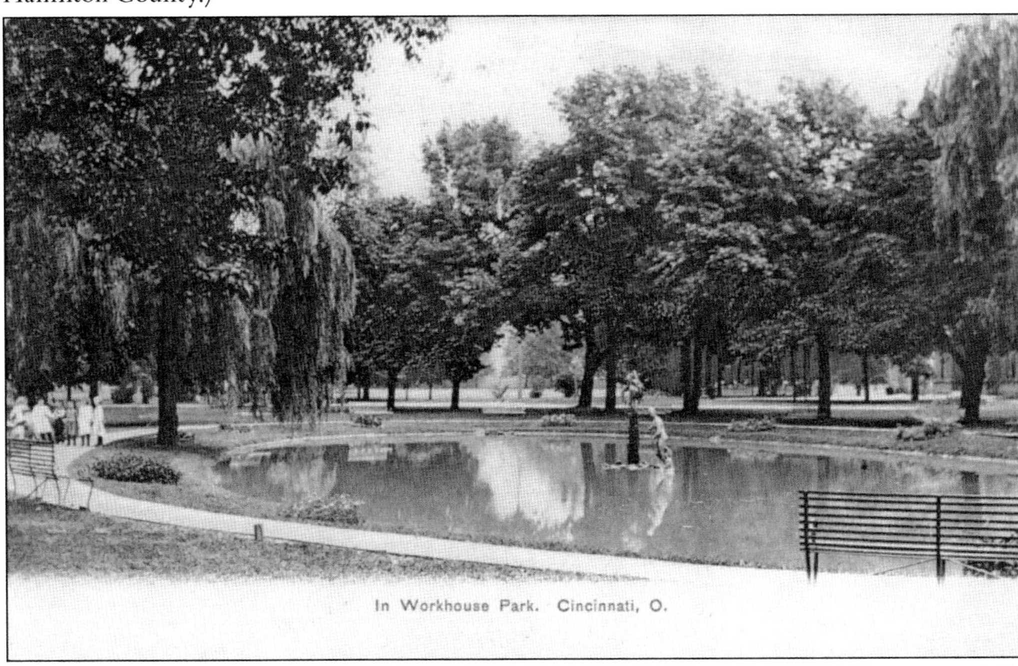

The conditions inside of the Cincinnati Workhouse were anything but pleasant. Thankfully, for those visiting and for those being released, there is a bit of beauty just outside of the old walls. Today, this park features a memorial statue honoring World War I soldiers. (From the Collection of the Public Library of Cincinnati and Hamilton County.)

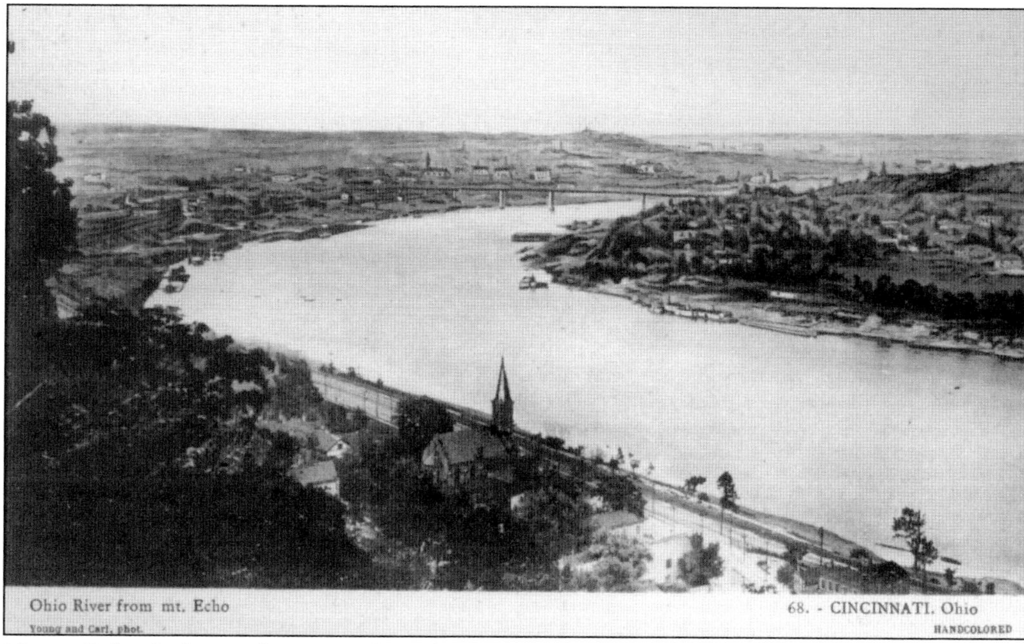

Mount Echo Park, on the west side, refuses to die. Opened in 1908 on the site of an old dairy farm, it features one of the finest views of the city skyline and river. However, due to funding issues and a devastating landslide, the park was closed for many years before being reopened in 1985. (From the Collection of the Public Library of Cincinnati and Hamilton County.)

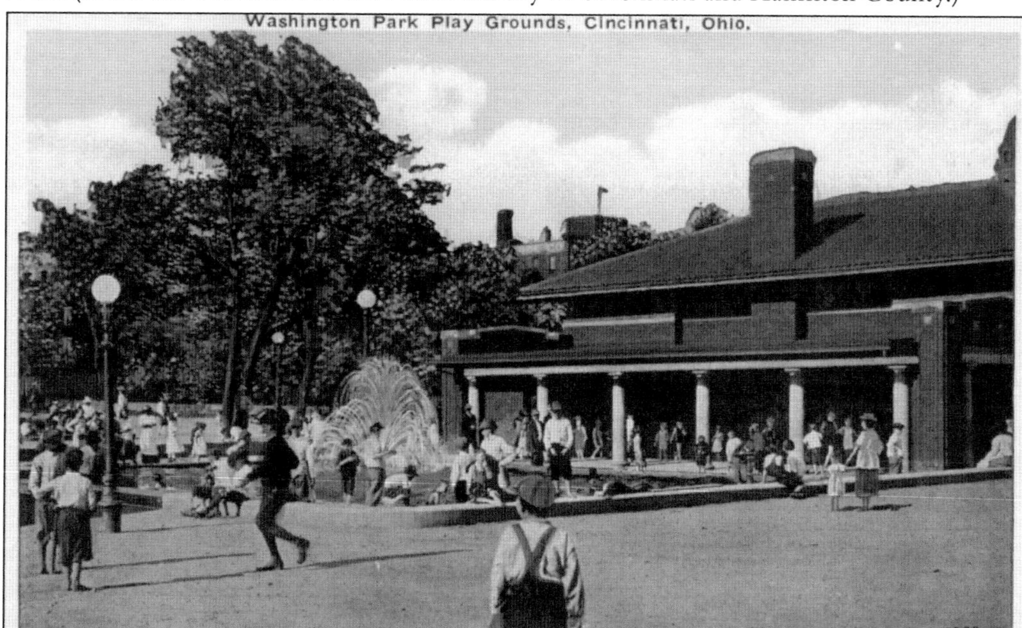

The modern Washington Park was built over the site of four 19th-century cemeteries. The first was Presbyterian, followed by an Episcopalian, a German Protestant, and a Civil War cemetery. Over the years, construction has occasionally unearthed forgotten graves or tombstones. In 2010, renovation dug into more than 50 grave shafts. (From the Collection of the Public Library of Cincinnati and Hamilton County.)

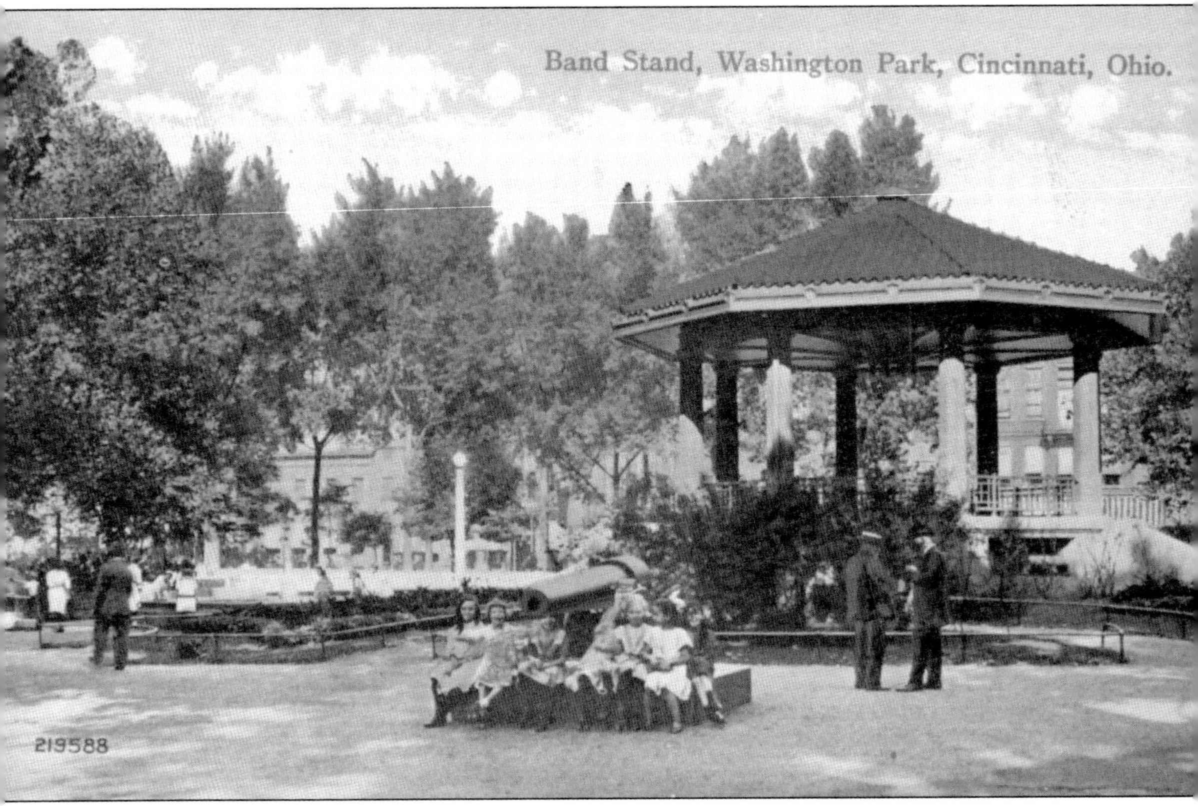

Washington Park does not look like this today. As the surrounding neighborhood of Over-the-Rhine deteriorated over the years, descending from a working-class German neighborhood to a poverty-stricken area, the once idyllic park across from Music Hall became less and less hospitable. In 1888, the park attracted nearly a million visitors for events celebrating the city's centennial. In 2012, it is a haven for drug dealers, the homeless, and other unsavory elements of society. It was nearly the scene of chaos in 1911 after a dispute over a bench turned into a brawl that resulted in the dispatching of several patrol wagons to calm a potential riot. In the midst of the confusion, one policeman was struck by a blackjack. Police officer William Crowley had his gun drawn on miscreant Joseph Farmer. Farmer told the policeman, "Now Bill, I've always been a good friend of yours. Don't treat me that way." Officer Crowley reflected upon their long friendship and lowered his gun. As soon as he did, Farmer punched him. (From the Collection of the Public Library of Cincinnati and Hamilton County.)

Five

A Trip to the Zoo

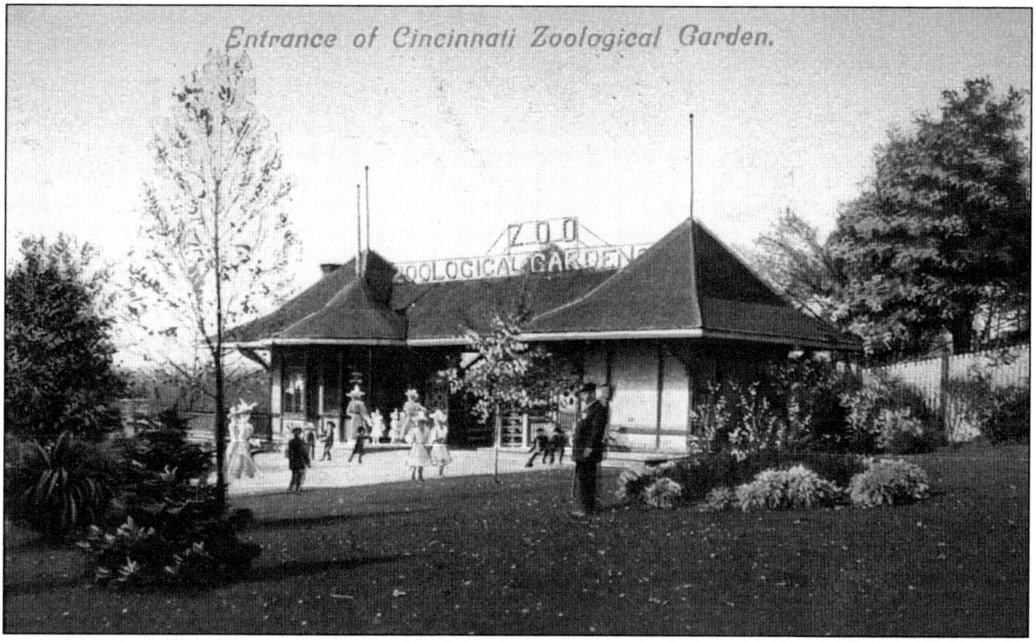

One of the city's most beloved landmarks is the Cincinnati Zoo and Botanical Gardens. The zoo features nearly 2,000 different animals of more than 500 species in a magnificent 65-acre park. It is celebrated for its work in conservation and breeding endangered species. (From the Collection of the Public Library of Cincinnati and Hamilton County.)

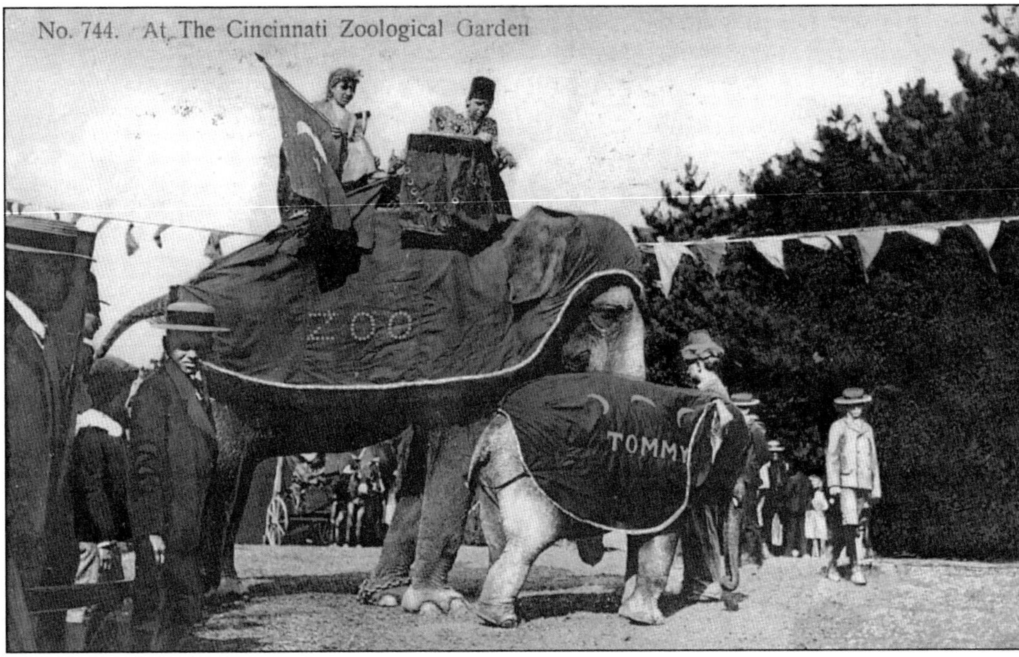

Generations of Cincinnatians and visitors to the city have loved a day at the zoo. The path leading up to this happy Sunday outing in 1907, with a thrilling ride on an exotic elephant, began with, of all things, caterpillars. (From the Collection of the Public Library of Cincinnati and Hamilton County.)

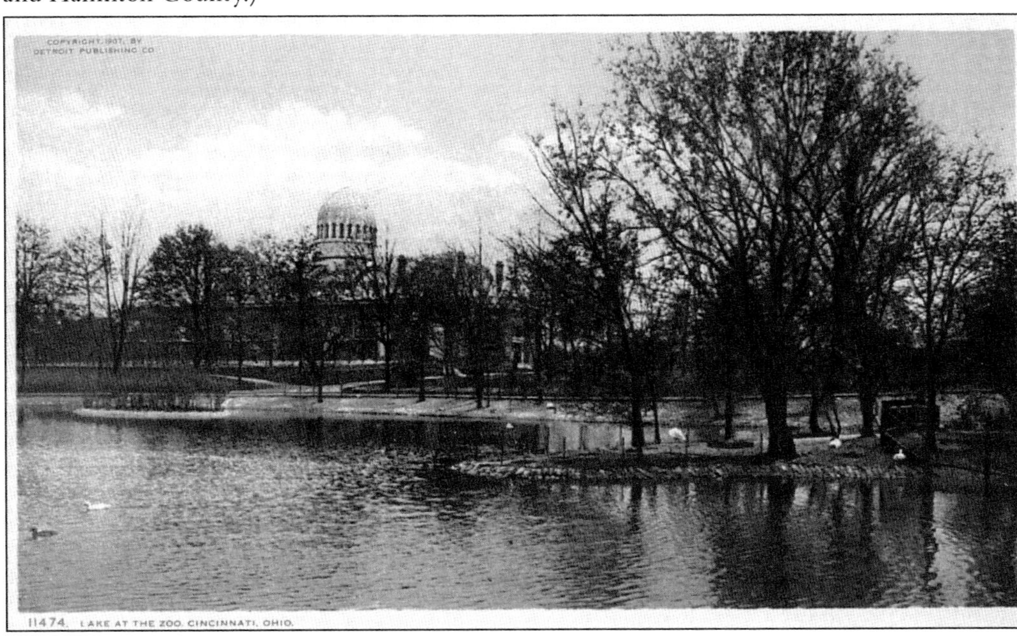

In 1872, a swarm of caterpillars destroyed much of the vegetation in Cincinnati. German immigrant and industrialist Andrew Erkenbrecher imported birds to eat the caterpillars. This could have resulted in an ecological disaster, but instead it led, three years later, to the forming of the Cincinnati Zoological Gardens, the second-oldest public zoo in the nation. (From the Collection of the Public Library of Cincinnati and Hamilton County.)

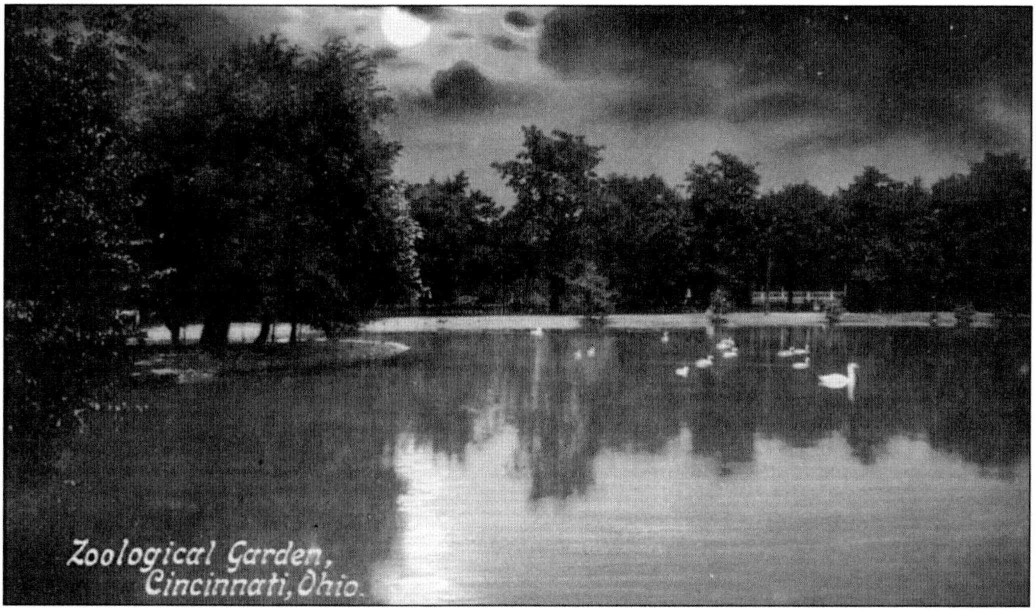

There was originally a great deal of controversy as to where exactly the new zoo should be located. Both Eden Park and Burnet Woods were unacceptable, so a remote cow pasture known as Blakely Woods was finally chosen, in out-of-the-way Avondale. As seen in this night view, the transformation from field to park went very well. (From the Collection of the Public Library of Cincinnati and Hamilton County.)

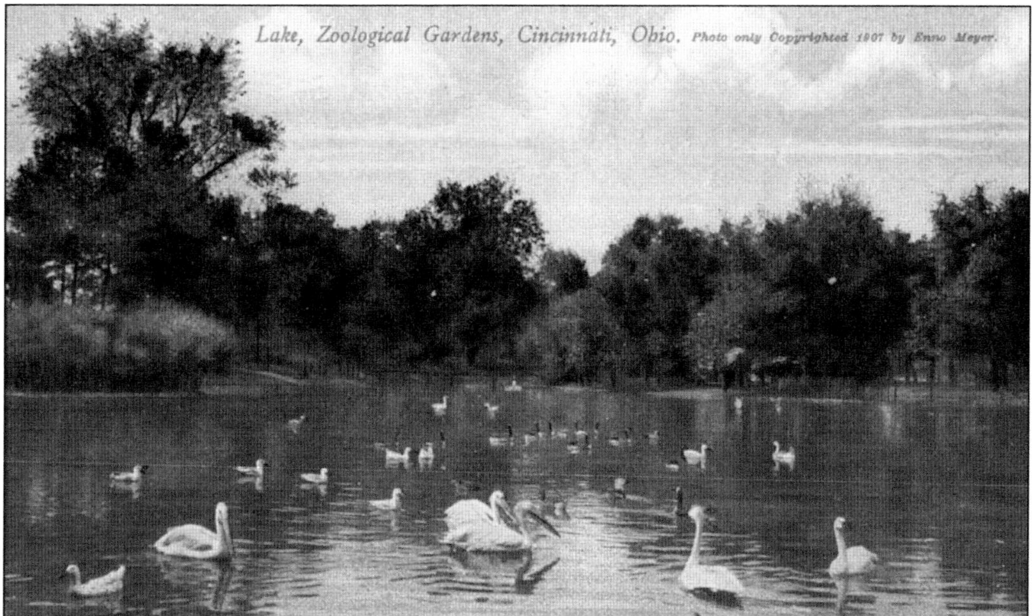

Adolph Strauch, who designed the idyllic grounds of Spring Grove, gave assistance and trees to the new zoological garden. Despite its beauty, the zoo was often in financial peril before being rescued by wealthy donors. Oliver M. Gale jokingly stated that its early days "read like the *Perils of Pauline*." (From the Collection of the Public Library of Cincinnati and Hamilton County.)

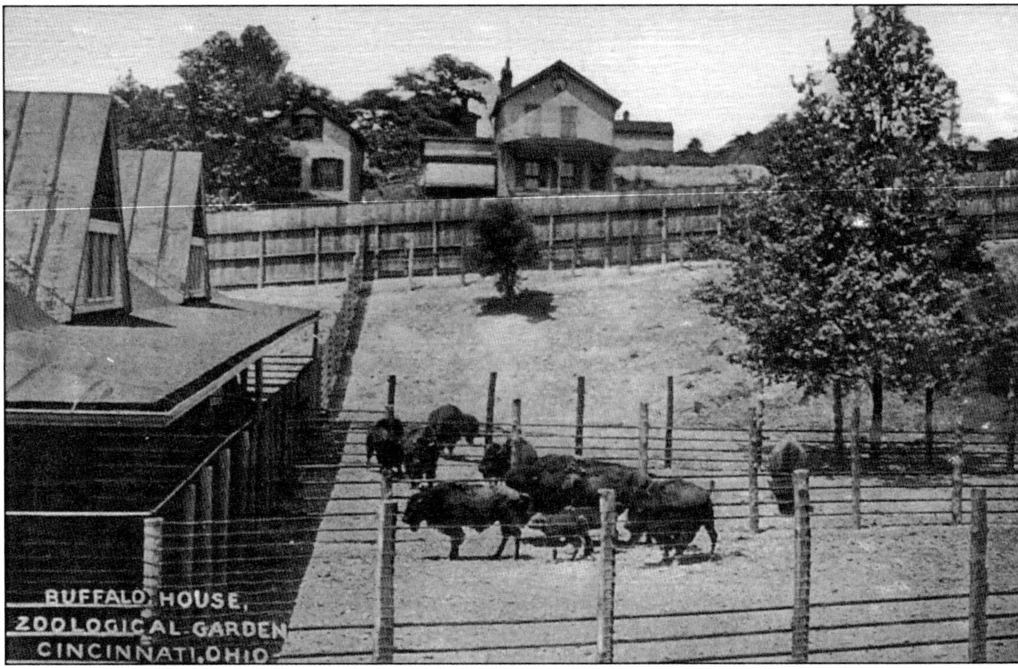

In 1903, the zoo created a large enclosure for the great symbol of the American west, the buffalo. At the time, the zoo also had the largest buffalo in captivity in its collection. Only in Cincinnati would this proud example of the quintessential American animal be named Bismarck. (From the Collection of the Public Library of Cincinnati and Hamilton County.)

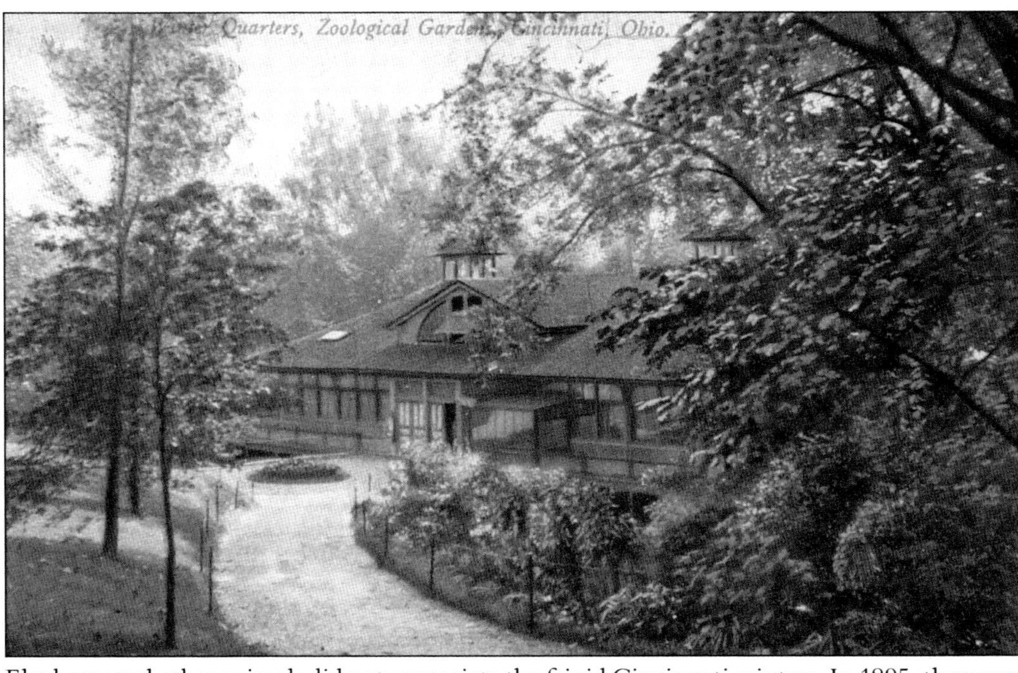

Elephants and other animals did not appreciate the frigid Cincinnati winters. In 1895, they were accommodated by a special building to ensure their safety and comfort. (From the Collection of the Public Library of Cincinnati and Hamilton County.)

This curious postcard shows the care that the zookeepers used when transporting their charges. The sides of the wagon are too high for the animal to jump out of and padded so the giraffe does not get injured from fright. In 1911, one zoo giraffe, Alice, who was named after Pres. Theodore Roosevelt's daughter, died from fright during a particularly violent thunderstorm. (From the Collection of the Public Library of Cincinnati and Hamilton County.)

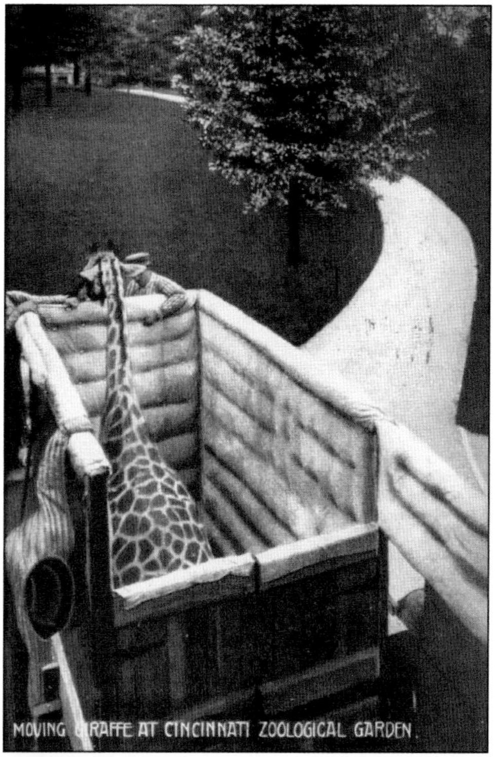

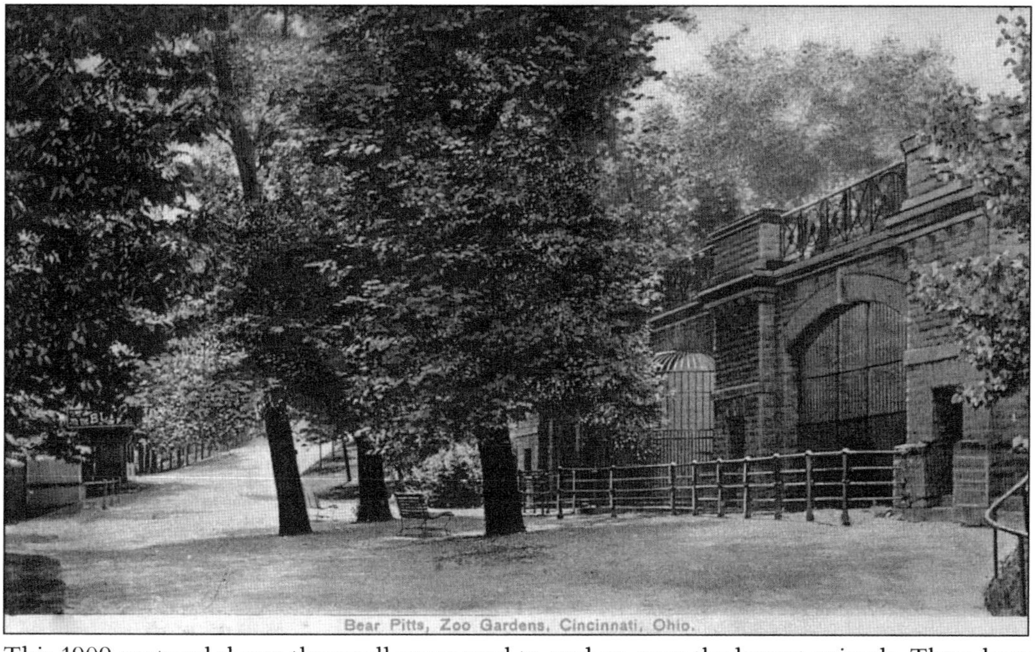

This 1909 postcard shows the small cages used to enclose even the largest animals. Three bear pits were placed side by side, giving the animals a mere 22-foot-by-24-foot area. The design, by James McLaughlin, was inspired by a similar enclosure in Hamburg, Germany. Today, the animals are given adequate room to move about. (From the Collection of the Public Library of Cincinnati and Hamilton County.)

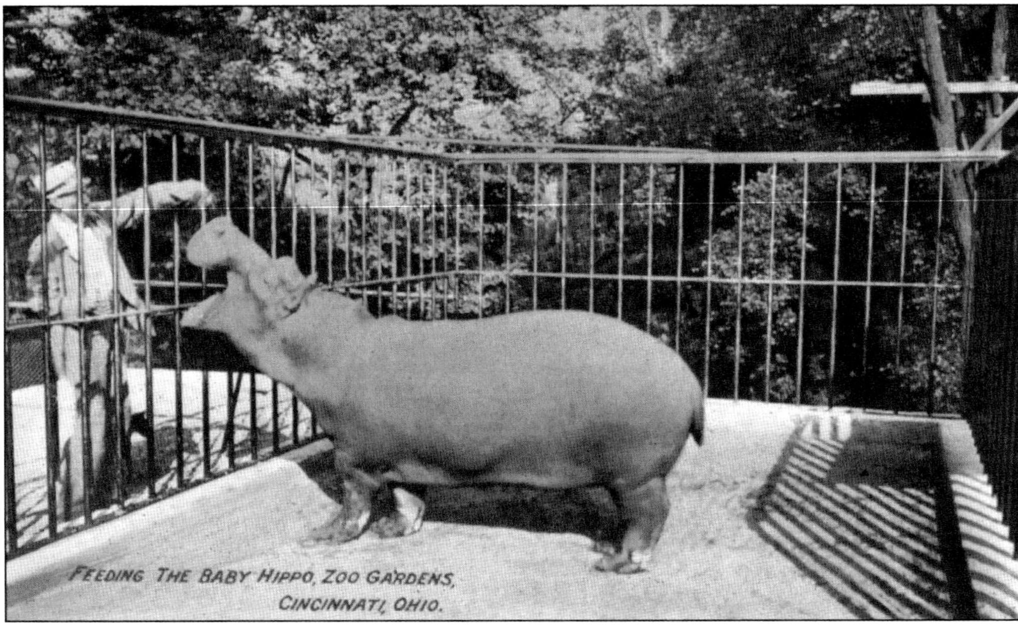

Today, feeding a baby hippopotamus would send a zookeeper into fits. However, in the first two decades of the 1900s, it was considered the fashionable thing to do at the zoo. This hippopotamus here, the famed Zee-kowe, was the largest hippopotamus in captivity at the time. People fed him all sorts of things, including a tennis ball. (From the Collection of the Public Library of Cincinnati and Hamilton County.)

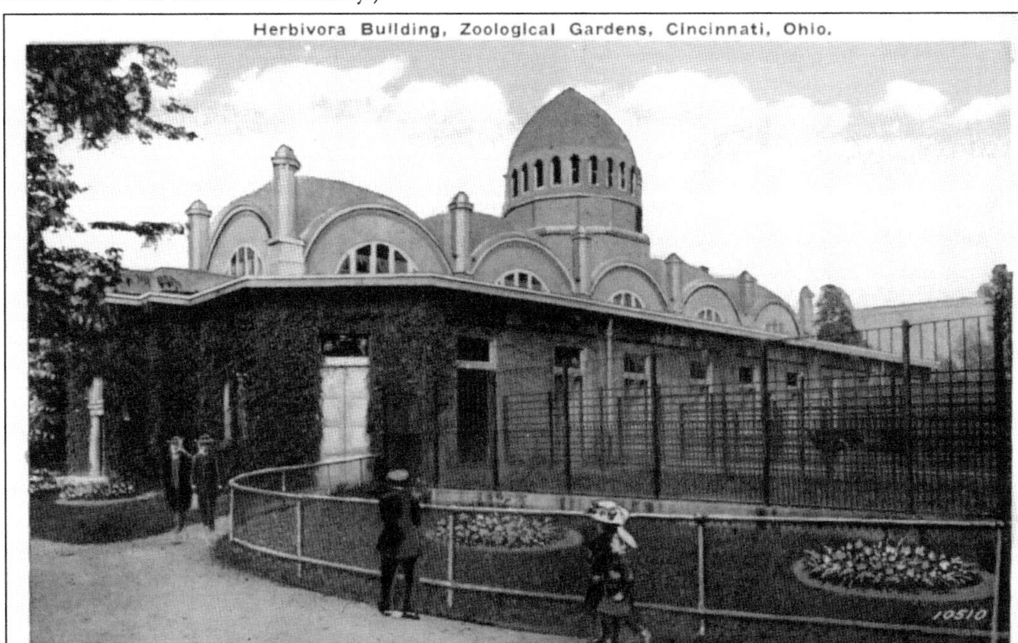

A landmark within a landmark, this herbivore building, now called the Elephant House, was designed by architects Alfred O. Elzner and George M. Anderson to resemble the Taj Mahal. Opened in 1906, it was, at 75 feet tall, the largest animal enclosure in the world for a time. (From the Collection of the Public Library of Cincinnati and Hamilton County.)

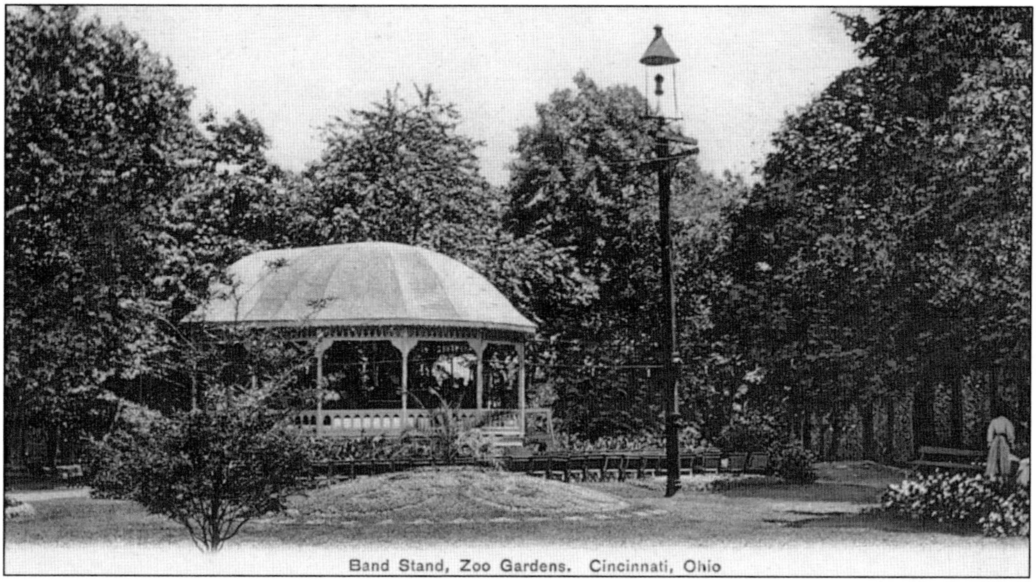

In 1920, this bandstand became an opera stage, but the grand opening almost did not occur. Before the scheduled performance, the workmen went on strike. However, the dispute was settled, and the new stage was ready just before the deadline. Ironically, the first opera performed was *Martha*, the name of the last passenger pigeon that died at the zoo. (From the Collection of the Public Library of Cincinnati and Hamilton County.)

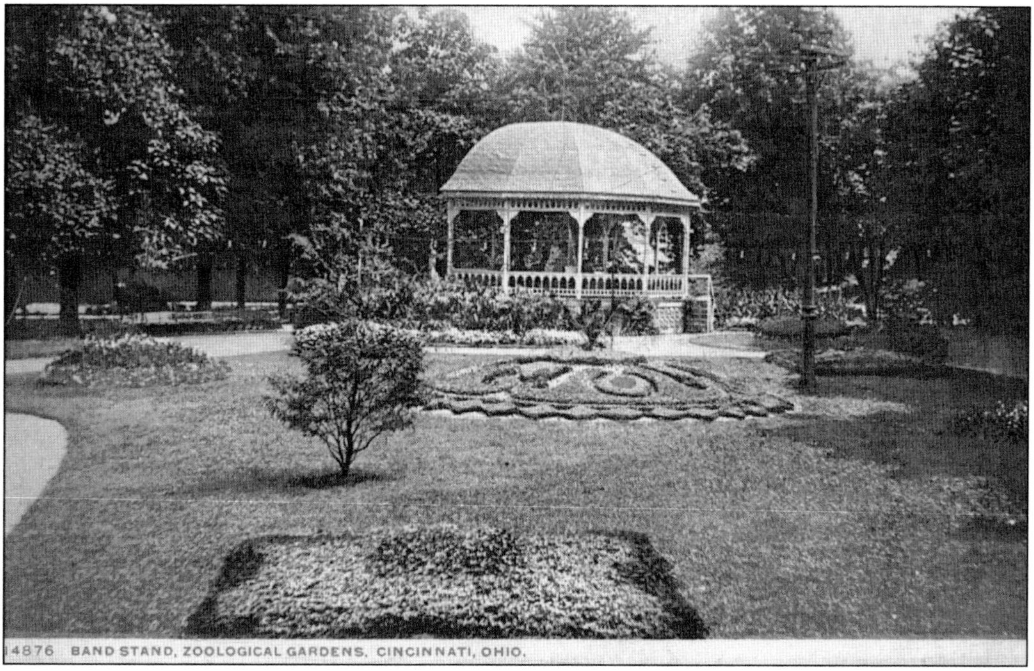

Performing grand operas at the zoo was originally designed as a diversion. Between acts, there was a 45-minute ice-skating performance. Sometimes, the animals would "comment" on the music by making noise. The peacocks loved to shriek their shrill calls, turning a diva's aria into a duet. In 1972, the opera moved to the more sedate Music Hall. (From the Collection of the Public Library of Cincinnati and Hamilton County.)

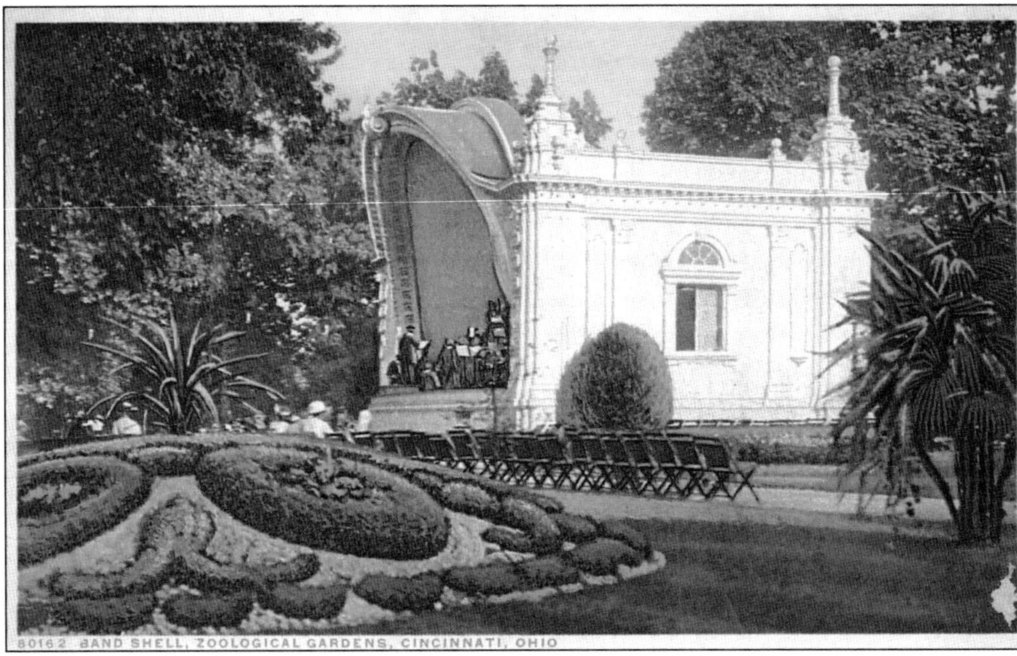

Opera was not the only music heard at the zoo. Since its beginnings, all manners of musical entertainment were offered to attract visitors and make the experience more enjoyable. One could not only dance to popular orchestras, but could also hear such treats as Swiss yodelers. (From the Collection of the Public Library of Cincinnati and Hamilton County.)

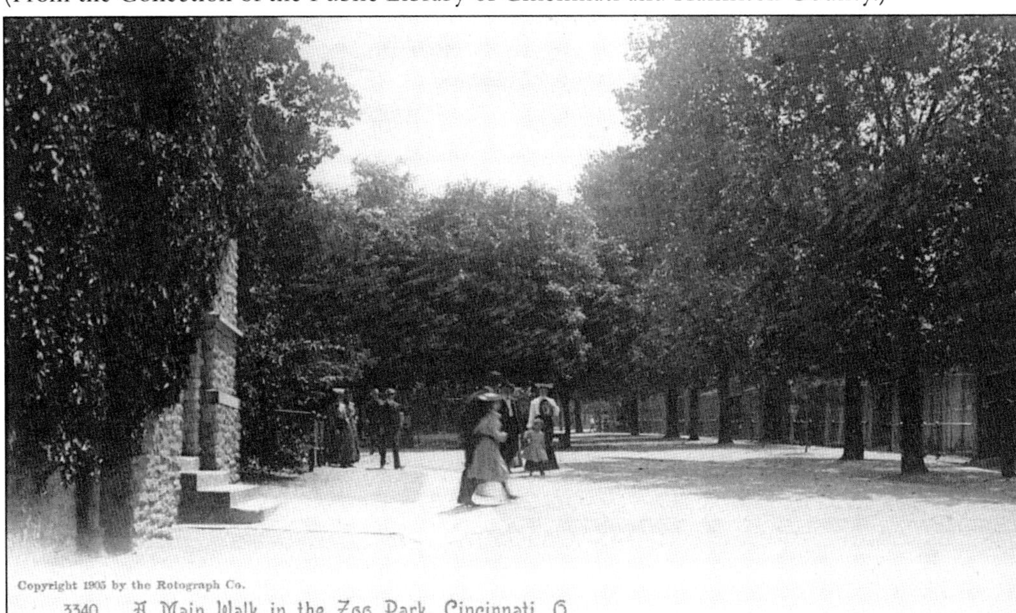

The most solemn exhibit at the zoo commemorates the terrible day in 1914 when the passenger pigeon became an extinct species. An attendant found the last surviving pigeon, Martha, lying at the bottom of her cage. The zoo had offered $1,000 for anyone who could provide a male to mate with her, but because of overhunting, there were none left. (From the Collection of the Public Library of Cincinnati and Hamilton County.)

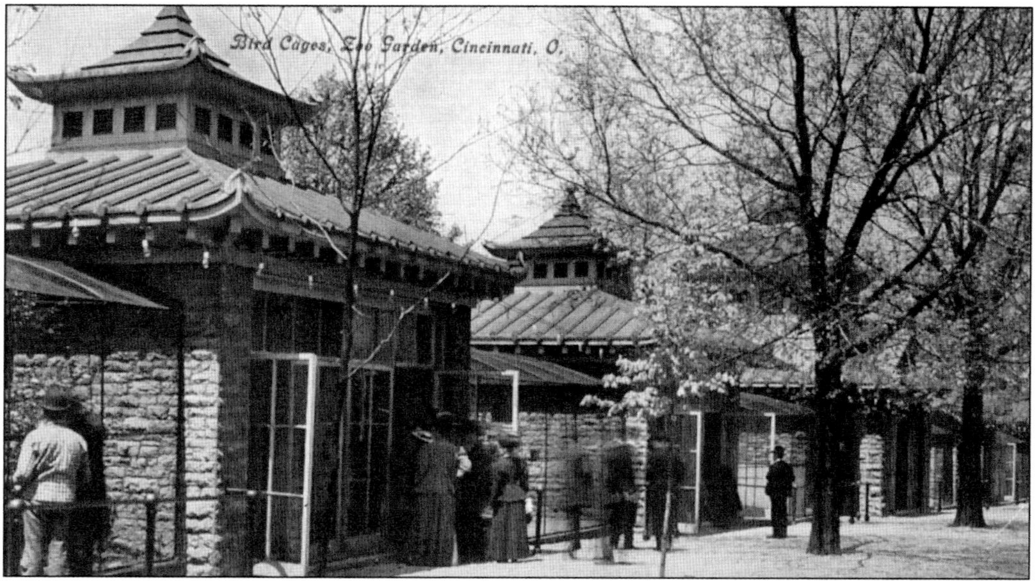

In September 1914, Cincinnatians were surprised to read in their newspapers, amidst news of war in Europe and the election of a pope, an account of a dead bird. Passenger pigeons were once so numerous that they darkened the sky. As the last pigeon, Martha, lay dying, director Sol Stephens had a rope fence erected so that the species could end in silence. (From the Collection of the Public Library of Cincinnati and Hamilton County.)

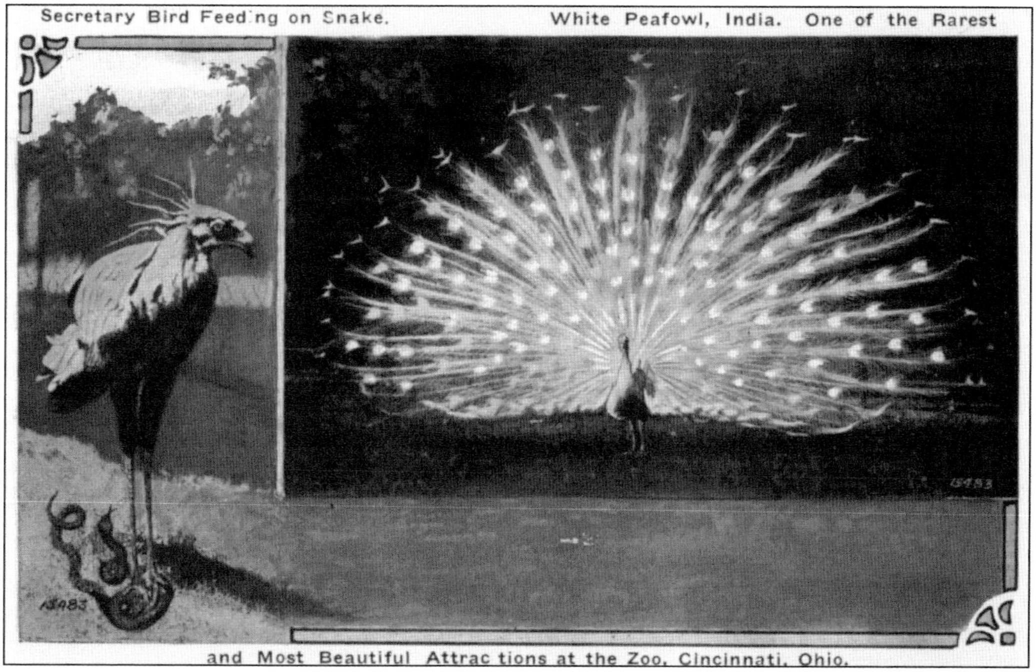

The Cincinnati Zoo was founded as a haven for caterpillar-eating birds and later was the site where the last passenger pigeon died. Justifiably showing pride in the zoo's avian residents, this 1925 postcard depicts the secretary bird, which graces the coats of arms of South Africa and Sudan. Here, the bird has met a snake, renewing an old animosity. A peafowl is also shown on the card. (From the Collection of the Public Library of Cincinnati and Hamilton County.)

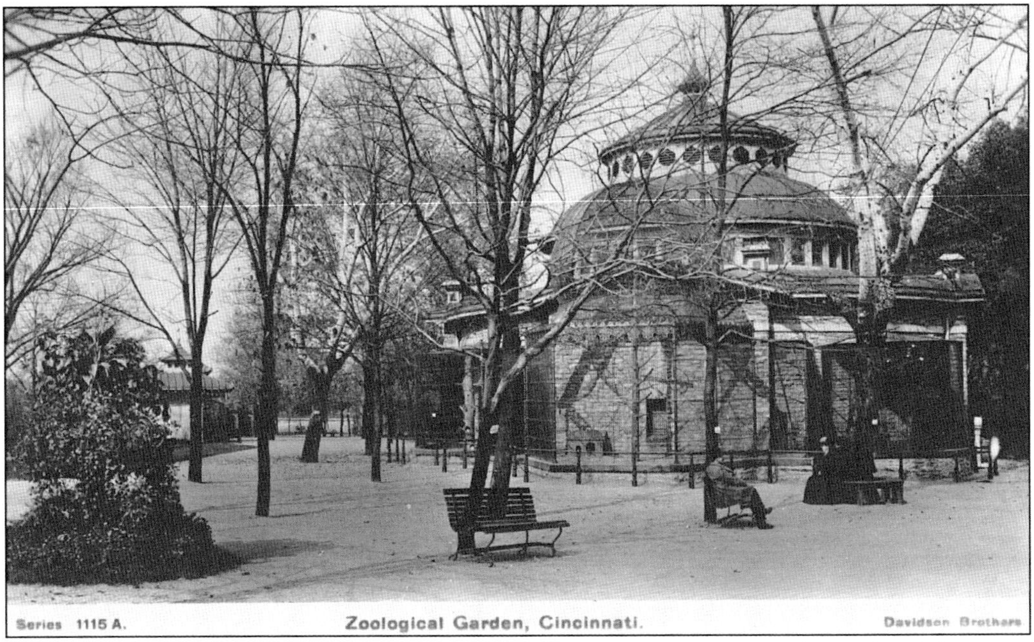

The oldest zoo building in the country is the current Reptile House. Based on a sketch by James McLaughlin, this Moorish-style edifice was built in 1875 to house monkeys. In the 1960s, it was nearly razed, but it luckily survived the board of supervisors vote. (From the Collection of the Public Library of Cincinnati and Hamilton County.)

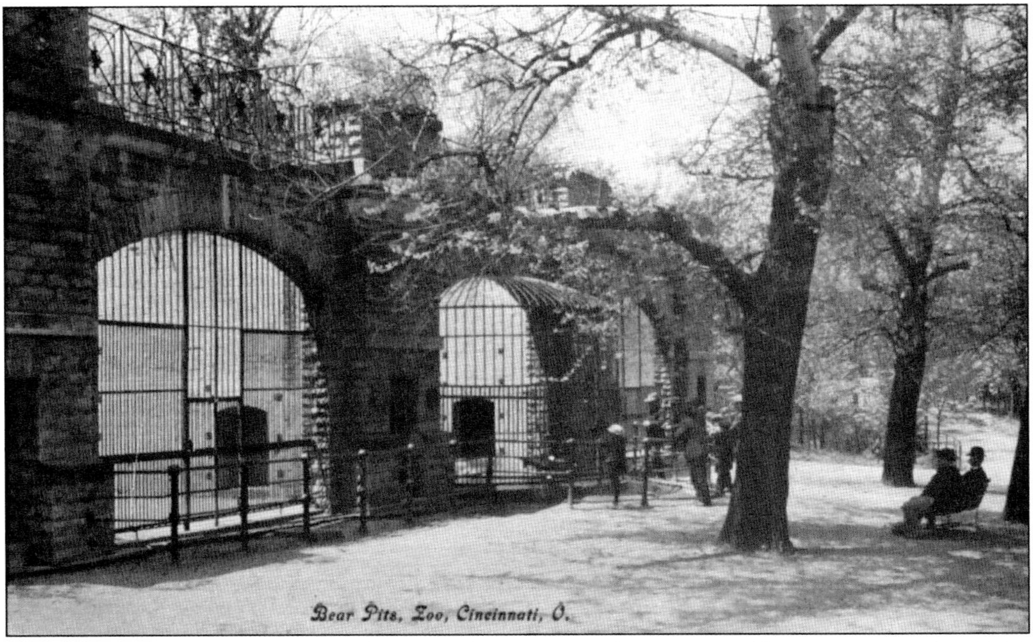

Working with wild animals is always a dangerous and unpredictable occupation. In 1886, attendant Mathias Hathoeffer wandered too close to the grizzly bear cage while sweeping. The male bear lunged forward and grabbed him and was joined quickly by the female grizzly. Attendants and patrons were able to pull Hathoeffer away, but he later died in the hospital from the mauling. (From the Collection of the Public Library of Cincinnati and Hamilton County.)

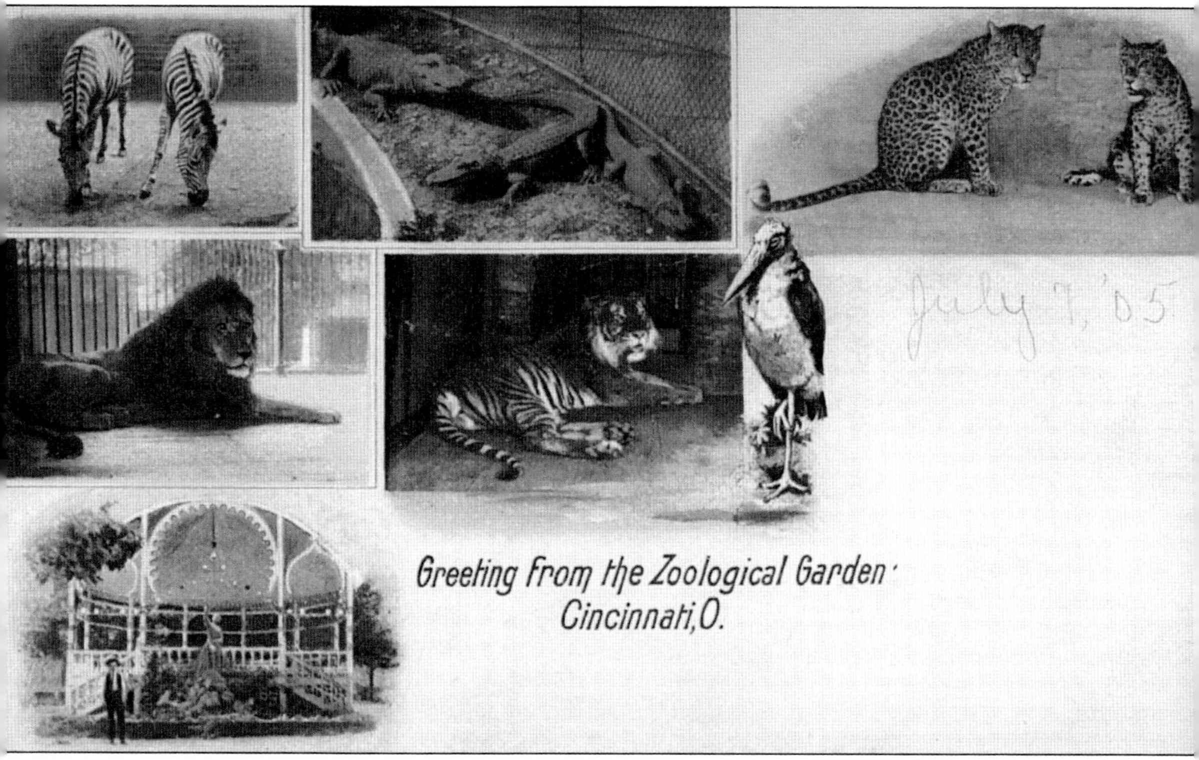

Visitors to the zoo on September 11, 1875, received a very unexpected "greeting" and had to flee for their lives. A lioness spotted a donkey pulling a cart by her cage. For some reason, the irate cat went berserk and literally crashed through the bars of her cage to attack the donkey. The burro later had to be euthanized after being severely mauled. Panicked zoo patrons fled as the deadly beast roamed free in the park. At one point, a squad of policemen managed to surround the dangerous creature, but they did not shoot. They were, as they explained later, frightened of repercussions from the animal rights activists of the time. The queen of beasts quickly escaped the police and soon local men were flocking into the park for a rare chance to hunt a lion. Finally, the big cat was spotted and killed by a shotgun fired by local carpenter Pat McAvoy. (From the Collection of the Public Library of Cincinnati and Hamilton County.)

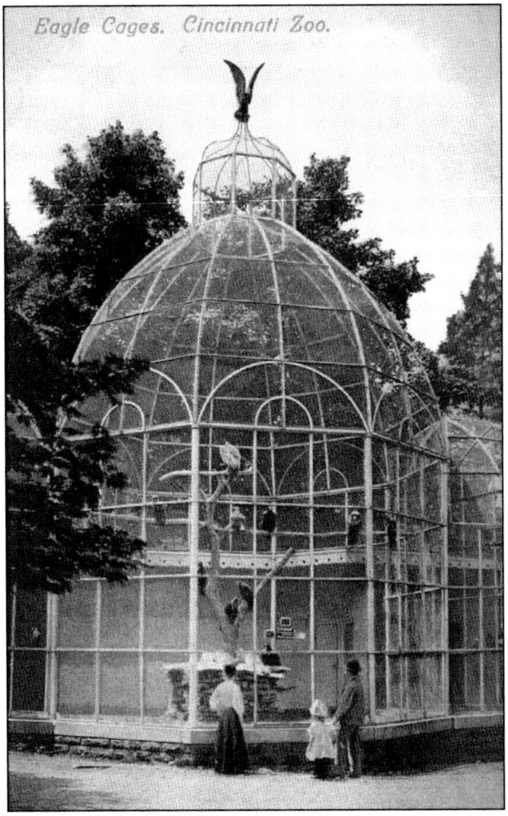

In August 2010, a zookeeper walked down fashionable Lafayette Avenue blowing a whistle and waving a dead mouse to entice an escaped hawk, Tex, back to its cage. The bird had flown away and was sighted by a resident. The gambit worked and Tex was recaptured. (From the Collection of the Public Library of Cincinnati and Hamilton County.)

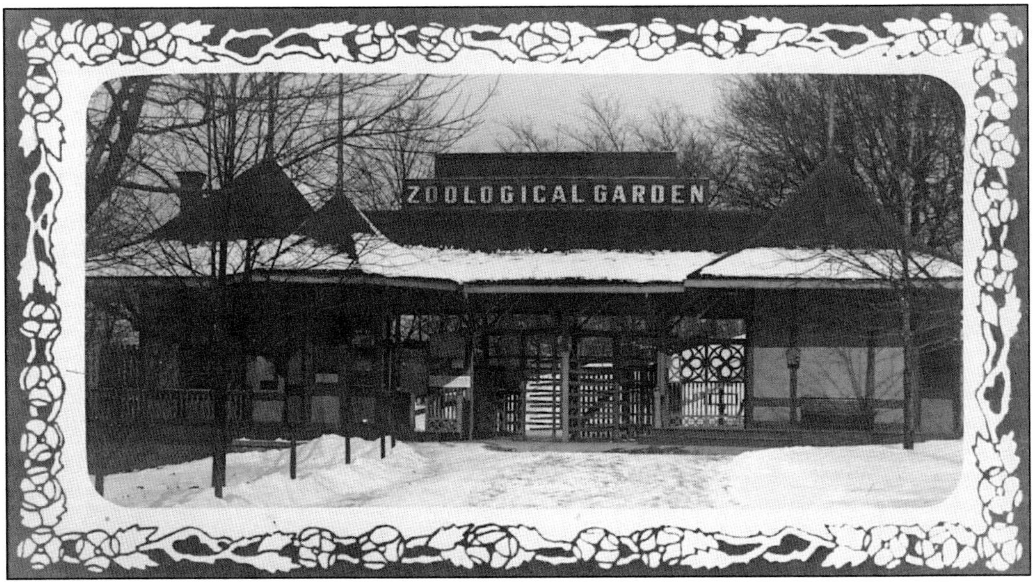

While more than a million people a year visit the Cincinnati Zoological and Botanical Gardens looking at animals, many do not notice that they are walking through a horticultural paradise. From bamboo to orchids, exotic plants are displayed along with the animals. At Christmastime, visitors flock to see the breathtaking Festival of Lights. (From the Collection of the Public Library of Cincinnati and Hamilton County.)

Six
A Day of Fun

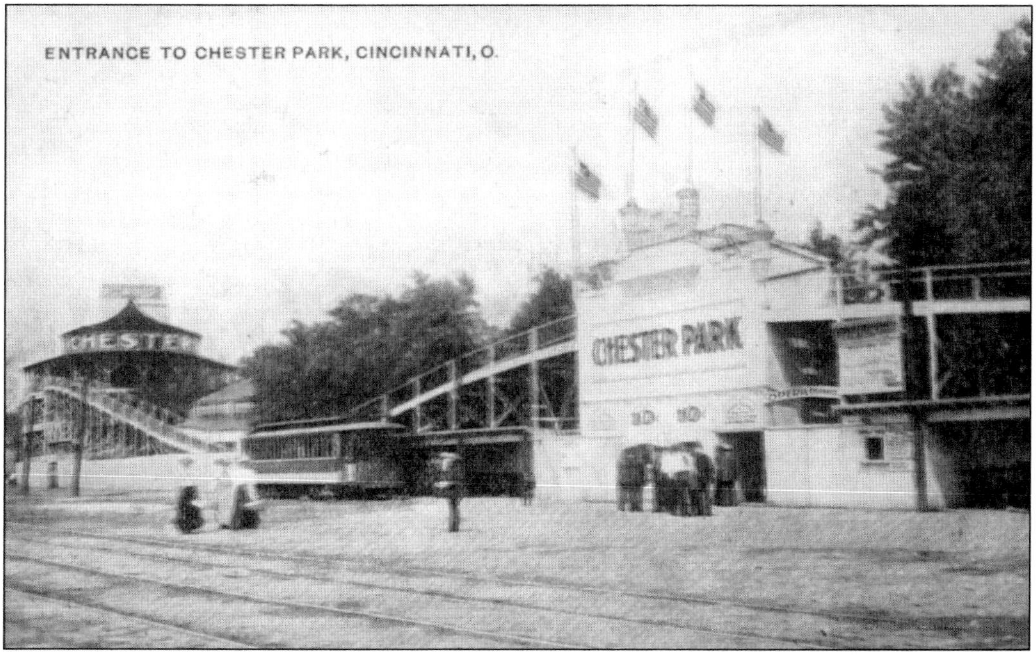

The first major amusement park in Cincinnati, Chester Park, opened on October 5, 1875, as a racetrack built on farmland. Twenty-one years later, the park was illuminated by electric lights. The name of the facility comes from a line in Walter Scott's poem *Marmion*: "Charge, Chester, charge!" (From the Collection of the Public Library of Cincinnati and Hamilton County.)

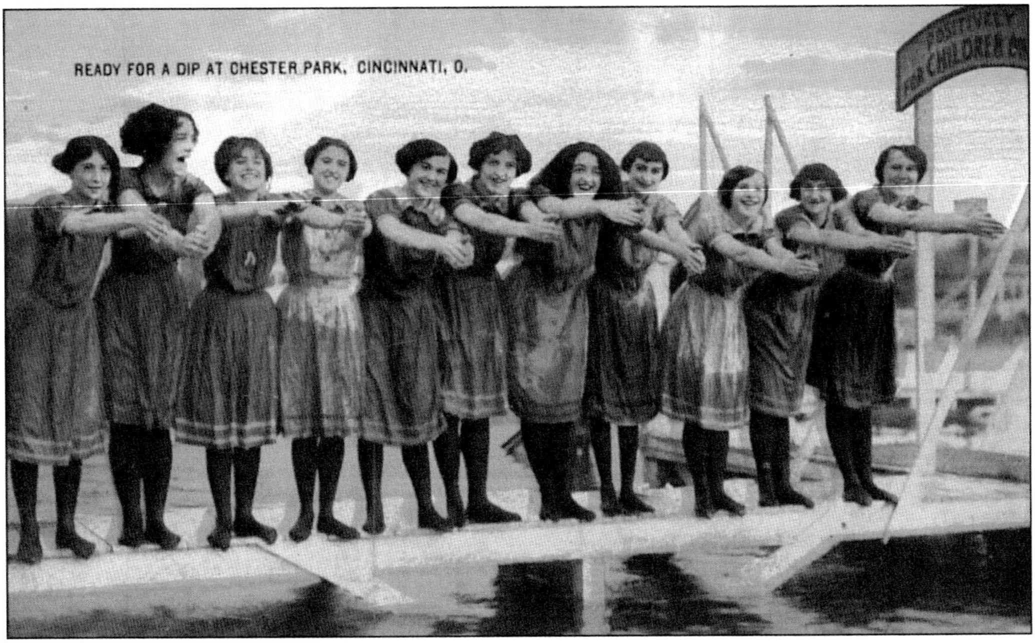

In 1861, the farmland that would later become Chester Park was converted into Camp Harrison. Training here was the 9th Ohio Volunteer Infantry, along with its new colonel, Robert McCook. The colonel did not have a uniform when the unit was formed and had to wear his stovepipe hat while drilling troops. Many of the soldiers would surely have liked to see *this* scene. (From the Collection of the Public Library of Cincinnati and Hamilton County.)

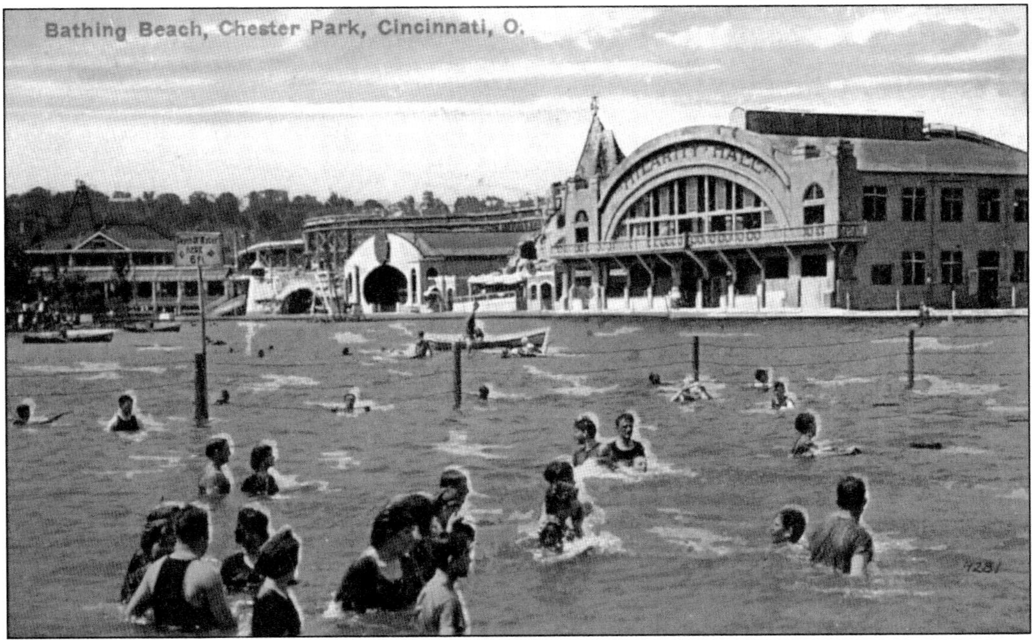

One of the most popular attractions of Chester Park was its enormous lake. Thousands of people would swim or boat in the muddy-bottomed lake in a day's time. There were even machines to create artificial waves. In the background is Hilarity Hall, a five-story funhouse. (From the Collection of the Public Library of Cincinnati and Hamilton County.)

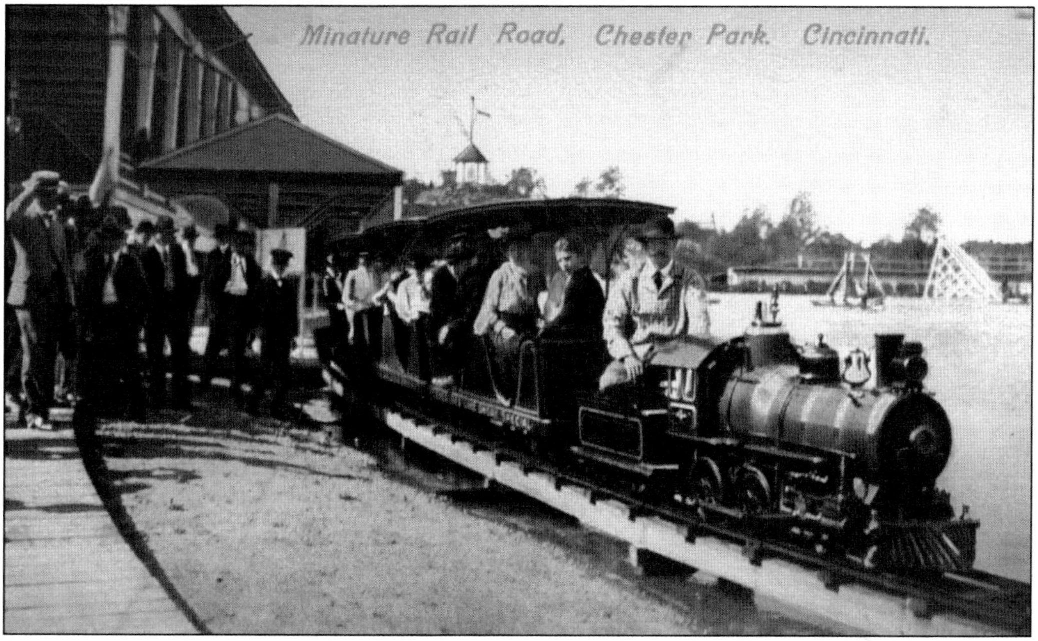

This miniature railroad gave tired patrons a chance to rest for a moment while taking a ride around the length of the lake. In 1904, the lake was temporarily converted to saltwater to make people feel as if they were swimming in the ocean. The park used 100,000 gallons of fresh water each day. (From the Collection of the Public Library of Cincinnati and Hamilton County.)

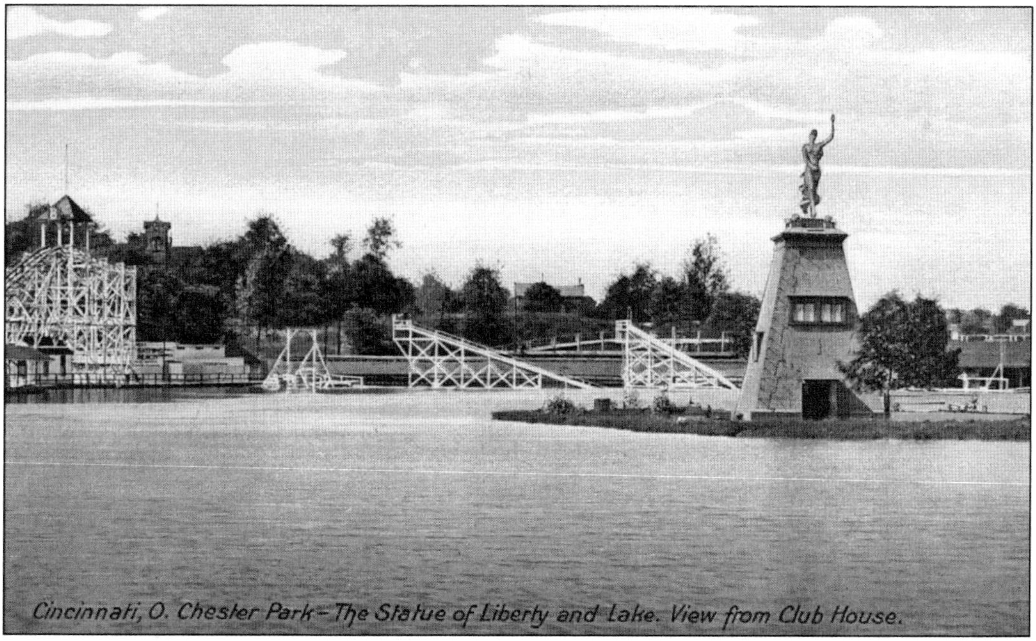

One of the biggest events ever held at Chester Park was a boxing match between John Sullivan and Dominick McCaffrey. Many of the 15,000 attendees made no secret that they were well armed. When it was time to render the decision, the frightened referee caught the next train downtown and telegraphed the decision to the waiting fans. Sullivan was the victor. (From the Collection of the Public Library of Cincinnati and Hamilton County.)

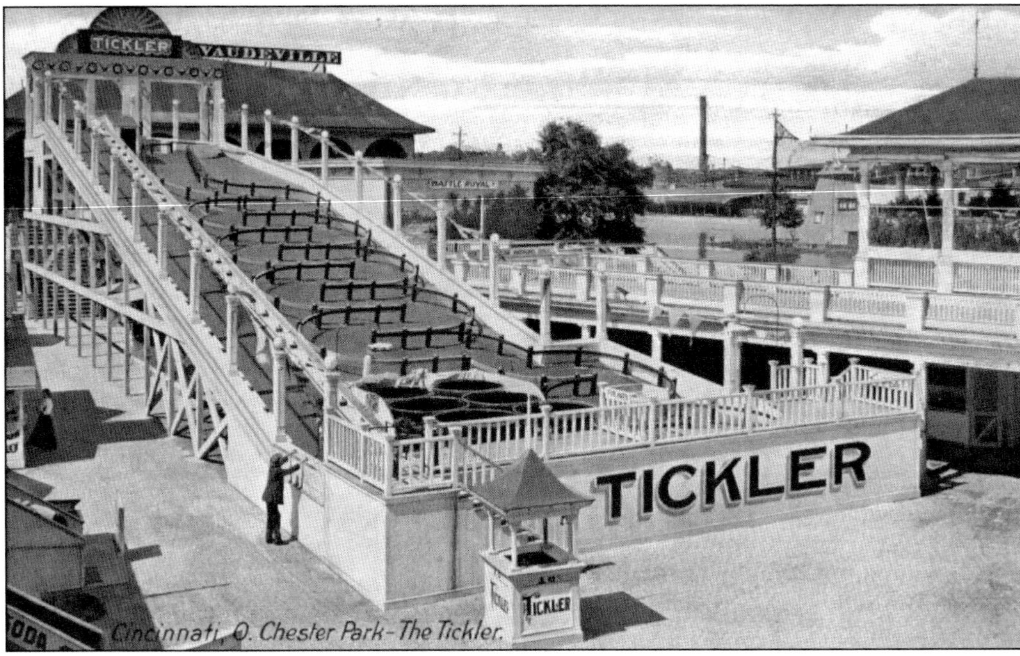

One of Cincinnati's worst fires began on August 11, 1911, when some wires crossed in a storeroom underneath this ride. The fire began at 6:00 p.m., between the afternoon and night crowds. It spread rapidly, eventually reaching M.B. Farrin's lumberyard. The blaze took the Vaudeville Theater and some rides, causing $100,000 in damage. (From the Collection of the Public Library of Cincinnati and Hamilton County.)

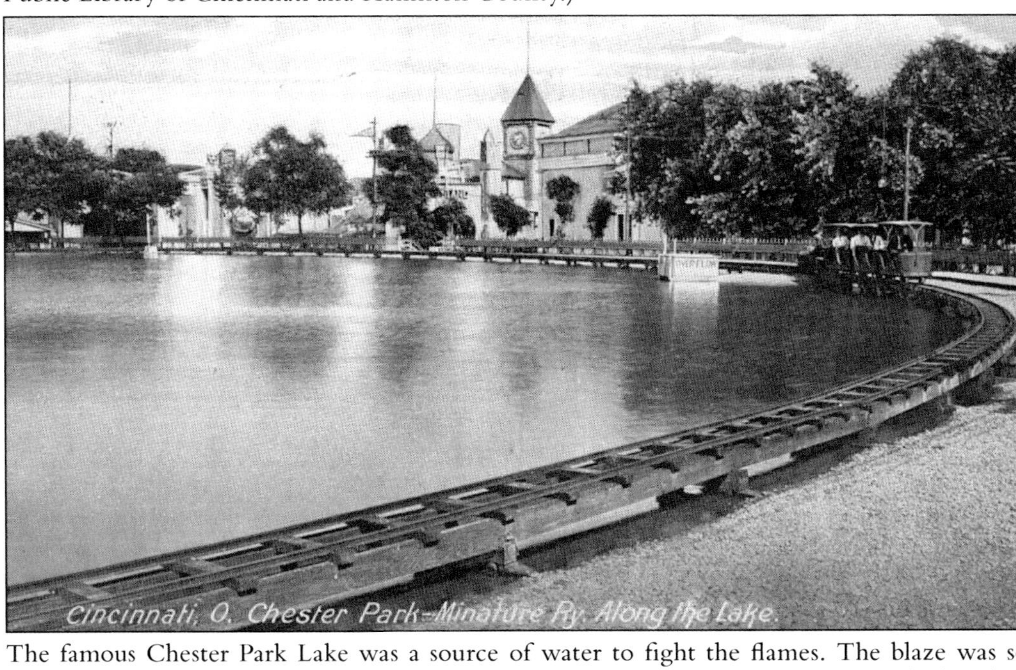

The famous Chester Park Lake was a source of water to fight the flames. The blaze was so powerful that the next day, machinist William Wilkerson found 40 pennies that had melted into one big glob. Wilkerson was a longtime employee who had worked at the park for decades. (From the Collection of the Public Library of Cincinnati and Hamilton County.)

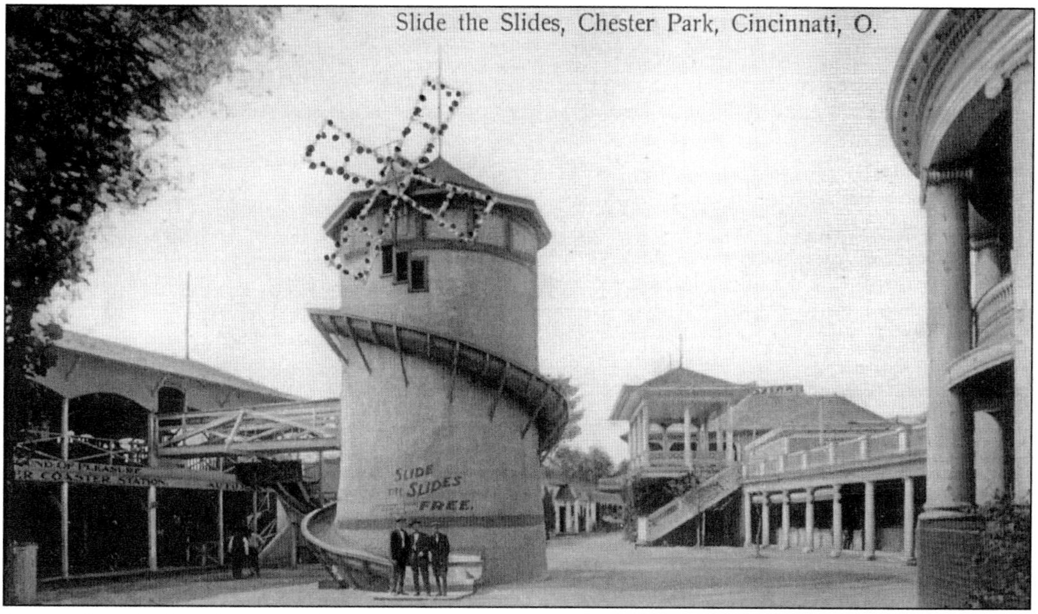

In a rather foolish business decision, the park initiated a contest to find a new name for the attraction in 1929. The winner was Rainbow Park. Unfortunately, the new name did not help the sagging attendance brought on by the banning of beer sales under Prohibition. In 1932, the original name was restored, but by then it was too late. (From the Collection of the Public Library of Cincinnati and Hamilton County.)

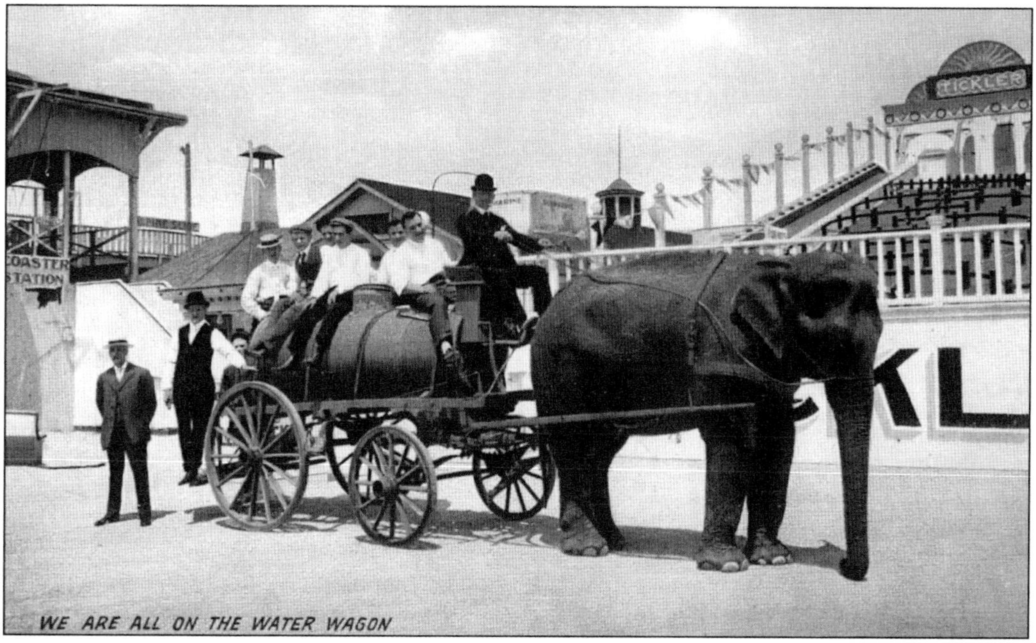

Unlike the demise of old Coney Island, which was commemorated with a massive fireworks display, on August 18, 1932, the beloved Chester Park closed its doors silently. The park had lost attendance during Prohibition and could not afford to pay an $1,800 water bill. Ironically, the site is now occupied by the Cincinnati Water Works. (From the Collection of the Public Library of Cincinnati and Hamilton County.)

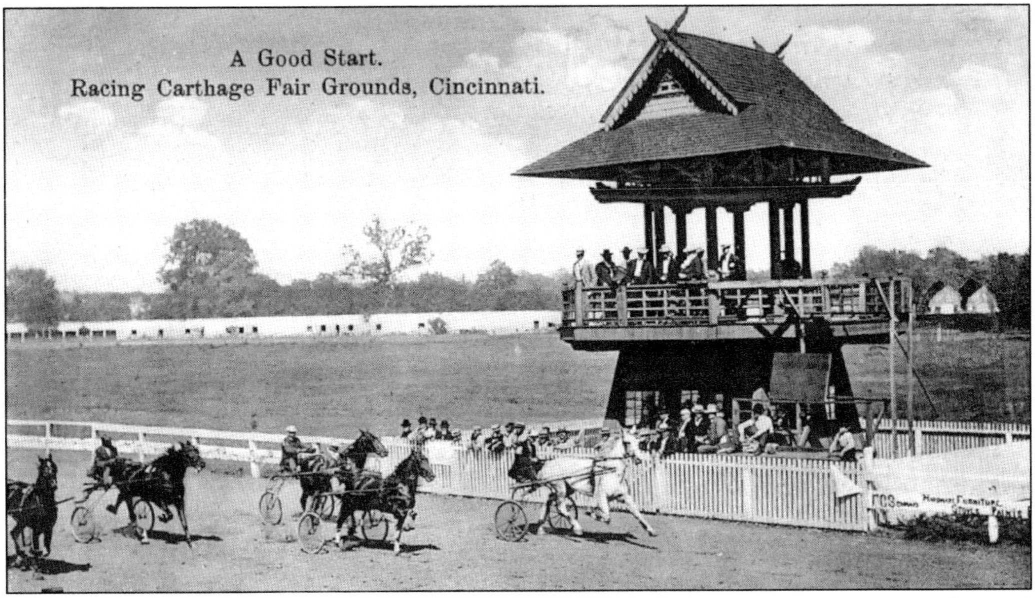

It is shocking to recall that the Carthage Fair (now the Hamilton County Fair) once banned Germans. In 1917, US marshal Michael Devanney declared the fair and a half-mile area around it as "restricted territory" to enemy aliens under Woodrow Wilson's Proclamation 1364 declaring war with Germany. Germans who wished to enter needed a permit signed by Devanney. (From the Collection of the Public Library of Cincinnati and Hamilton County.)

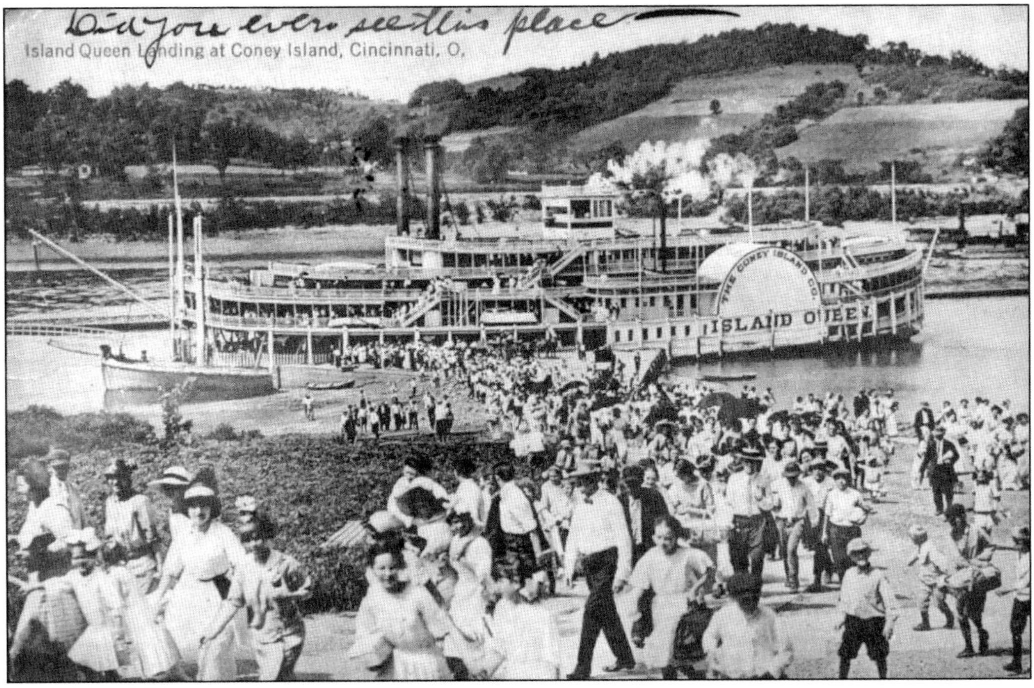

Upon boarding the *Island Queen* at the public landing, children would scurry up to the fifth deck and cover their ears as the captain blew the whistle on the way to Coney Island. On the voyage home, the top deck was abandoned by exhausted youngsters and taken over by lovers enjoying the moonlight. (From the Collection of the Public Library of Cincinnati and Hamilton County.)

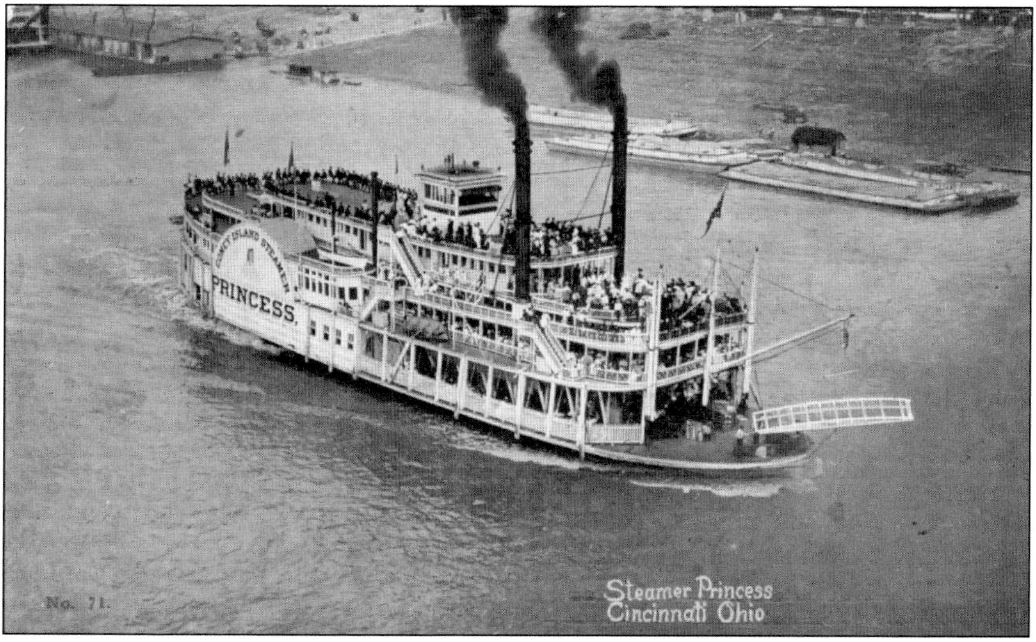

In its heyday, two steamboats carried passengers off to a day of fun at Coney Island. Originally known as the *Torrence*, this restored boat became known as the *Princess*. After it was renamed, the owners had the image of an Indian princess painted on the wheel box. (From the Collection of the Public Library of Cincinnati and Hamilton County.)

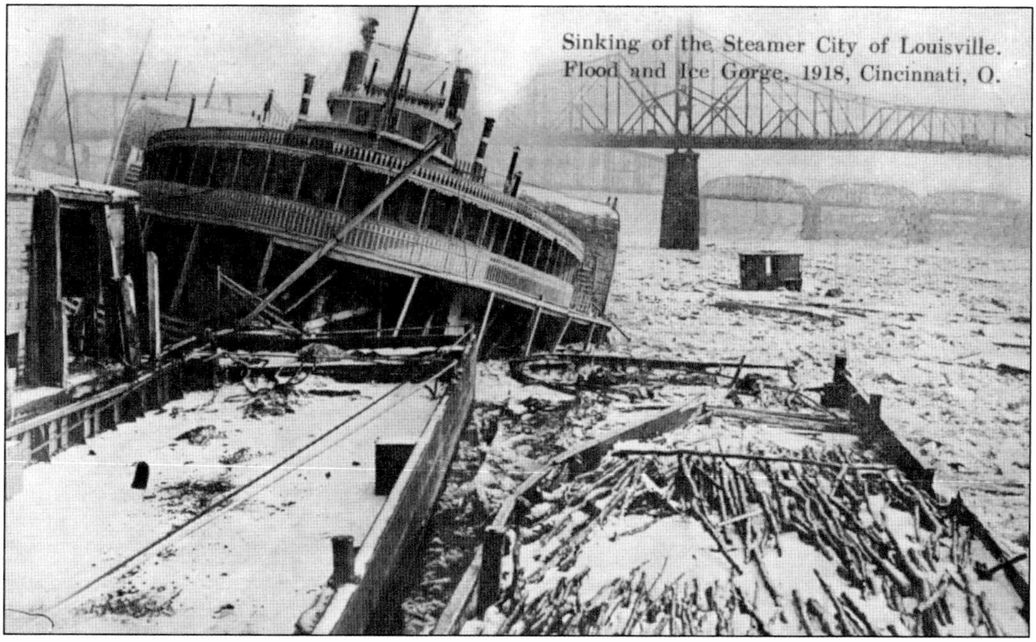

The winter of 1918 was brutal, with two-foot-thick ice crushing the hulls of steamboats. Both Coney Island boats were secured, but a historic prison ship, the *Success*, broke away from its mooring and smashed into the *Island Queen*. Both ships then crashed into the *Princess*, knocking her into the ice. The hull was ripped, and the *Princess* sank. (From the Collection of the Public Library of Cincinnati and Hamilton County.)

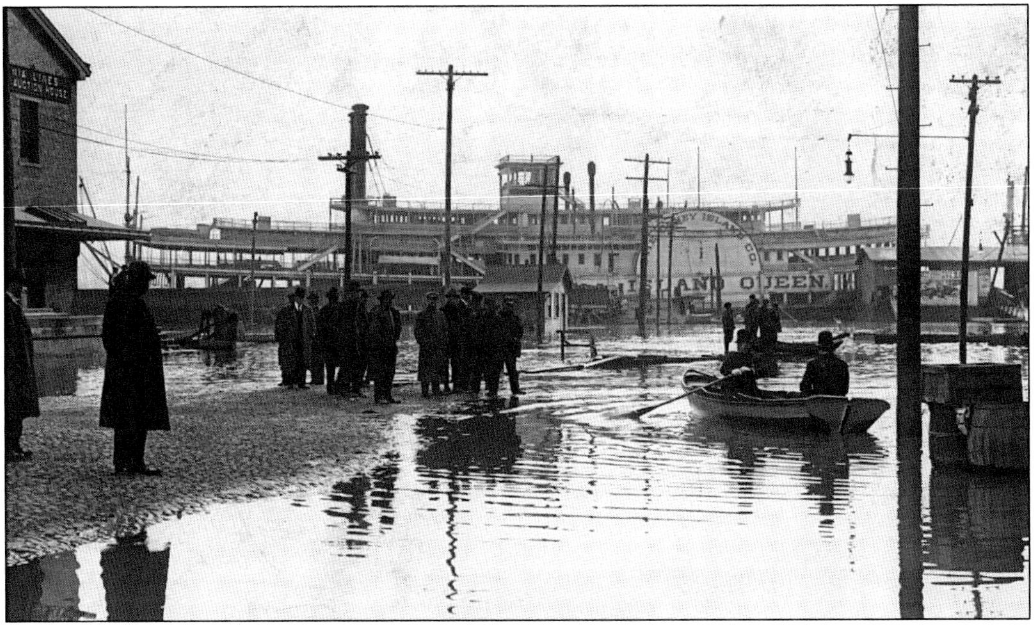

The first *Island Queen* steamboat is safely moored during the flood of 1913. This steamboat survived both the flood and the ice flow of 1918. But it caught fire and sank in 1922. The second *Island Queen* lasted until it exploded while being repaired in 1947. With that tragedy, the nostalgic days of steamboats serving Coney Island ended forever. (From the Collection of the Public Library of Cincinnati and Hamilton County.)

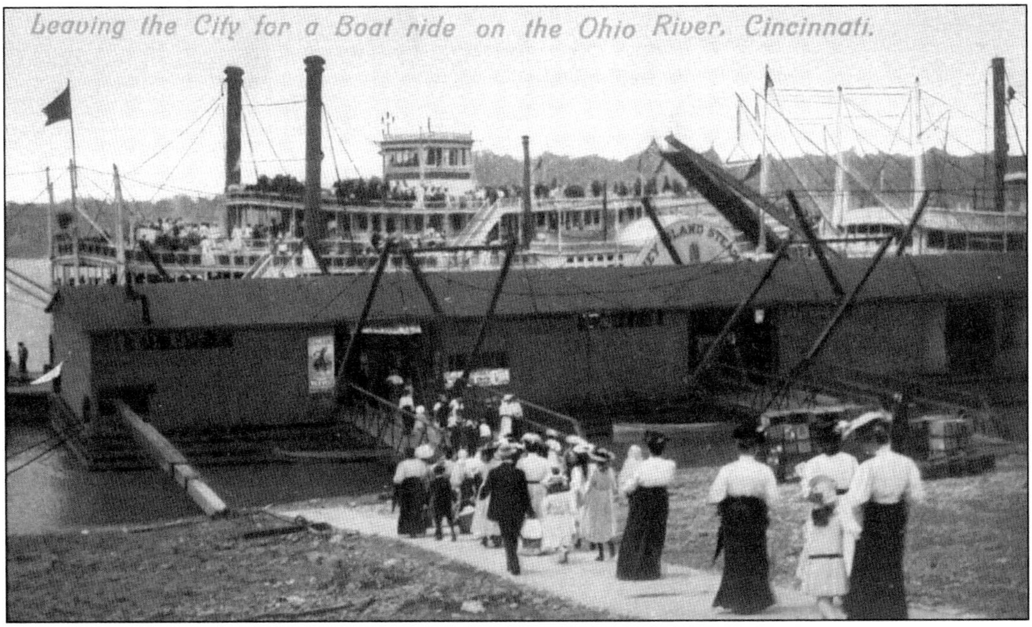

The association between the park and steamboats began in James Parker's era, when he rented out his facility to a church group. The faithful chartered a steamboat to take them from the city to the park. When the facility was later sold to a steamboat captain, the long connection between riverboats and Coney Island was set. (From the Collection of the Public Library of Cincinnati and Hamilton County.)

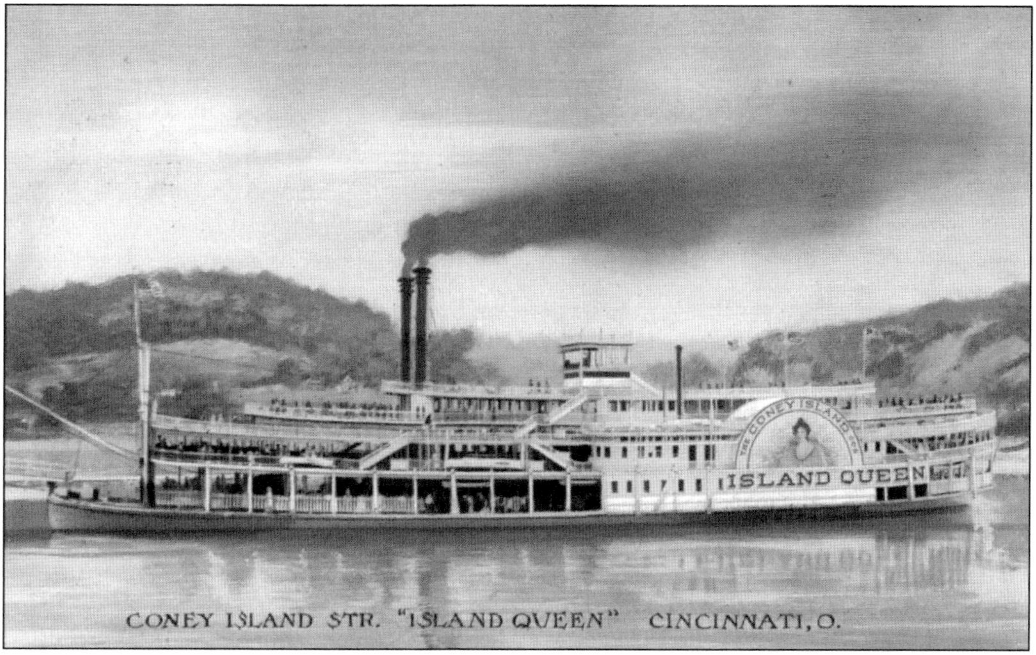

The name of the *Island Queen*, the most famous of the Coney Island steamboats, was chosen by contest. Two women suggested the same name and thus split the grand prize of $100. (From the Collection of the Public Library of Cincinnati and Hamilton County.)

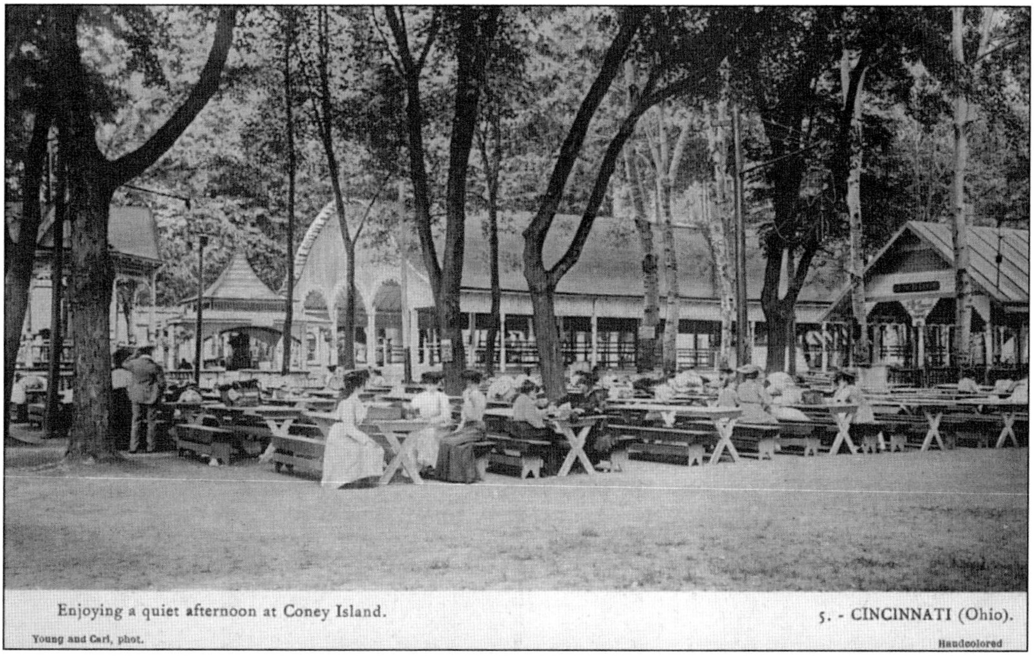

Cincinnati's most famous amusement park began in 1867 when farmer James Parker planted an apple orchard near the banks of the Ohio. As it grew into a wonderful place for city dwellers to have picnics and escape the smog and heat of the city, Parker saw his opportunity, naming his ground Parker's Grove and charging admission. (From the Collection of the Public Library of Cincinnati and Hamilton County.)

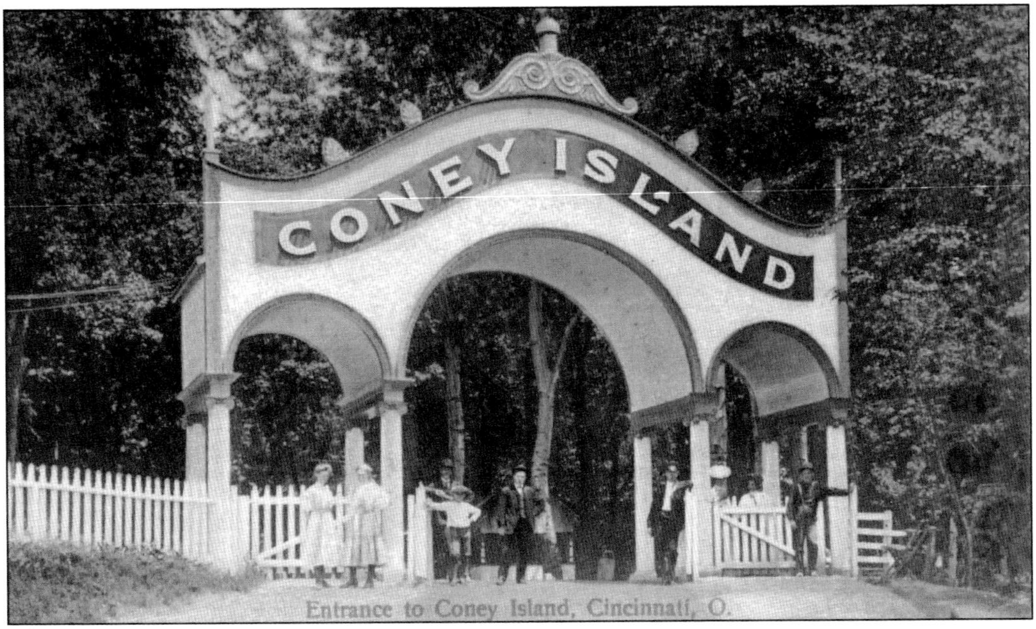

The original Parker's Grove opened on June 21, 1886. Advertisements enticed visitors to visit "Ohio Grove, Coney Island of the West," where they could witness a "balloon ascension by a lady aeronaut . . . grand display of fireworks . . . free music, free dancing." To further amaze visitors, it was promised that there were "electric lights everywhere." (From the Collection of the Public Library of Cincinnati and Hamilton County.)

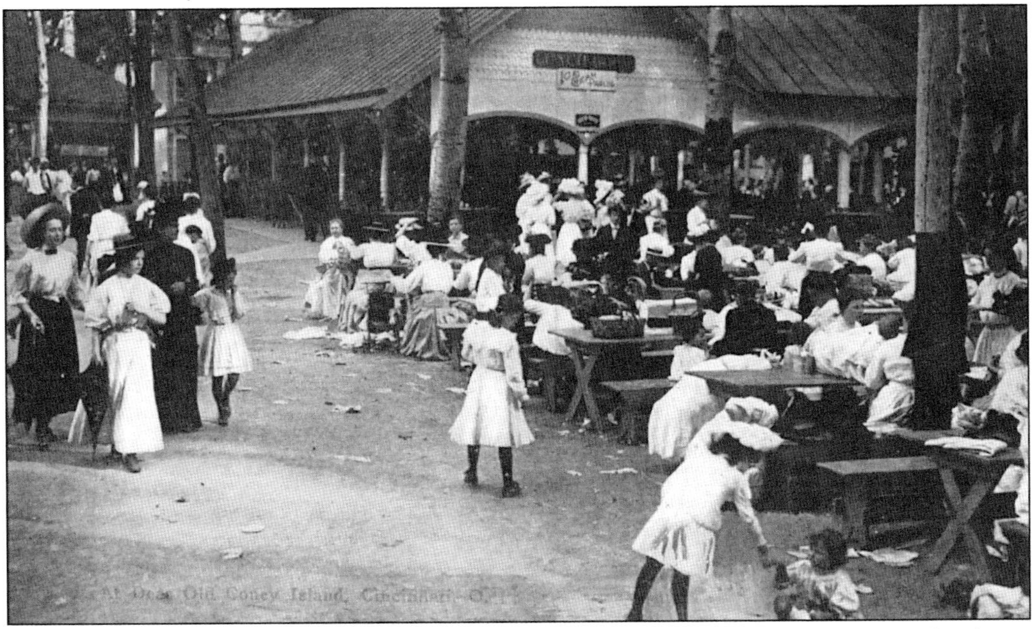

Parker supplied more than just apples at his new park. He also erected a shelter and a dance hall. Knowing that young folks would enjoy going on rides, he included Coney Island's first breathtaking thrill ride—a merry-go-round powered by a mule. People flocked to Parker's Grove, and their money brought about more improvements as well as new problems. (From the Collection of the Public Library of Cincinnati and Hamilton County.)

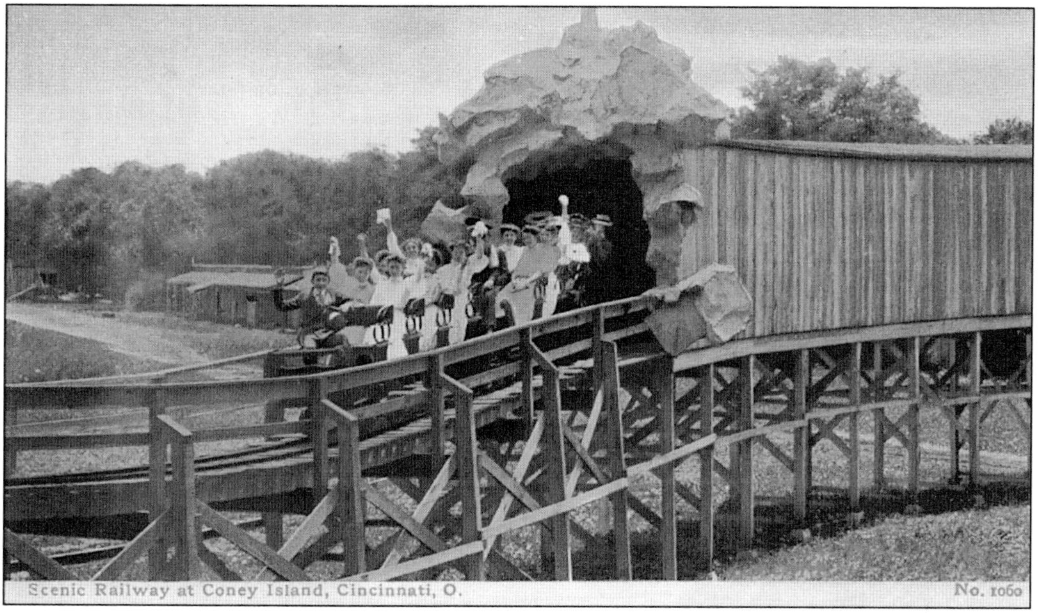

Parker's Grove was a rather rough place to be on a weekend night. As the facility catered to a drinking clientele, as many as 50 fights could break out during the course of an evening. When the park became Coney Island, alcohol sales were suspended and a more family-friendly environment was created. (From the Collection of the Public Library of Cincinnati and Hamilton County.)

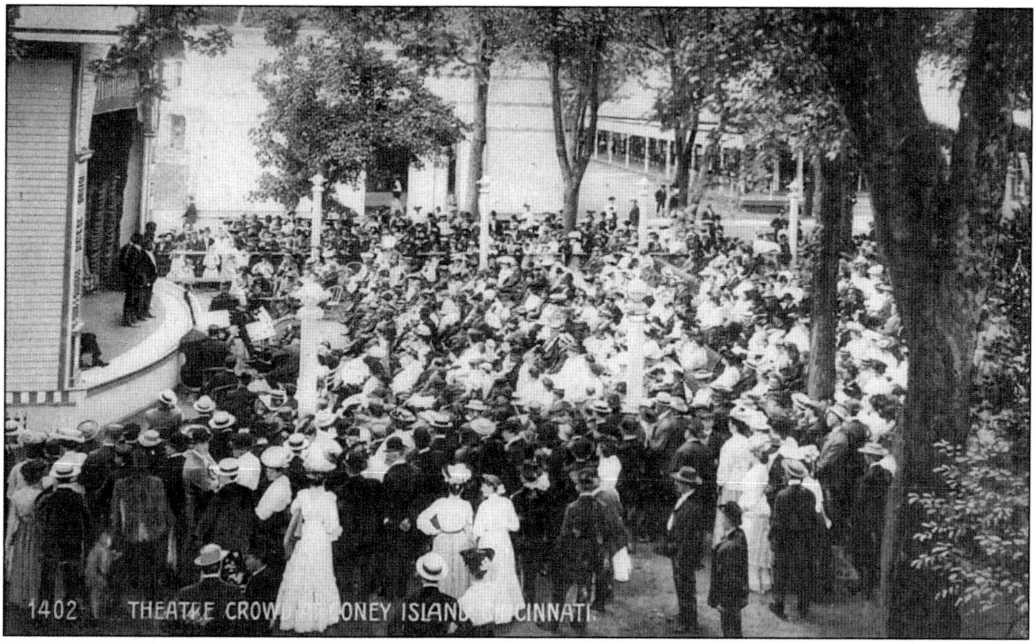

The influx of people, sometimes acting in rowdy ways, created difficulties, as drinking would often lead to fights. Parker's greatest problem, as the crowds grew ever larger, was angry complaints about pickpockets. Also, the Ohio River flooded in 1883 and 1884, causing damage to his growing business. Exhausted, Parker sold his park to steamboat captain William McIntyre for $17,500 in 1886. (From the Collection of the Public Library of Cincinnati and Hamilton County.)

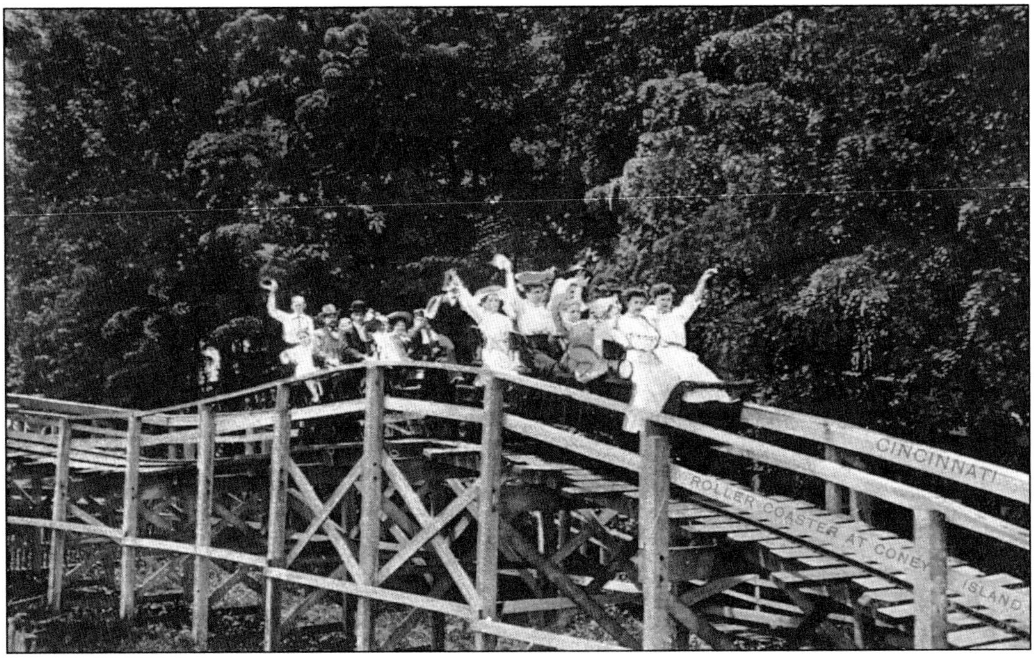

In 1886, new owner William McIntyre brought a new ride, a roller coaster, to the ever-expanding park, which by then included a bowling alley and a shooting gallery. Coney's most famous roller coaster was the Clipper, later named the Shooting Star, which boasted a drop of 102 feet and speeds in excess of 90 miles per hour. (From the Collection of the Public Library of Cincinnati and Hamilton County.)

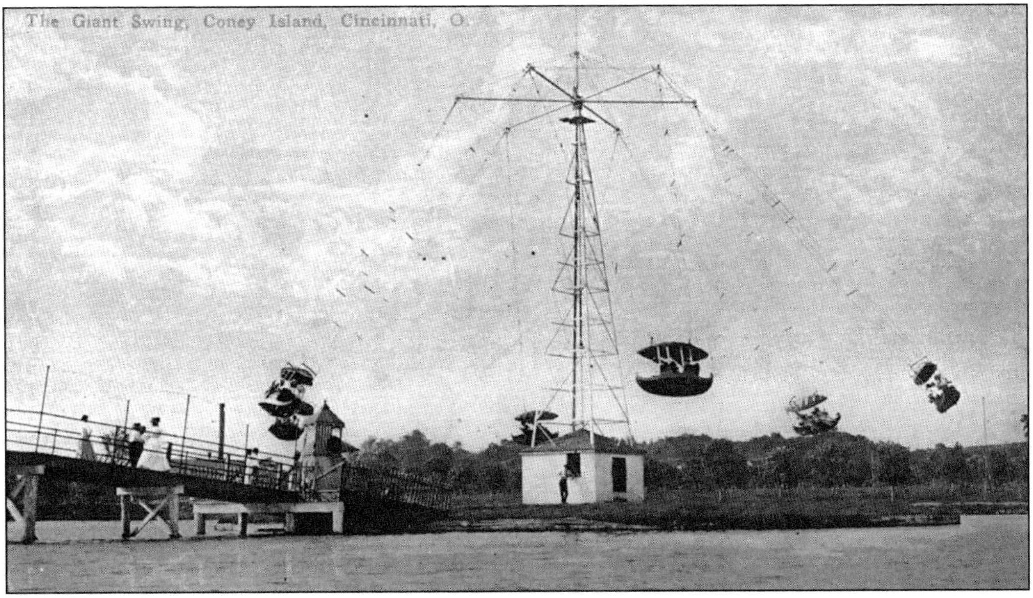

The origins of the name Coney Island, derived from Brooklyn's Luna Park, come from Celtic mythology and means "Rabbit Island." The original island is located in Ireland's Lough Neagh in County Armagh. The myth states the lake was formed when the giant Fionn mac Cumhaill dug out some earth to toss at an enemy in Scotland. The dirt fell short but became the Isle of Man. (From the Collection of the Public Library of Cincinnati and Hamilton County.)

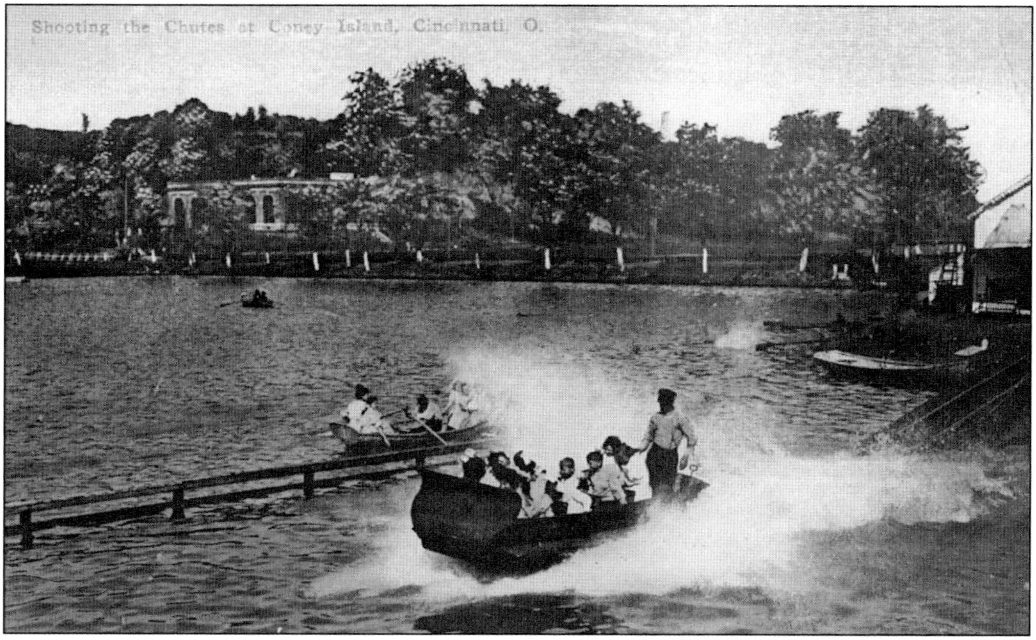

Another romantic legend explains the name of the original Coney Island in Ireland differently. Just before a battle, Dermot, the chieftain of the O'Neill clan, became gravely ill. Coney was a healing woman who tried unsuccessfully to cure him. To escape the wrath of his followers, she was hidden on an island in the lough that is still known as Coney Island. (From the Collection of the Public Library of Cincinnati and Hamilton County.)

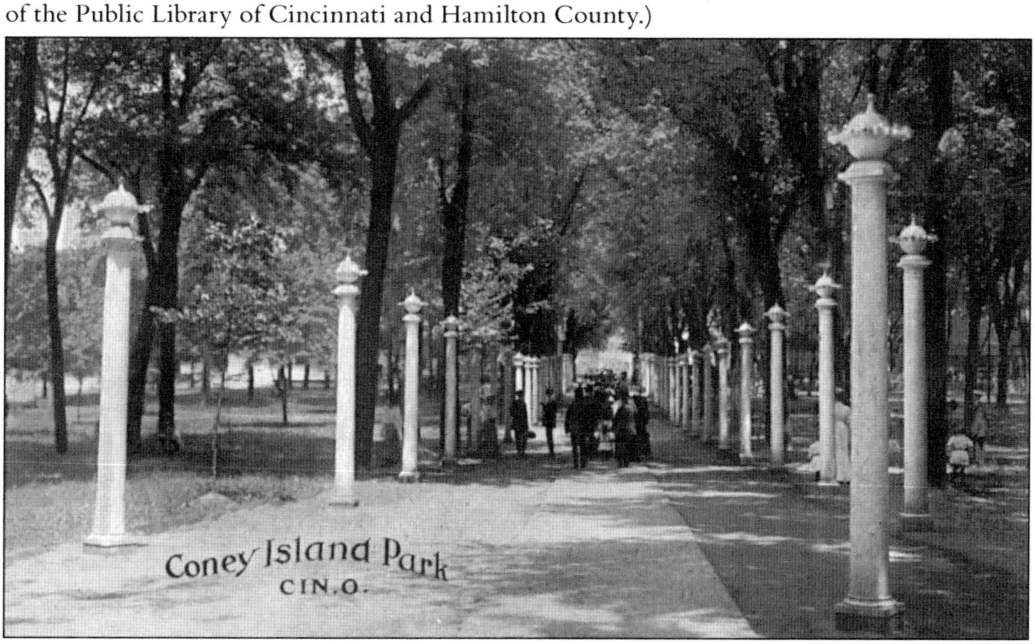

Coney Island is reportedly home to a number of ghosts. Many have reported seeing an elderly couple in Moonlight Gardens reliving their fondest moment as they dance to unheard music. Moonlight Gardens has also been seen covered in an unearthly fog even when everywhere else is clear. Indian war chants have also been heard at night. (From the Collection of the Public Library of Cincinnati and Hamilton County.)

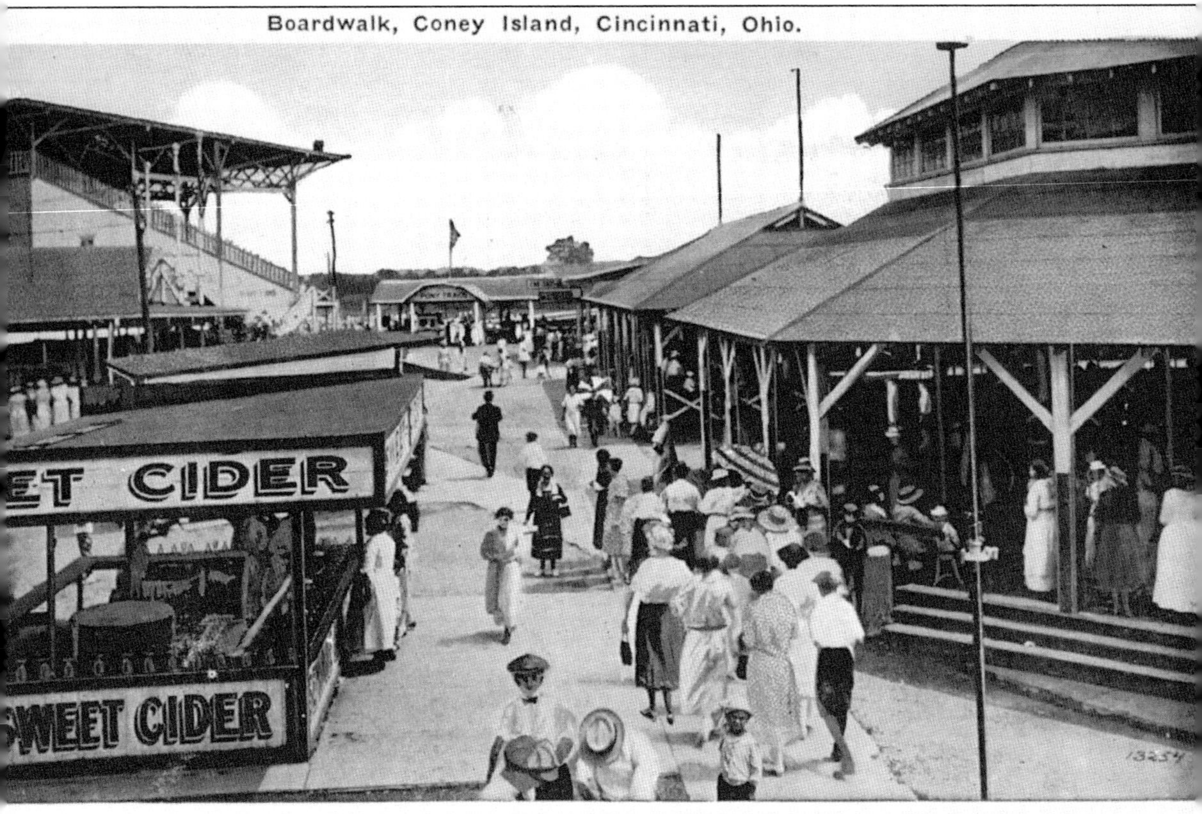

Today, it is hard to believe that in the "good old days," Coney Island was not open to everyone, as the park was racially segregated. Civil rights activists, including councilman Theodore Berry, who was later the first African American mayor of Cincinnati, and Rev. Maurice McCrackin, fought Coney Island management for the admittance of African Americans. However, integration did not come easily. Once, a car was parked in front of the gate to prevent African Americans from entering. Blacks wishing admittance were often told that the facility had been "reserved." Ethel Fletcher sued the park and won. In 1955, when the city stated that it might not renew the license of Coney Island, the park finally relented and integrated. Sunlight Pool, however, remained segregated. In 1961, protestors returned and demanded to be admitted to the pool as well as the park. Twenty-seven civil rights protesters were arrested as they attempted to go swimming in the whites-only pool. Finally, management opened access to the pool to everyone. (From the Collection of the Public Library of Cincinnati and Hamilton County.)

Seven

ZINZINNATI

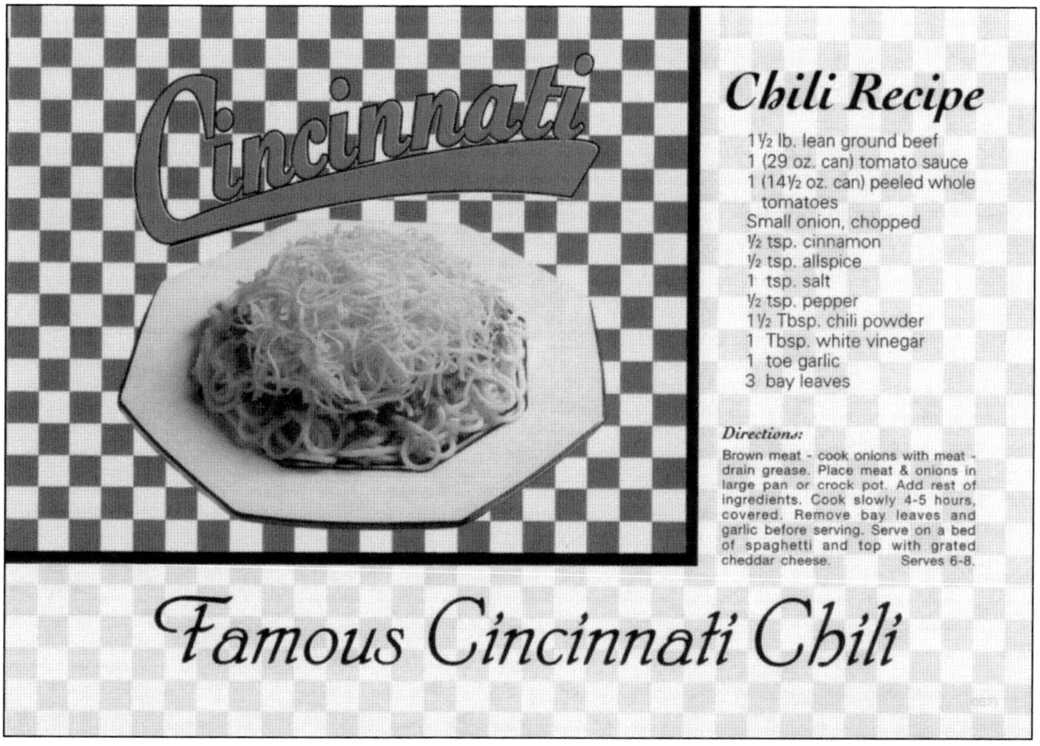

If a person has not tried Cincinnati chili, he has not really been to the Queen City. Unlike the hot Southwestern variety, Cincinnati's mild chili is made with such ingredients as cinnamon and even chocolate. It began in 1922 when Macedonian immigrants Tom and John Kiradjieff served their special recipe on hot dogs at their Empress Restaurant, which was next to a burlesque theater. (Image copyright SFI, Inc., www.souvenirfactory.com.)

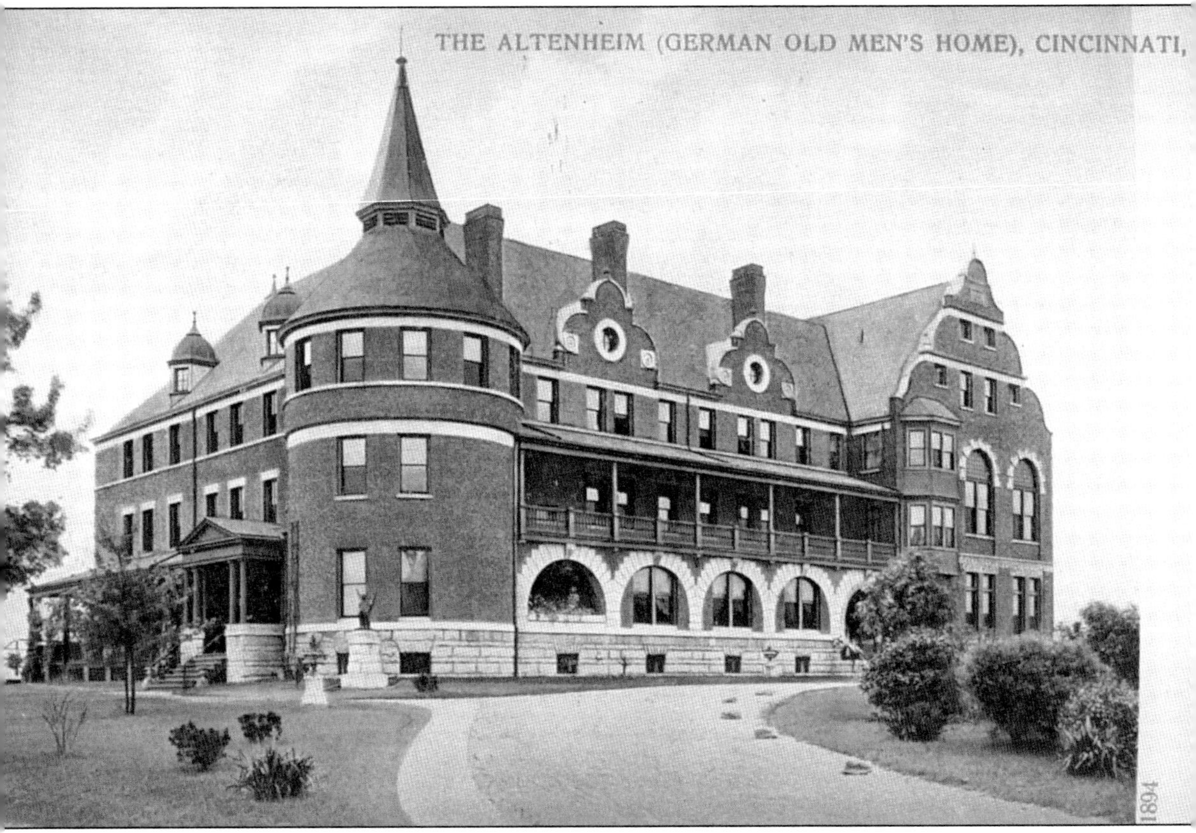

This German facility, the Altenheim, in the hospital district of Avondale, is more famous for what happened next door. In 1907, a disgruntled employee from construction work on the new City Hospital decided to strike a blow against his employer. On the site was a shed containing 250 pounds of dynamite, securely locked with a padlock. He did not attempt to break the lock, but rather stole some oil, poured it over the building, and set it ablaze. The explosion was heard as far away as Lockland and northern Kentucky. The Altenheim looked as though it had been shelled and every resident inside was injured by flying glass. Amazingly, no one died from the blast, but a woman in Walnut Hills reportedly succumbed from shock upon hearing the blast. The construction company was found to be negligent, as the law required that no more than 100 pounds of dynamite could be stored in one location. (From the Collection of the Public Library of Cincinnati and Hamilton County.)

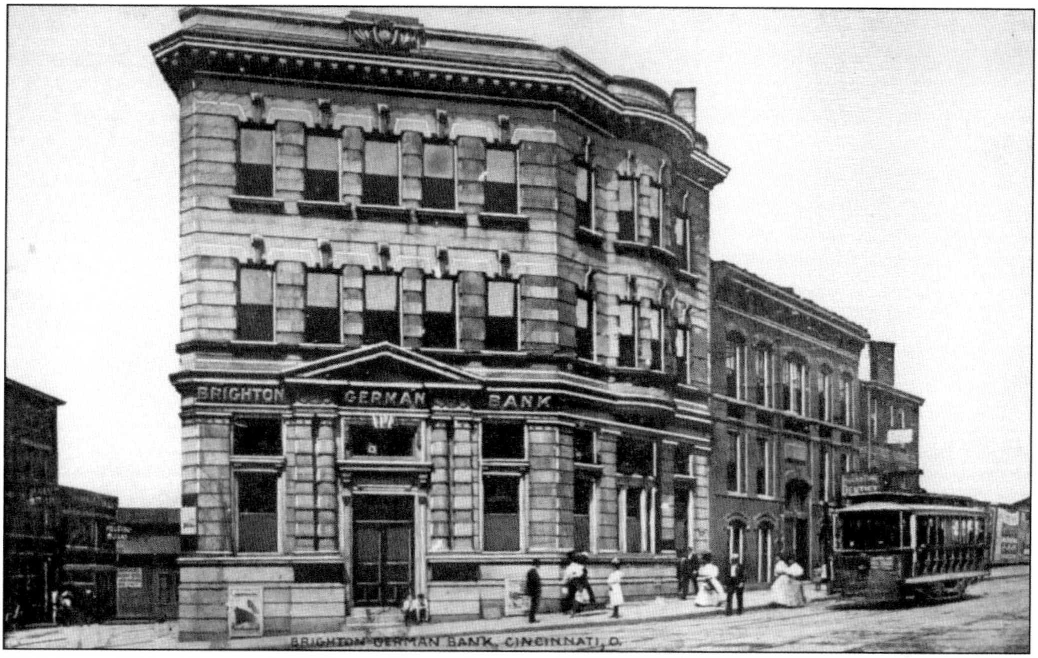

This beautiful old stone building still stands in Brighton but is no longer a bank. In 1899, safe manufacturer Max Mosler organized the Western German Bank here. The stone building was on the site of the former Brighton House. The word "German" was removed from the title during World War I. The bank did not survive the Depression. (From the Collection of the Public Library of Cincinnati and Hamilton County.)

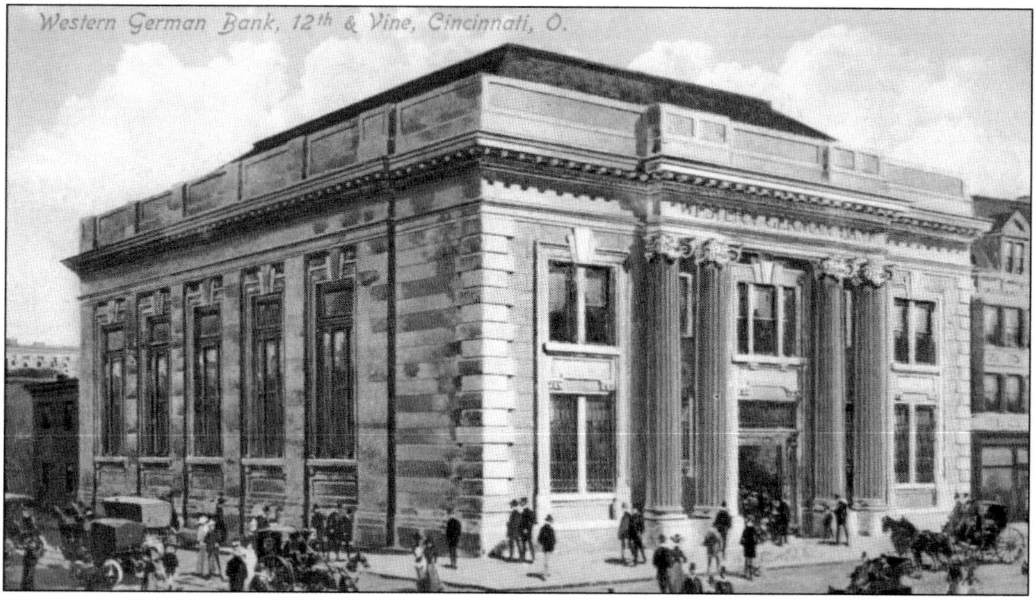

German immigrant Rudolph Tietig designed this stately bank building, the Western German Bank, in 1887. Once a landmark of the German community, the building has since deteriorated. Tietig designed numerous other great buildings in Cincinnati, including the original Rockdale Temple and the College of Engineering Building at the University of Cincinnati. (From the Collection of the Public Library of Cincinnati and Hamilton County.)

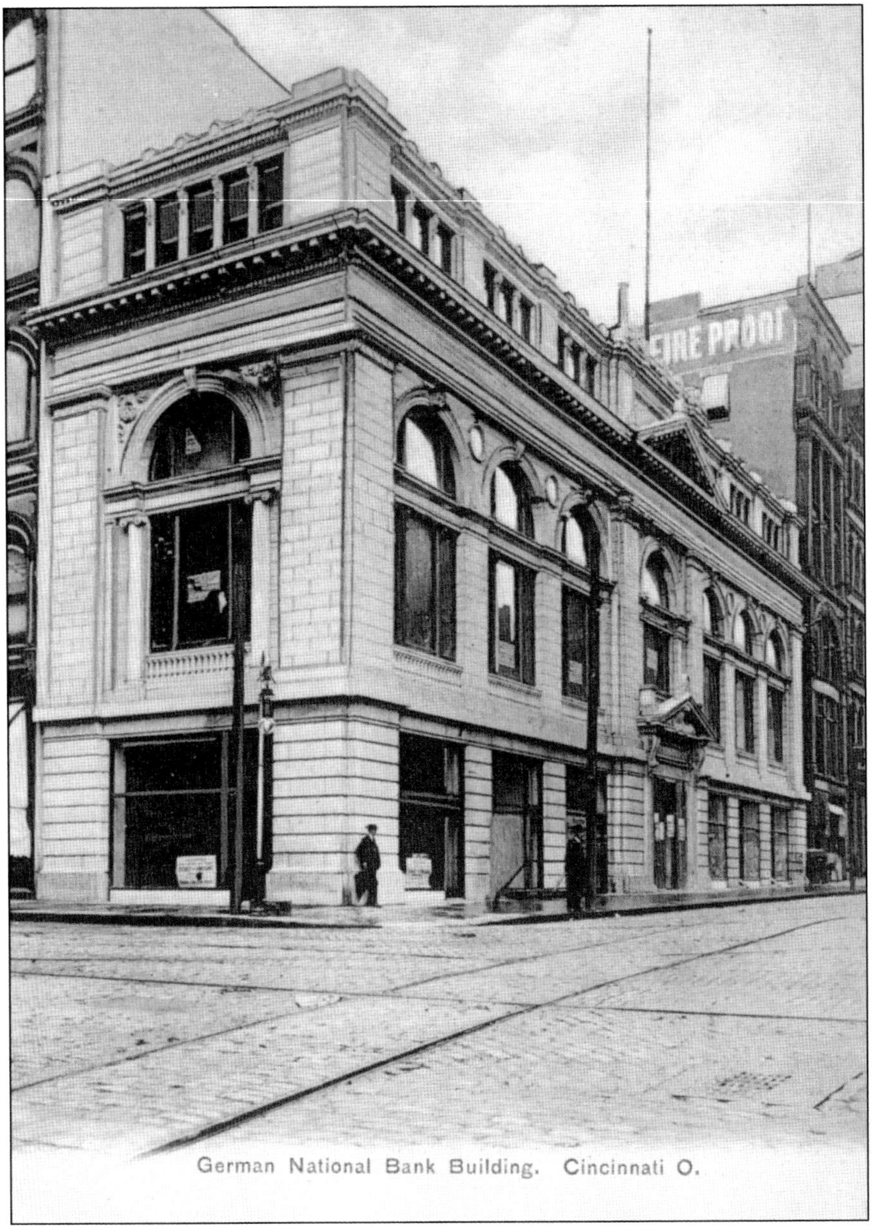

The Western German Bank was one of the many casualties of anti-German prejudice during World War I, with the word "German" in the name being replaced with the more American "Lincoln." Before the war, Cincinnati had one of the finest German-language programs in the nation. Even one school that served the African American community taught German. Critic Edward Colston stated, "I do not think it decent or proper to teach the matter in German textbooks to American children. If it were not for the profanity of it I'd say teach them to hell with the Kaiser and Hohenzollerism [the policies of the ruling dynasty of Germany]." With the Ake Law, the teaching of German to schoolchildren was outlawed, but in Cincinnati, the change was slow to come. Nonetheless, some songbooks had the words and music to "America the Beautiful" literally pasted over traditional German songs. (From the Collection of the Public Library of Cincinnati and Hamilton County.)

This German Protestant church, built in 1868, gave the name Gabriel's Corner to this intersection. The steeple displays an image of the angel Gabriel blowing his horn. The original angel was blown down in 1960. As it was suspected that it had been looted from a besieged Mormon church in Illinois in 1846, it was sent to Utah. (From the Collection of the Public Library of Cincinnati and Hamilton County.)

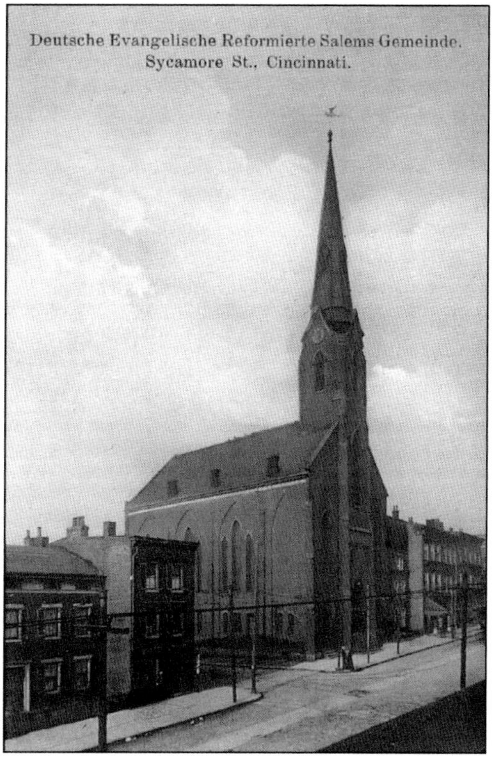

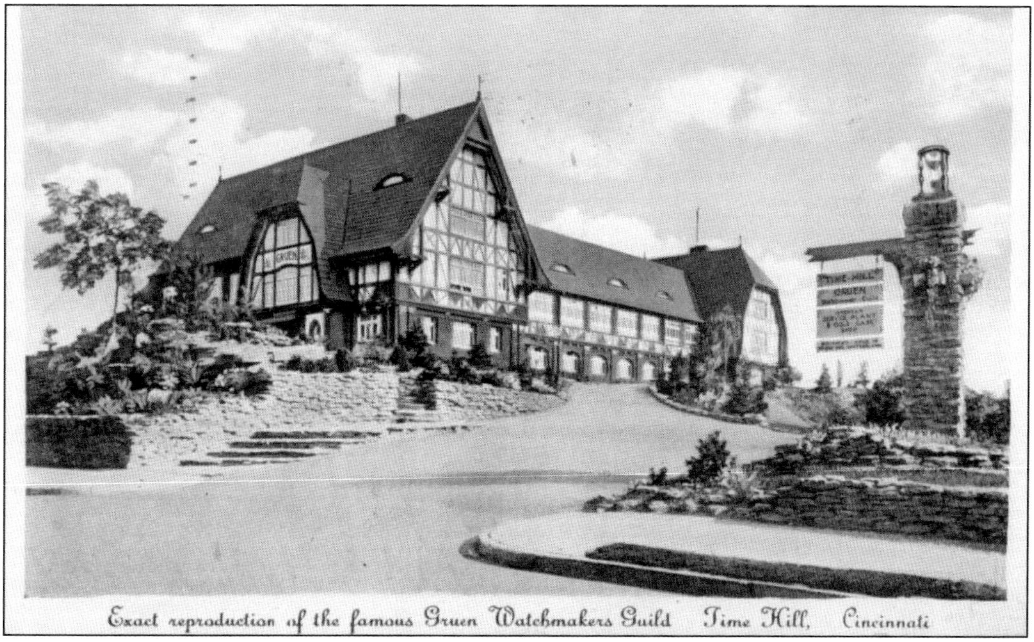

On what was known as Nanny Goat Hill, Fred Gruen built Time Hill, a watch factory in the style of a medieval Belgian guildhall. Gruen was one of the first to use radio for timekeeping. Powerful antennas on the building were in contact with the US Naval Observatory. During World War I, the company donated its equipment to the government. (From the Collection of the Public Library of Cincinnati and Hamilton County.)

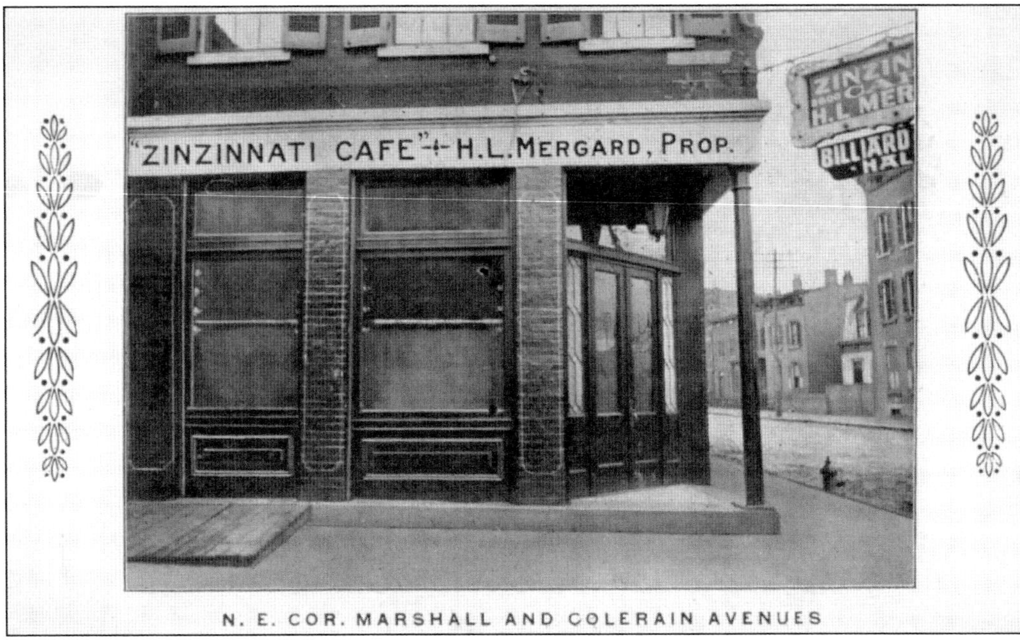

Camp Washington, the neighborhood where the classic Zinzinnati Café once stood, has always been a working-class area. In the settler days, Riddle's Station, a stockade to defend against Indian attack, was located there. Later, it housed an encampment for training soldiers destined for the Mexican-American War. The first Ohio State Fair was held here in 1850. (From the Collection of the Public Library of Cincinnati and Hamilton County.)

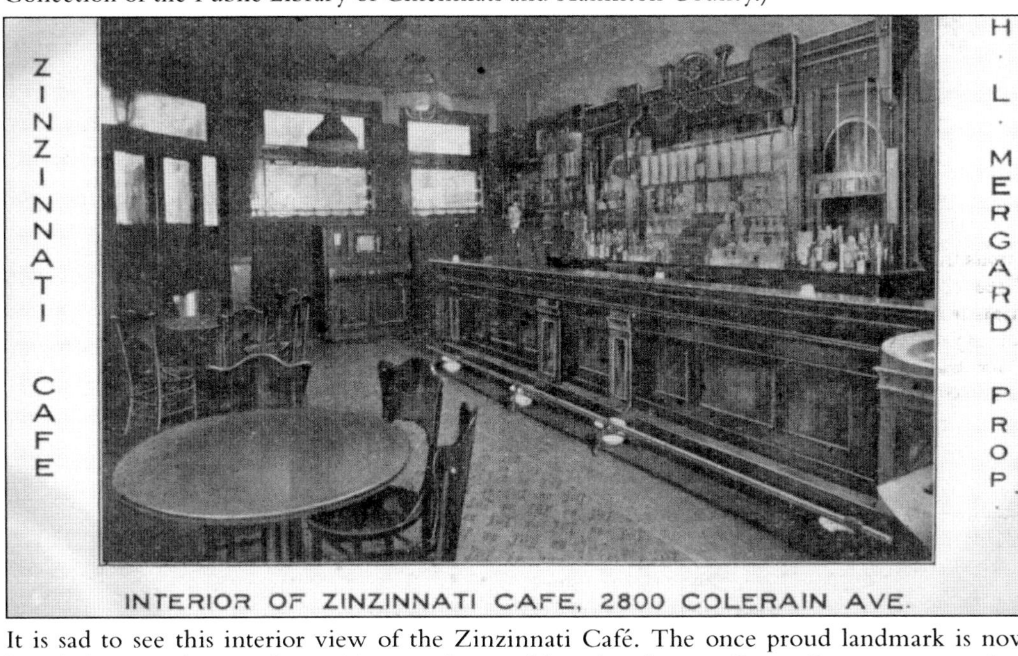

It is sad to see this interior view of the Zinzinnati Café. The once proud landmark is now boarded up, with even the writing on the outside painted over. Once, German was spoken here amidst laughter and rounds of local beer. Many of the patrons were workers from nearby slaughterhouses, the men who put the "pork" in "Porkopolis." (From the Collection of the Public Library of Cincinnati and Hamilton County.)

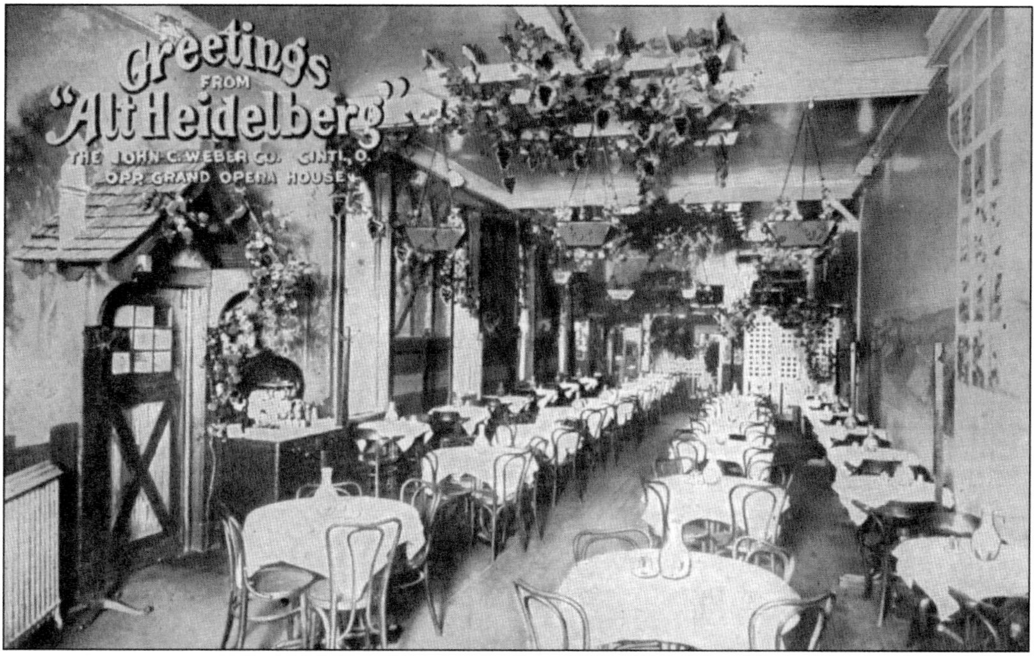

The Alt Heidelberg, or "Old Heidelberg," was one of the most luxurious and popular German restaurants in its day. In 1957, it turned away from its German heritage, renaming itself as the more Mediterranean-sounding Isle of Capri. (From the Collection of the Public Library of Cincinnati and Hamilton County.)

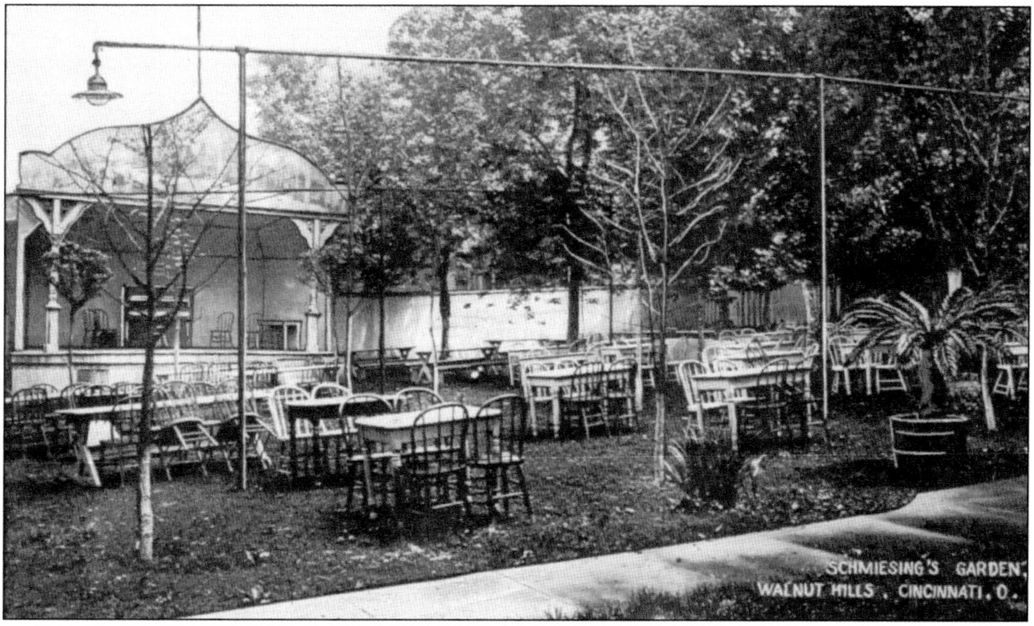

German culture in Cincinnati was exemplified by the beloved biergarten. Fred Schmiesing's German Biergarten was considered to be the finest such establishment on the east side. Located in Walnut Hills on Blair Avenue near Gilbert Avenue, the restaurant featured—on top of dining and beer drinking—bowling, billiards, dancing, and even live concerts. (From the Collection of the Public Library of Cincinnati and Hamilton County.)

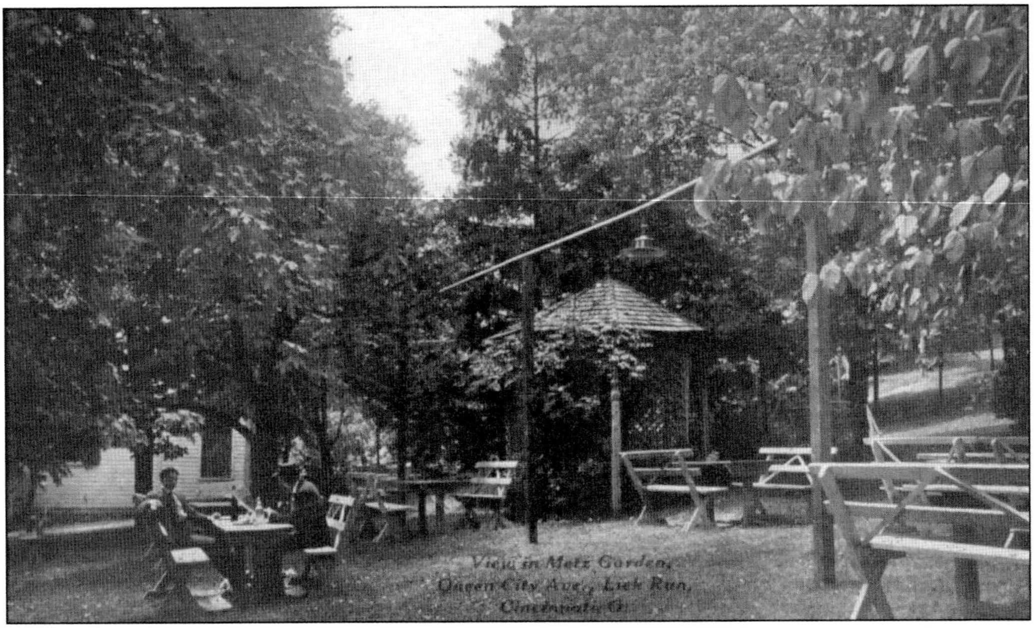

One of the few people who prospered from James Gamble's Westside railroad was Phillip Metz. The Metz family was from Hayna in southern Germany, an area famous for its wine. The Metz Wine Garden attracted visitors from out of town and local people who rode the train and spent a pleasant day drinking wine and enjoying the view. (From the Collection of the Public Library of Cincinnati and Hamilton County.)

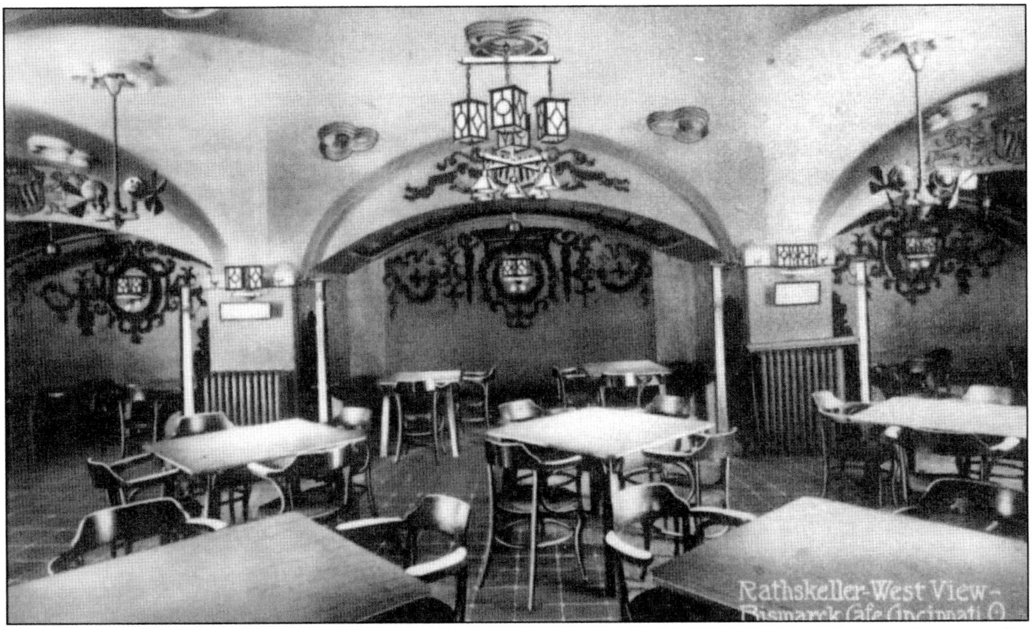

The largest and most prestigious German restaurant in Cincinnati around 1900 was the celebrated Bismarck Café. It was originally located on Vine Street, but in 1904, it moved to Walnut Street in the bottom of the Mercantile Library Building. This new location gave it a better position to compete for the evening theater crowd. (From the Collection of the Public Library of Cincinnati and Hamilton County.)

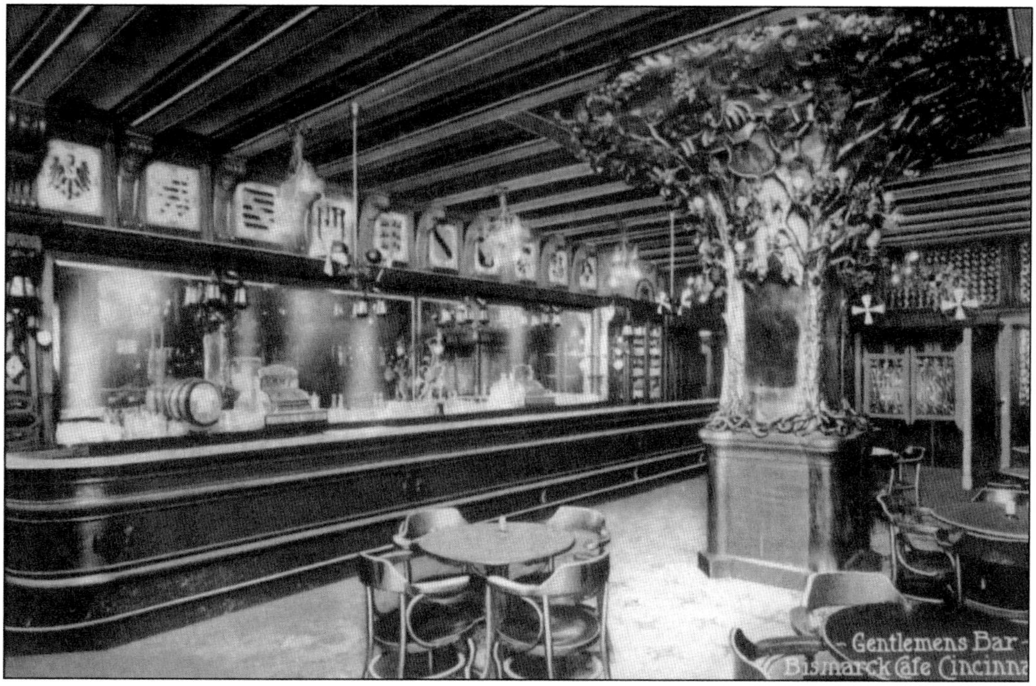

The Bismarck was so large that it had three dining rooms, one for ladies, another for gentlemen, and a separate grill. Owned by the Ehrman Catering Company, the restaurant could boast that its chef, Carl Ehrman, once prepared food for the emperor of Germany. (From the Collection of the Public Library of Cincinnati and Hamilton County.)

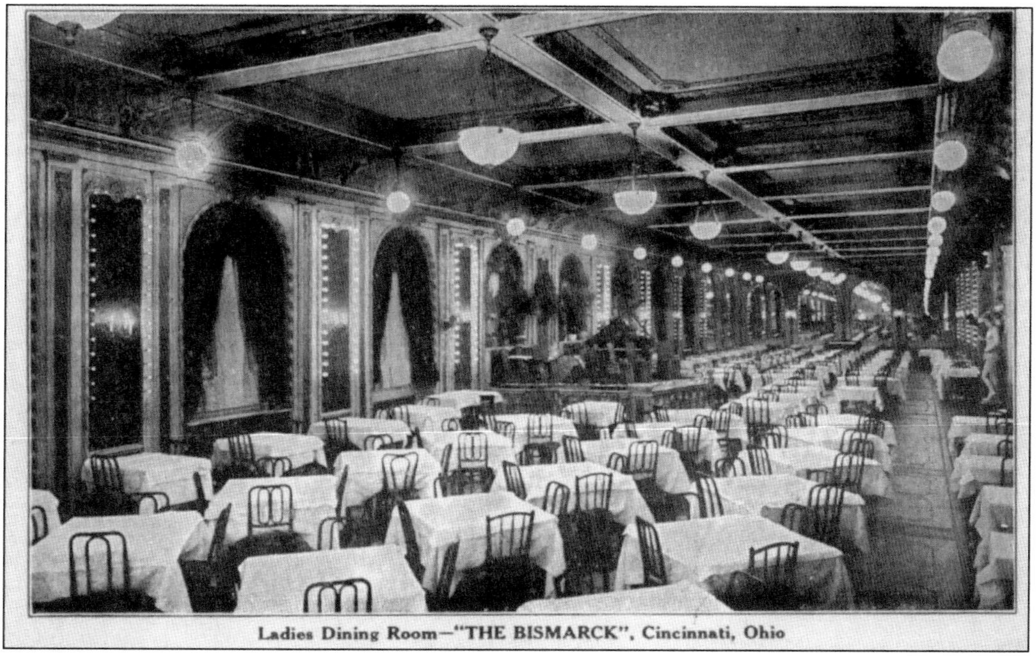

Ladies had their own private dining area in the popular Bismarck Café. For many, a night at the theater downtown would not be complete without a meal at the Bismarck. The establishment had a staff of 150. (From the Collection of the Public Library of Cincinnati and Hamilton County.)

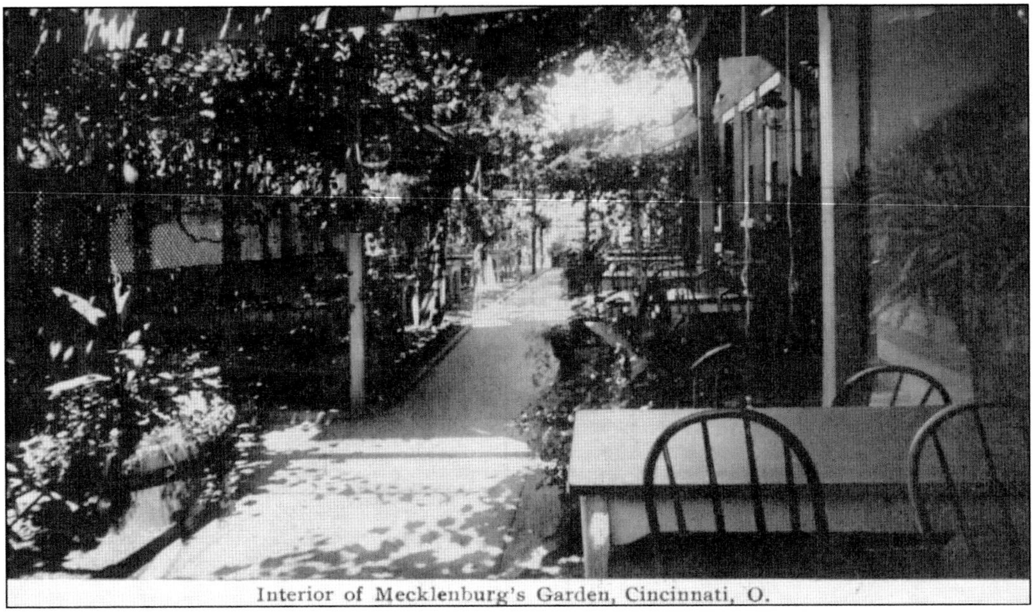

A few German *biergartens* still exist in Cincinnati. Hidden away on streets near the University of Cincinnati is this charming German restaurant, Mecklenburg's Garden, which once provided lessons to German immigrants on how the American political system worked, having candidates run in mock elections for such mythical offices as Kloppenburg or Schnuttenkratzer. (From the Collection of the Public Library of Cincinnati and Hamilton County.)

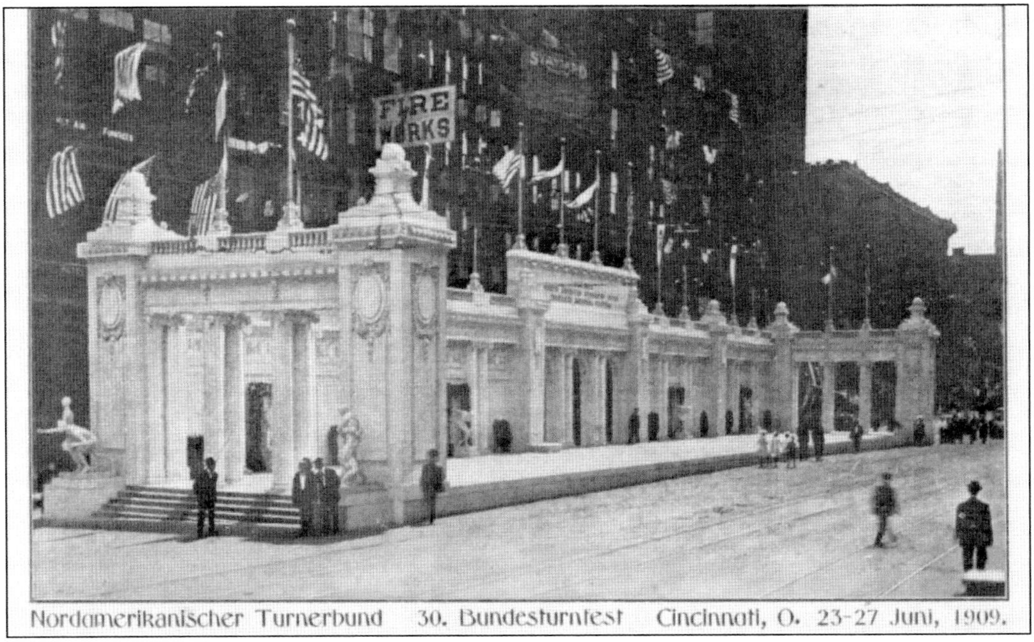

The oldest American branch of the Turner Society was founded in Cincinnati in 1848. Members were mainly political refugees from failed revolutionary movements in Germany in the 1840s. Knowing the feel of living under harsh rule without rights, the Turners became involved in the abolitionist movement. This caused violence in Philadelphia in 1854 and later in Cincinnati and Columbus. (From the Collection of the Public Library of Cincinnati and Hamilton County.)

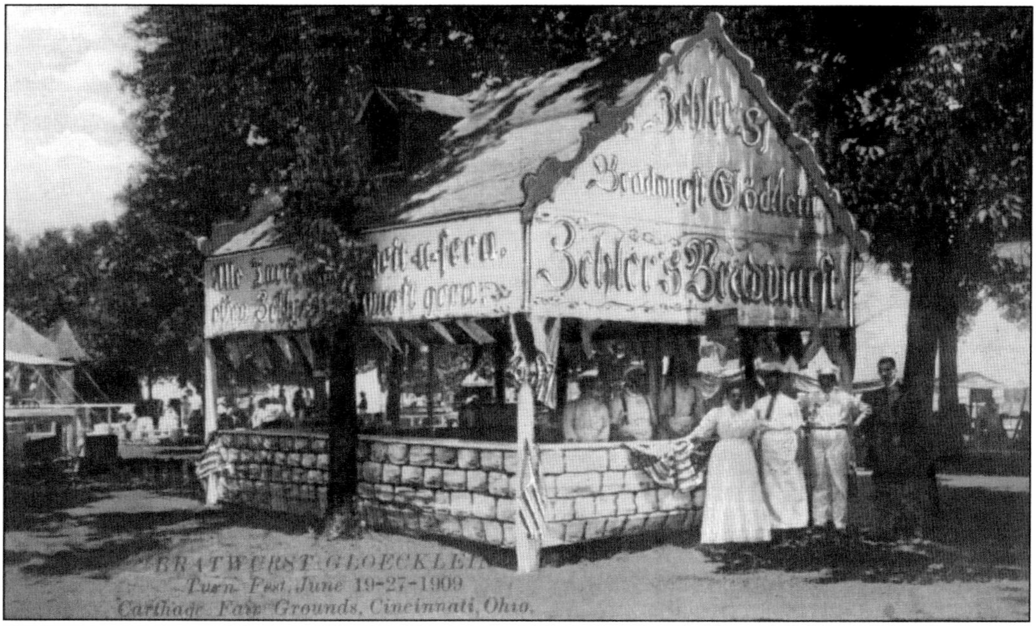

Looking like a scene from a Grimms' fairy tale, this is part of the 1909 Turnerfest. Most visitors who flocked to Cincinnati from all over the nation preferred to stay in the more luxurious hotels in the downtown area. However, for the more daring among them, there was an encampment on the grounds of the Carthage Fair. (From the Collection of the Public Library of Cincinnati and Hamilton County.)

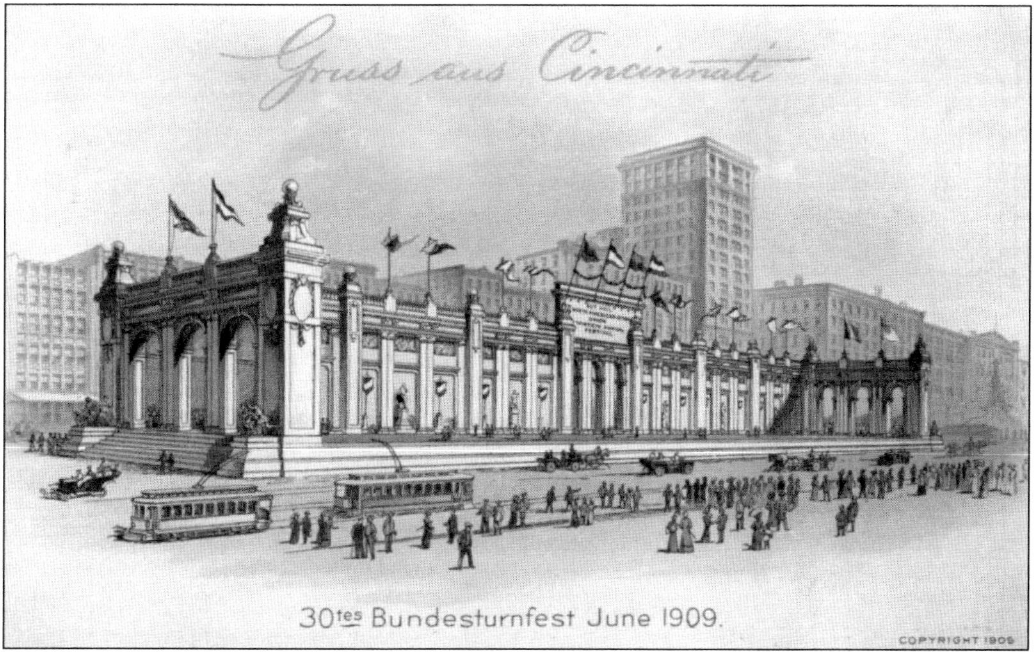

The festival instructor for this cultural and athletic event was Nicholas Seuss. Originally from Sparneck, Germany, Seuss was later the city's supervisor of parks and playgrounds. In this capacity, he invented a game called kick baseball, which is now known as kickball. (From the Collection of the Public Library of Cincinnati and Hamilton County.)

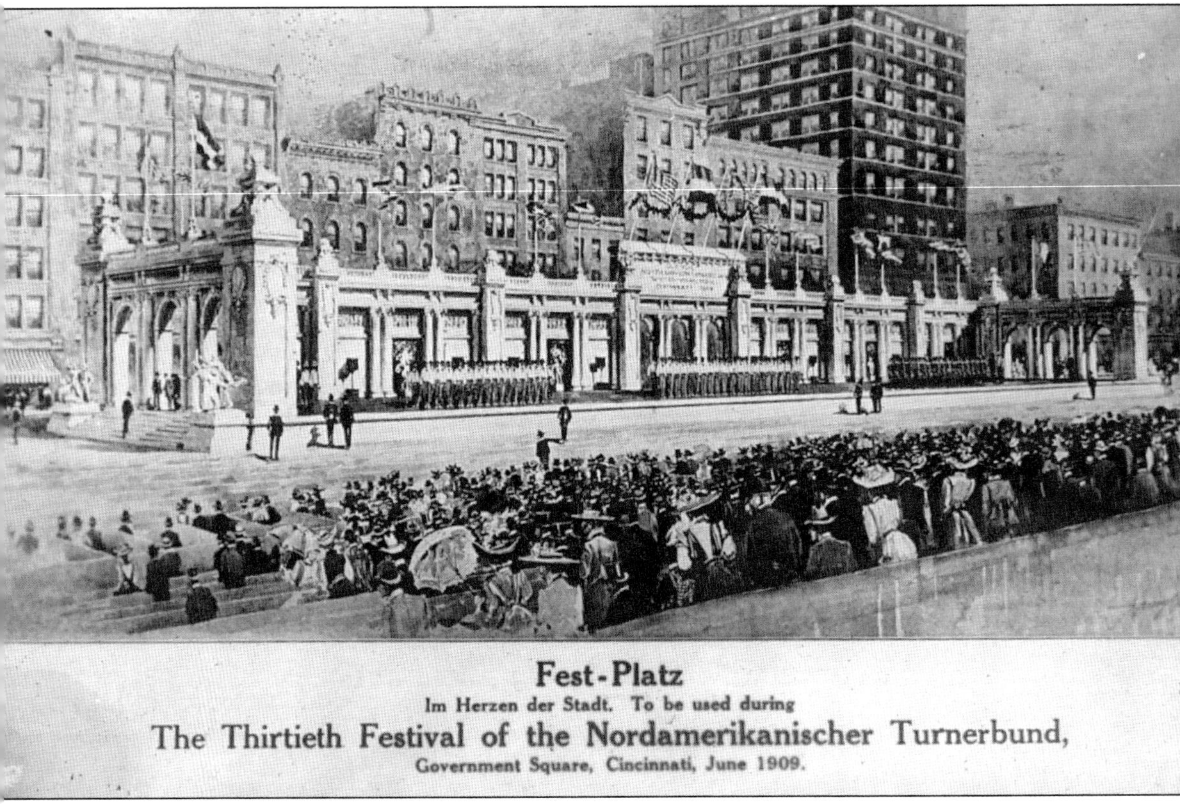

The festival of the Nordamerikanischer Turnerbund in Cincinnati in 1909 was orchestrated by one of "Boss" Cox's closest lieutenants, August Hermann. Earlier Turnerbunds in different American cities had ended in violence when groups such as the anti-immigrant Know Nothings attacked the "white shirts." Such violence had occurred in Cincinnati on Election Day in 1855, leading to complete street warfare, including immigrants barricading streets into Over-the-Rhine and shooting a cannon at their attackers. By 1909, attitudes had changed. That meeting was arranged and hosted by August Hermann, who later owned the Cincinnati Red Stockings. Hermann addressed the crowd by saying, "Gut heil," or "good health." The group was also welcomed by the acting mayor, John Galvin, who proclaimed that the German Cincinnatians "made up our best blood and sinew . . . our best people, and our best citizens." Pres. William Howard Taft was scheduled to appear but was detained in Washington. (From the Collection of the Public Library of Cincinnati and Hamilton County.)

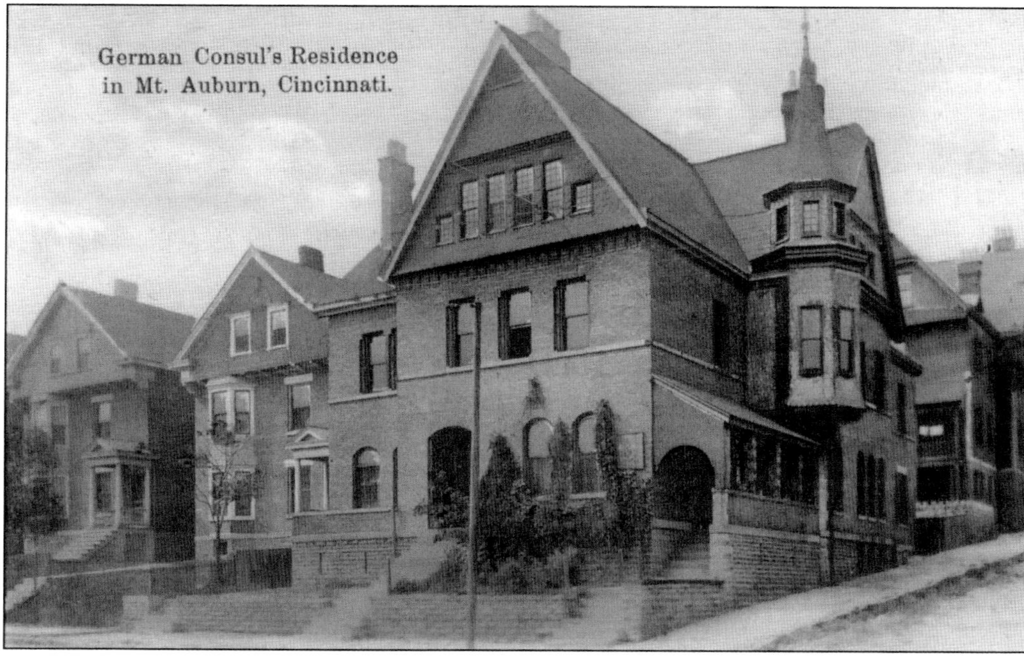

The German population in Cincinnati was so large that the German government actually had a consular office in the city to handle the needs of its people. The house of the consul is seen here, located up the hill on Mount Auburn. (From the Collection of the Public Library of Cincinnati and Hamilton County.)

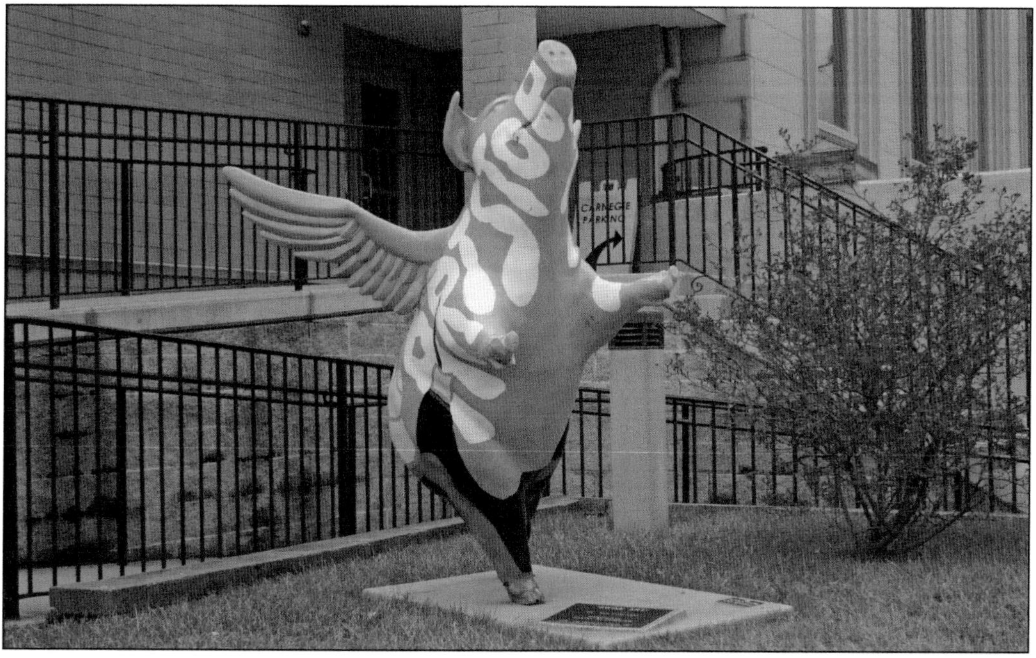

In 2000, Cincinnati celebrated the new millennium by engaging in a whimsical artistic project celebrating its 19th-century history as "Porkopolis." Inspired by Chicago's Cow Parade, the city instituted the "Big Pig Gig." Pig statues decorated by local artists, many with Lewis Carroll–inspired wings, graced the entire city. (Photograph by Doug Weise.)

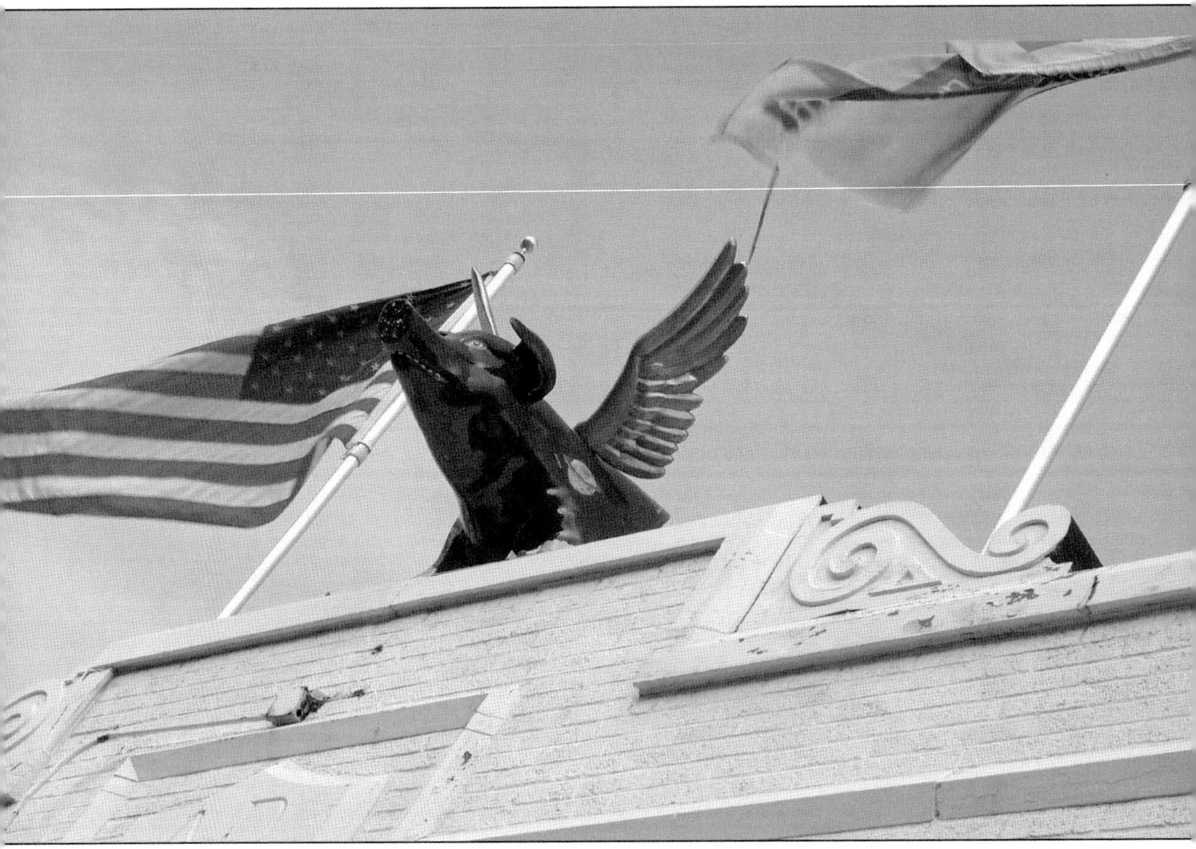

The "Big Pig Gig" was a temporary landmark, but parts of it can still be enjoyed. After the event was completed, many of the statues were auctioned off, such as this one, now located on Spring Grove Avenue. The history of flying pigs in Cincinnati is a tumultuous one. In 1988, the gateway sculpture to the riverfront park Sawyer Point featured statues of winged pigs emerging from the smokestacks of a steamboat. This commemorated Cincinnati's history as both a major port and as "Porkopolis," the largest pork producer in the nation. Some city council members wanted the pigs removed, feeling that they were undignified. Thankfully, after heated debate, the rest of the council determined that a city must have a sense of humor. Twelve years later, the winged-swine image was adopted by the "Big Pig Gig." Many of the statues can still be seen throughout the city on businesses and other buildings. The little pig seen here had better get those wings a-flappin'—he is perched on top of a sausage company. (Photograph by Doug Weise.)

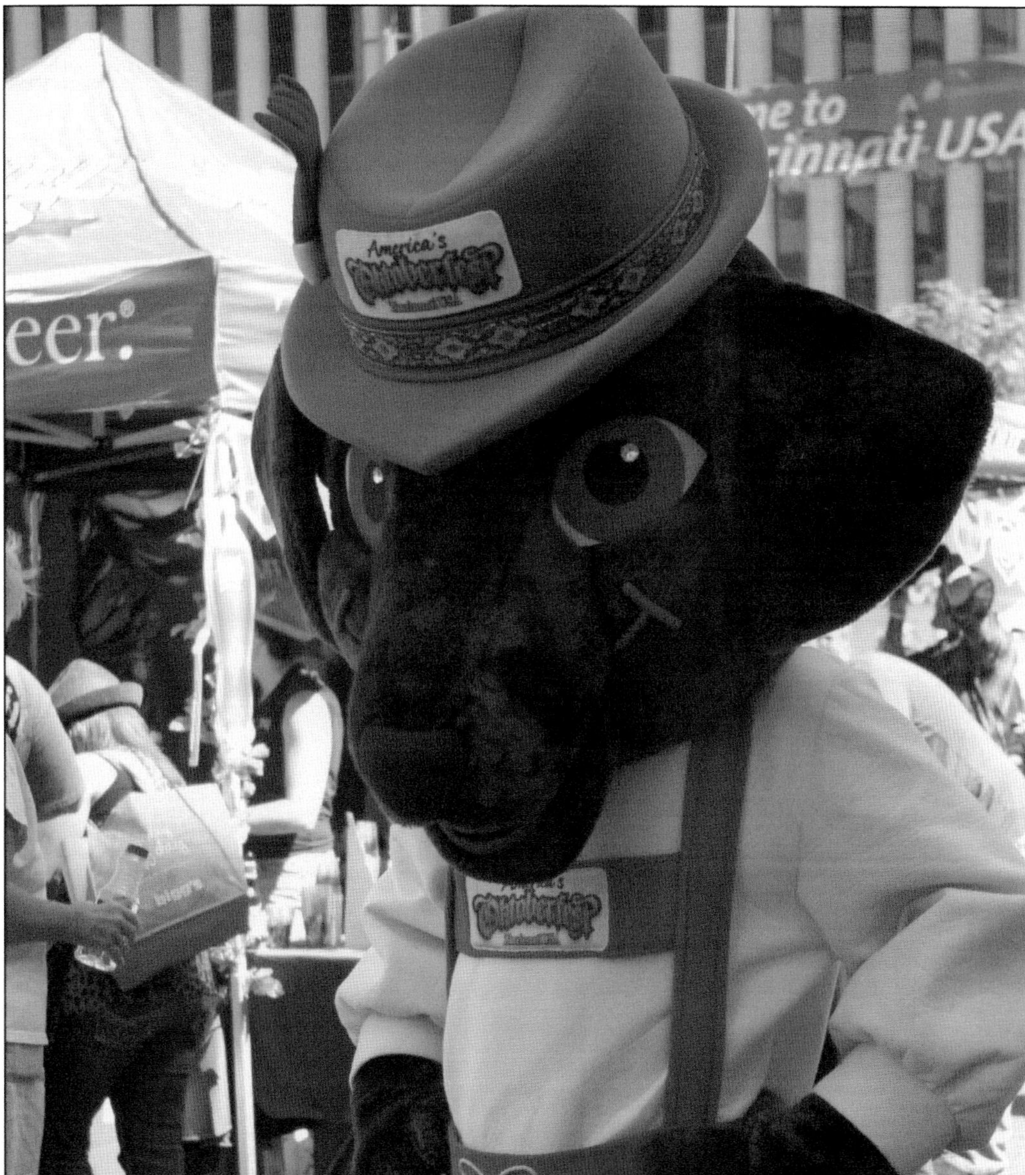

Fritz, the Oktoberfest *hund*, dances in Fountain Square to one of Cincinnati's most unusual landmarks, the Chicken Dance event. Cincinnati's Oktoberfest, the largest in North America, includes the annual Chicken Dance, and it is in this esteemed category that the Queen City holds the world record. The dance is done in the shadow of the Tyler-Davidson Fountain, which has a connection to Bavaria's Oktoberfest. Munich's statue *Patrona Bavariae* was created by three men, including Ferdinand von Miller. His son Ferdinand helped to create the *Genius of Waters*. "The Chicken Dance," composed by Swiss musician Werner Thomas, was originally called "Der Ententanz," or "The Duck Dance." It became a staple of Oktoberfests starting in Tulsa, Oklahoma. Cincinnati's dance is hosted by celebrities, ranging from the crown prince of Bavaria, in 1994, to Weird Al Yankovich, five years later. In 2004, a world record for the largest such dance was set under the leadership of rock singer Vince Neil of Mötley Crüe. Thus, Cincinnati ventures boldly into the future—chicken dancing. (Photograph by Doug Weise.)

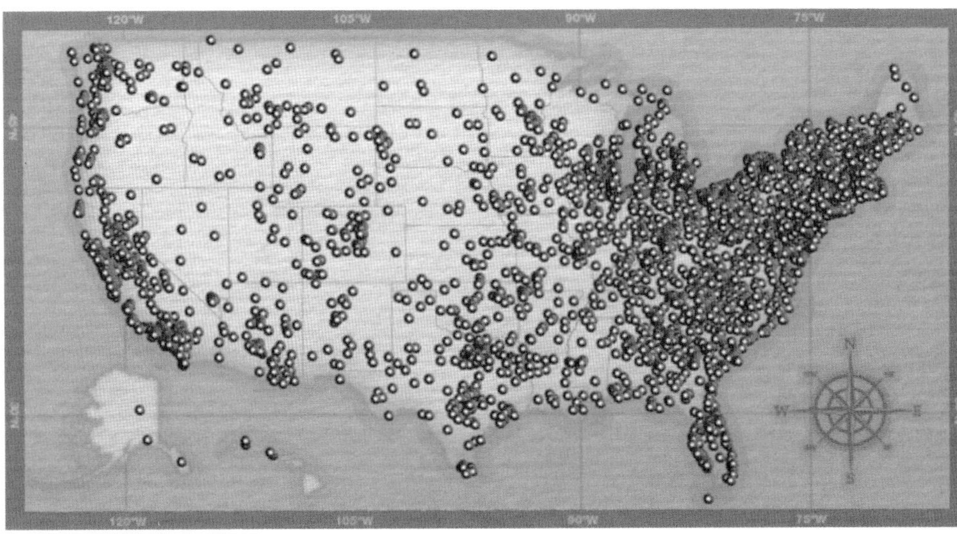